The Exile

Also by Roland Perry:

Programme for a Puppet (fiction)
Election Sur Ordinateur
Hidden Power: The Programming of the President

ROLAND PERRY

The Exile

BURCHETT:
REPORTER OF CONFLICT

First published 1988 by
William Heinemann Australia
(a division of Heinemann Publishers Australia Pty Ltd)
81 Abinger Street, Richmond, Victoria 3121

Designed by Lynda Patullo
Jacket design by Lynda Patullo
Author photograph by Ziggy Gruzauskas
Typeset in 11/13 pt Garamond
   by MacKenzie Typesetting (Vic) Pty Ltd, Melbourne
Printed in Sydney
   by Macarthur Press Pty Ltd

National Library of Australia
   cataloguing-in-publication data:

Perry, Roland, 1946–
   The exile: Burchett: reporter of conflict
   ISBN 0 85561 106 5.

   1. Burchett, Wilfred, 1911-1983. 2. War
   correspondents – Australia – Biography.
   3. Journalists – Australia – Biography.
   I. Title.
070′.92′4

For Angela

Contents

Preface

The inspiration for this book came while I was reading the morning papers in my local cafe, Picasso, on Kings Road, London in late September 1983. The obituaries for Wilfred Burchett in *The Times*, *Financial Times* (he was a correspondent for both) *Guardian* and *Herald Tribune* were amazing.

His extraordinary life struck me immediately as suitable for a book and a film. Until then my impressions had come from just one of his thirty-odd books – *My War with the CIA* (which he wrote for Cambodia's Prince Sihanouk in the early 1970s) – and other media glimpses of Burchett as a passportless exile who had had some influence in the Vietnam war.

He appeared to be like the American John Reed, who had been romanticised by Warren Beatty in his film 'Reds', and a similar treatment seemed appropriate for Burchett. The research, however, uncovered something different, more fascinating, intriguing and complex.

Many but not all of the people I interviewed fell into two camps: those on the left who wanted to mythologise Burchett in the Ned Kelly tradition, and those on the right who would do everything to destroy his reputation.

Somewhere between and beyond these rigid positions was the real Burchett story.

Some stood out for their help and supply of information. (On occasions this was not helpful to their own positions on the subject.) I am grateful in particular to Winston Burchett, who made available private correspondence, his unpublished diary, 'The Timid Adventurer', his mother's diary and other files, Professor Gavin McCormack, Dr Ben Kiernan, Roy Turner, Harvey Cooper, Vessa Burchett, George and Peter Burchett, Stephanie Alexander, Mavis Robertson, Rupert Lockwood, Joe Waters, Rainer Burchett, John Halliday, Russell Spurr, Jim Cardinal, Jack Grossman, Judge Robert Taylor, Tibor Meray, Edwin Morrisby, Ken Gott, Denis Warner, Peggy Warner, Robert Manne, Jack Kane, Molly Gray, Kevin Davis, George MacArthur, Sam White, Ed Hymoff, Walker Bud Mahurin, Paul

Kniss, Terry Tobin, Creighton Burns, Ronald Payne, John Miller, Martin Page, Henry Keys, Frank Robertson, Christopher Dobson, Donald Rochlan, General Farrar-Hockley, Phillip Greville, Howard Handleman, Ruth Karen, Douglas Pike, Heuston Kennedy, and Margot Traill.

I am also indebted to innumerable sources, including many who did not wish to be mentioned, and several in intelligence agencies – west and east – who could not. The most useful information came from representatives or files or both from Australia's intelligence services, Australia's former Department of External Affairs, especially in connection with Burchett's near defection in 1953, British Intelligence, French Intelligence, Soviet and Bulgarian Intelligence, the CIA, and the Wilfred Burchett archive at the La Trobe Library, Melbourne.

The complete transcript of the trial *Burchett* v. *Kane* (NSW Supreme Court, October 1974) was, of course, essential source material for this book.

Many thanks to my editor, Jane Arms, and especially to the film director Tim Burstall with whom I am writing a TV series based on *The Exile*. His overview on the story was invaluable.

Roland Perry, 1987

PART
ONE

Sue or be damned

1. The Hiroshima Scoop

The siren caused thousands of Japanese to run for cover in homes, tin huts and ditches as the steady drone of two planes was heard flying over the city. Using binoculars, local authorities checked the planes and judged them harmless American reconnaissance aircraft, which had often been seen in the past weeks. The all-clear was sounded. On that summer's day, 6 August 1945, locals returned to their daily toil.

At 8.20 am one of the planes returned. The authorities noted it, but assumed that it was doubling back for more photos. This time it was higher. The alarm was considered then abandoned.

Then it struck.

A blinding flash like lightning was followed by scorching heat. An explosion accompanied a cyclone of hot wind that flattened every building and structure within fifty kilometres. Tens of thousands of people evaporated in the blast. Not even their ashes remained.

A pillar of black smoke was speared by a scarlet thread that glowed until it went red. On the ground there was a charred desert of collapsed buildings. The city of Hiroshima had vanished.

Australian journalist Wilfred Burchett listened to the radio crackle of a speech by President Truman that announced the successful trial of a powerful new bomb. Neither Burchett nor any of the American marines in the midday chow line on the recently conquered island of Okinawa realised that they were less than 650 kilometres from the site of the first atomic weapon blast, which had hit Hiroshima a few hours earlier. Okinawa was being prepared as a springboard for an invasion of Japan scheduled for November 1945. But now, as the message from the president was repeated, the Americans began to wonder if it was necessary. Would this bomb mean that the war was at last over?

The news meant something else to Burchett. He wanted to see Hiroshima. As a thirty-three-year-old professional war correspondent, his name had been made on exclusive stories from the Pacific and Asian war zones. He had sent his first successful dispatch to the London *Daily Express* on 23 December 1941, when the Japanese bombed Rangoon and opened the way for the invasion of Burma a few weeks later. He became the paper's man in the region and never looked back. Unlike most of his colleagues, he had never been trained on a paper.

The war had created a unique opportunity for Burchett. He was a loner with the initiative to roam the war zones of South-East Asia and China. He had grown accustomed to fending for himself under rough, even primitive, conditions while tramping Australia's outback as an itinerant worker during the Depression. His lean physique was not exceptional, and the only immediate hint of strength was a pair of outsized hands that had been shaped in his youth in building and carpentry work. Long treks had made his legs muscular, and his outback experience sustained him in going that extra stretch for a story.

While reporting the Pacific war, for instance, Burchett would even hitch a ride with a dive bomber from an American aircraft carrier in order to get an overview of an island invasion as the Allies pushed towards Japan. This way his stories were worth ten times those of his rivals. Burchett's dispatches would reach Fleet Street two weeks before those from correspondents who travelled with invasion forces at a beach head.

He would also go to painstaking lengths, such as noting promotions among the American naval ranks and sending them a congratulatory telegram. When he wanted a favour – a quick flight here or an exclusive story there – he would get it. A touch of ruthlessness, too, pushed him into the front ranks of professionals. When the *Express* wanted a reporter transferred to the island-hopping operations of the US in 1944, it cabled its office in Chungking. Burchett picked it up first and was on his way before his more senior *Express* colleague – who also wanted the Pacific job – knew about the request.

Within a week of Hiroshima's destruction, Burchett set out for Japan with the US 4th Marine Regiment, the same unit with which he had landed for the invasion of Guam. He soon realised that making it to the A-bomb site would mean summoning all his cunning and courage. General MacArthur had made Hiroshima off-limits to all correspondents and, although many wanted the story, they were nervous of travelling through a hostile country that had yet to officially capitulate.

The initial hint that the natives might be less dangerous than anticipated came when the American armada arrived in Tokyo Bay on 30 August. Emperor Hirohito had demanded a calm and dignified acceptance of defeat, and the reality of the atomic bomb's awesome power had sapped the nation's resistance.

After some early trepidation, Japanese from the naval barracks town of Yokosuka were soon bartering with the invaders, who had behaved civilly towards them. The atmosphere encouraged Burchett to catch a train to Tokyo with Chicago *Daily News* correspondent Bill McGaffin, who had been sent to Japan to witness the surrender ceremony on the US battleship *Missouri*. They were the only foreigners aboard the train, which was packed with curious and fearful locals. Burchett's exceptional facility with languages – he had taught himself French, German, Spanish and Russian – proved helpful. He had been studying a US military manual and had already memorised useful Japanese phrases, which eased the tension. The locals were more surprised than ferocious.

Both men felt most uncomfortable when passing through what once had been the most densely populated area in the world. Allied bombing had flattened the area. But now that the fighting had ended, green growth was already pushing through the ashes.

With his mind on a third book he was shaping on his Hermes typewriter, Burchett found a seat and began scribbling in a notepad. There were, he wrote, 'hundreds of shacks improvised from rusted, corrugated-iron remnants of factories which had been reduced to shambles of concrete rubble, twisted girders, and shattered, rusty machinery'.

His mind turned to Hiroshima. If this was what regular bombing could do, what would the results of a nuclear blast look like?

He and McGaffin tried to book in at the Imperial Hotel, but it had been taken over by American correspondents who had landed with General MacArthur's airborne troops a few hours ahead of the marines. Only the Dai Ichi hotel was available. They booked in and found that cigarettes were acceptable currency. Later they dined at the hotel, and Burchett flirted with the wary waitresses with his fumbled, yet persistent attempts at their language. He was not destined to win a beauty contest, but his gregariousness gave his looks a rugged charm, especially among Asians, who often found other Europeans aloof. Where other Australian males had the reputation of ranking women below drinking and sport, Burchett seemed genuinely interested in them. Although he had been reared in the Australian bush, his manner and bearing had been overlaid with nearly a decade of expatriation. His accent was recognizable as Australian, but it had acquired a mid-Atlantic, senatorial tone.

By the end of a convivial evening, in which a sizeable quantity of sake had been downed, Burchett was making fair conversation with the girls. One of them seemed particularly enchanted with him and, amid much giggling, agreed to a secret assignation in his room. She stayed with him until dawn, and Burchett's communicative powers went up another notch. He learned that he could catch a daily train to Hiroshima, and that he could perhaps get help from Domei, the official Japanese news agency.

The next morning at breakfast, Burchett declined the offer

from McGaffin to join him on a walk through the city for a piece on the atmosphere. Burchett explained with a nod and a wink that he still had the girl in his room. McGaffin believed him, for he had known Burchett for two years in the Pacific. His reputation with women was legendary.

When McGaffin left, Burchett hurried to the Domei agency's foreign desk and asked about going to Hiroshima. A startled Japanese journalist told him that no one was visiting the city: 'Everyone is dying there.' It made the mission urgent. Burchett pressed further, and the journalist agreed to buy him a return ticket in exchange for taking food and cigarettes to Nakamura-san, the Domei correspondent in Hiroshima.

Nakamura had only one method of getting a message to Domei's Tokyo office – by the laborious use of a Morse hand-set – but it was good enough for Burchett, who told the journalist he might be trying to push through a story from Hiroshima.

Burchett met McGaffin back at the Dai Ichi. McGaffin asked where he had been, and Burchett replied that the girl had taken him sightseeing.

The two correspondents returned by train to Yokosuka, and Burchett buried his face in a book of short stories by Jack London. If there was the slightest opportunity, Burchett would be reading – usually fiction, such as that of London or H.G. Wells. If not, he would be at work on his own book or story. He had developed the discipline of the long-distance traveller and writer.

Later they joined all their Allied colleagues at a Yokohama hotel, which acted as press headquarters. Burchett drank heartily long into the night with several friends, including compatriot Henry Keys, who also worked for the *Daily Express*. They swapped heroic and hilarious stories from the war.

Burchett, always great company among his correspondent buddies, consumed more alcohol than anyone, but as usual demonstrated an exceptional constitution by becoming merry but not drunk.

He and Keys retired to a shared room where Keys showed Burchett an urgent cable from the *Express*'s Editor, Arthur Christiansen. It read: 'I set the greatest store by the *Daily Express* being first in the world to run the full story of Hiroshima.'

Burchett confessed his obsession to get the story, but Keys was adamant that he wanted it too. The telegram had been sent to him, and he had already done considerable research into the blast, including a raid on the Domei files. The agency had covered the story over the three and a half weeks since the bomb had struck. Burchett tried to sell him the idea of covering the *Missouri* ceremony, but Keys wouldn't have it. In the end, the two weary reporters tossed a coin. Burchett won, and Keys sportingly sat down with him to hatch a plan to create the story first for the *Express*. Keys would monitor Domei for Burchett's story, which he would file to Fleet Street from Yokohama's press centre.

At five the next morning, an Allied press officer knocked on their bedroom door. They were due to leave with the other 253 journalists going to the *Missouri*. The officer heard loud groaning and hurried in. Burchett was lying on his back acting ill. Keys was applying hot towels to his stomach. When the anxious officer asked what was wrong, Burchett mumbled something about diarrhoea. He was exempted from the ceremony. When the officer had left, the two Australians congratulated each other. Keys gave Burchett a bulletless Colt .45 automatic pistol and wished him luck.

Burchett used the hotel's rear fire-escape to evade the watchful eye of the press officers and his colleagues. He caught a train to Tokyo, and at six was pushed into another over-crowded train, destination Hiroshima.

Meanwhile, Keys reached the deck of the Missouri where he was greeted by a rival from the London's *Daily Mail*, New Zealander Lachie McDonald.

'Where's Burchett?' was McDonald's suspicious opening remark. When told that he had diarrhoea, McDonald laughed disbelievingly and wanted to know what he was really up to. It wasn't like Burchett to miss one of the big stories of the war, unless he was after something bigger.

The train trip to Hiroshima was expected to take a day. At first, Burchett was wary. The carriages were full of newly demobilised troops, and he had been careful to hide his pistol belt, gun and military cap. He clutched an umbrella borrowed from the hotel manager, in the hope that despite wearing jungle greens, he would be taken for a neutral foreign civilian, like the handful of White Russians, Swedes, Swiss and Portuguese seen in Tokyo.

It was standing room only outside compartments for the first six hours, and he was the object of curiosity for the sullen troops, who stared at him. Burchett, steeped in the Australian tradition of sharing and 'mateship' he had learnt in the Depression while jumping trains, offered cigarettes to those nearby. This broke the ice, and soon the Japanese were all smiles as they pressed him to accept bits of fish and hard-boiled eggs. They had been allowed to take as much food and drink away from their barracks as possible. Most carried rifles wrapped in blankets.

Burchett managed to communicate that scars on his leg had come from an attack by a Japanese plane in Burma, and this eased the tension further.

The crowd thinned, and Burchett wedged his way into a compartment and found a comfortable seat, much to the displeasure of Japanese officers.

'They were the most unhappy collection of men I have ever seen,' Burchett wrote of that experience. 'They still carried their swords; many of them had pistols and short samurai swords as well. There was a muttering and fingering of sword hilts as I perched myself on the edge of a seat. An officer in the seat shrank away as if I were a carrier of plague germs and barked something at me, which I didn't understand. They settled down to stare gloomily at the floor or into space, their hands clasped over their sword hilts.'

Burchett spotted another European – who turned out to be an American priest – and sat next to him. He was a prisoner-of-war who had been taken to Tokyo to explain to Allied troops how they should behave in Japan. He was now being returned to Kyoto to be locked up again until all POWs were liberated. The priest warned Burchett not to be effusive with the officers, who would take his smiles and enthusiasm as gloating over Japan's dishonourable capitulation, which was then being enacted on the *Missouri*. That gave Burchett pause, especially after Kyoto when the priest left the train.

Despite increased apprehension as the train passed through dark tunnels, Burchett arrived at Hiroshima ten hours later tired but unscathed. He was arrested by two black-uniformed police and taken to a makeshift tin and sandbag prison but released at dawn after more judicious use of cigarette bartering and explaining that he was a correspondent.

Burchett was five kilometres from the city centre and on the fringe of the destruction. He began following a tramline. He wrote:

'Walking through those streets I had the feeling of being transplanted to some death-stricken alien planet. There was devastation and desolation, and nothing else.

'Lead-grey clouds hung low over the waste that had been a city of a quarter of a million people. Smokey vapours poured from fissures in the soil. There was a dank, acrid, sulphurous smell. The few people in the streets hurried past each other without pausing or speaking, white masks covering their nostrils. Buildings had been pounded into reddish dust, solidified into ridges and banks by the frequent rains...

'No one stopped to look at me. Everyone hurried, intent on whatever it was that brought them into this city of death. In the centre I found that the buildings I had seen from the distance were outlines only, having been gutted by the fire which swept through after most of the city had disappeared in a pillar of dust and flame.'

Burchett found police at another temporary station in a solid bank, which had remained intact, and they searched for Domei's Nakamura. Burchett took notes:

'From the third floor view to the horizon there was nothing but flat acres of ground, except for a few trees and some factory chimneys without any trace of the factories they had served. Like the younger trees, the resiliance of a well-made chimney, which permits considerable swaying, saved them.

'Among the buildings still standing was a church which closer inspection revealed had jumped into the air, twisted around and come to rest practically intact but crazily athwart its foundations, a metre from the ground. Low-level concrete bridges had also jumped off their piles, some spans landing back again, others dropping down into the river. All balustrades and stone facings from the bridges had disappeared. There remained only red dust and shattered remnants of the Emperor's palace and a large military barracks. There were no broken walls, large chunks of rubble, or blocks of stone and concrete; no craters as one usually sees in a bombed city.

It was destruction by pulverisation.

'Central buildings still standing had been directly beneath the bomb as it parachuted down. They were sheltered in a relative safety cone as the explosive force expanded outwards around them.'

The police brought Nakamura and an English-speaking Japanese girl to Burchett, and they were all driven to a former school that served as an emergency hospital. There Burchett witnessed something even more horrifying than the destructive power of the A-bomb on a city: the effect on humans. His subsequent report here caused a controversy, the ramifications of which were to last a lifetime...

'Stretched out on the filthy mats on the floor of the first room I entered were a dozen or so people in various stages of disintegration from what I later knew to be atomic radiation. The doctors assured me that they would all die unless American scientists had some antidote to the terrible wasting disease that had stricken thousands of people since the bomb was dropped.

'In room after room it was the same. All the victims were emaciated and gave off an odour which almost halted me at the first door. Some had purplish burns on the face and body, others had bunched, blue-black marks on their necks. The doctor in charge told me he was at a loss on how to treat his patients...

'"We know now that something is killing off the white corpuscles, and there is nothing we can do about it," the doctor said. "There is no way of replacing white corpuscles."'

After the hospital visit Burchett sat down in the rubble and wrote what he hoped would be one of the world's most momentous reports. Then Nakamura tapped out the 3,000 word story, word by word, on the Morse hand-set, which transmitted it to Tokyo.

Soon afterwards, Burchett was wandering the city when he bumped into a group of American journalists known as 'The Flying Circus'. They had been sent to Japan by the American State Department to write sanitised stories about the surrender, the occupation, Hiroshima and other events. Believing that they had the Bomb story to themselves because MacArthur had authorised their visit, they were not in a great hurry to fly to Hiroshima. A Japanese admiral wishing to absolve himself of guilt in the more unsavoury side of the Japanese war effort had persuaded the Americans to visit him in Kyoto en route to Hiroshima. The journalists were entertained lavishly and delayed a day.

They were surprised to see Burchett, whom most knew as a Pacific war reporting ace, and they were puzzled when he declined their offer to take his copy to Tokyo. Burchett told them that he had not completed gathering information.

In Yokohama, Henry Keys was worried. Tokyo had been placed off-limits to all Allied troops and correspondents. He had sent a Swedish-Japanese called Aczel to the Domei office, but Burchett's report had not come through. Finally one take – the first 200 words – was transmitted. It was not enough to make the big article the *Express* had in mind, although it was the on-the-spot verification the paper needed to authenticate the story. Keys was forced to act fast if his paper was to break the story. He gathered the research he had already prepared from Domei and began a feature article at Yokohama, just as the US 'Flying Circus' returned to the hotel press centre there. Keys gleaned more information about Hiroshima's destruction from them and then finished the story, the introduction of which was Burchett's 200 words. Keys stood over the telex operator at the press centre until the last word was on its way to London. He generously but fairly gave the story the by-line 'Burchett', for it had been his. He had made the dangerous journey and taken all the risks. Without his eye-witness account the paper would have considered it unethical and unprofessional to have run the story.

The *Express* splashed it across page one and made it available free to every other agency and paper in the world. It said:

30th Day in Hiroshima.
Those who escaped begin to die victim of

THE ATOMIC PLAGUE
'I write this as a warning to the world'
DOCTORS FALL AS THEY WORK
Poison gas fear: All wear masks

Express Staff Reporter Wilfred Burchett was the first Allied reporter to enter the atom-bomb city. He travelled 400 miles from Tokyo alone and unarmed, carrying rations for seven meals – food is almost unobtainable in Japan – a black umbrella and a typewriter. Here is his story from –

HIROSHIMA, Tuesday. 'In Hiroshima, thirty days after the first atomic bomb destroyed the city and shook the world, people are still dying, mysteriously and horribly – people who were uninjured in the cataclysm – from an unknown something, which I can only describe as the atomic plague.

'Hiroshima does not look like a bombed city. It looks as if a monster steamroller had passed over it and squashed it out of existence. I write these facts as dispassionately as I can in the hope that they will act as a warning to the world.'

On the return train trip to Tokyo, Burchett visited Allied POW camps at Kyoto and Kobe and was delayed three days. He arrived back at the Japanese capital and was devastated to learn that only 200 of his 3,000 words had made it to Tokyo. Nevertheless, his spirits were lifted when Keys told him that Christiansen had given both men a bonus of 200 pounds for the scoop (which was later ranked as one of the top journalistic 'firsts' of the century).

Burchett was just in time for an American press conference at the Imperial Hotel, which was meant to refute his article.

Brigadier-General Thomas Farrell, the deputy head of the Manhattan Bomb project, explained that the bomb had been exploded high enough over Hiroshima to avoid any risk of radiation. Burchett, looking pale and unkempt after his harrowing trip, challenged Farrell's claims. A briefing officer took the questions and fielded them easily enough, for little was known about the after-effects of the bomb – radiation. The press was told that the bomb had been given 'the most exhaustive tests imaginable' in the Nevada desert. Radiation had been measured at acceptable levels after explosions at certain heights above targets. Burchett's 'radiation sickness' assertions were successfully denied.

Decades later, when the medium-term effects on the people

of Hiroshima had been researched, his report proved
accurate.

Hiroshima marked the end of fascism and World War II, and
the beginning of the Cold War between the west and the
communist world. Burchett became strongly pro-communist
in his views. He developed a passion for revolution, and his
romanticism was sustained by the Red Flag over East Germany,
Bulgaria, Hungary, North Korea, China, Laos, Vietnam, Angola
and Cambodia. Inevitably this brought him into conflict with
conservative powers in the US and Australia. His adversaries
labelled him a traitor and paid agent of communist
governments.

Burchett loved Australia and wanted to live there, but to
operate freely he had to crush his enemies, who had kept him
in exile for twenty years. The opportunity arose when a small
circulation right-wing magazine accused him of being a KGB
agent in late 1971. With Gough Whitlam's Labor government
in power a year later, the atmosphere seemed right for
Burchett to make a move. He sued the magazine and its editor
for defamation.

The trial, in October 1974, developed into the most
sensational and controversial court battle in Australian legal
history, as Burchett's extraordinary life was paraded before an
astonished world.

A trial victory for Burchett would mean the opportunity to
live luxuriously and unhindered in his homeland. Top legal
advisers told Burchett that if he won, many big publishers in
Australia and abroad could be sued for a fortune. A loss,
however, would mean permanent exile.

2. The Zenith

March, 1970

The Australian coast appeared like a low, white mist ahead of them, just distinguishable from the whorls of coral reef they had flown over for four hours since leaving Noumea. Wilfred Burchett smiled with nervous anticipation as the pilot of their Piper Navajo light plane gave the call sign 'Victor Bravo Yankee' to the coastal patrol and acknowledged the sight of landfall. This was the moment Burchett had pushed for for over 15 years since his passport had been lost in North Vietnam in 1955. He had put out feelers to diplomats in Moscow, CIA people in Korea, ambassadors in Cairo, and friends and colleagues in journalism everywhere from London to Melbourne. But the reply had always come back, 'Sorry, Wilf, nothing doing'. The Australian government did not want him to have access to his country of birth, or easy entry to the west. Burchett had once been fearful of confrontation. But now he was world famous. He had a petition containing scores of great names from Jean-Paul Sartre to Jane Fonda to back his efforts. If the government in Canberra would not forget the past, he would meet them head on.

A cork popped. Burchett turned to see journalist Bill Green grinning and pouring champagne. It frothed warm, but it was French and welcome. Green's paper, the Melbourne *Sunday Observer*, had sponsored Burchett's flight from Noumea, which provided it with good publicity and a scoop.

'It's been a long time, Wilf?' Green asked as he handed him a paper cup of bubbly. Burchett sipped and gazed out the plane window at the looming coastal sands of Queensland. He finished his drink.

'Twenty years,' he replied and gestured for another cup. Burchett wondered what Australia would be like after such a long break, but he was soon preoccupied with his Saturday afternoon reception at Brisbane airport. The crowd of a few hundred was hostile. People shouted abuse and waved placards that read: 'Burchett Back to Hanoi'; 'Burchett Traitor'; 'Burchett Better Red And Dead'.

He stepped from the plane and was booed. Police shepherded him through the passenger terminal to the guarded customs area. An immigration officer fumbled with Burchett's thick Laissez Passez, issued in Hanoi, which allowed him limited travel, mainly to communist countries. The officer demanded his birth certificate. It was enough for almost anyone to get into his country of birth, although Burchett claimed he was worried that it would not allow him to leave the country. That would be faced when he came to it in a few weeks' time. The officer asked no questions as he stamped the certificate and handed it back.

Burchett moved through the barriers to embrace his elder brother Winston, and shake hands with the tall, fair-haired criminal lawyer, Frank Galbally, who had taken on Burchett's cause. They were led into a room off the terminal lounge, where a mob of reporters and photographers had gathered. Galbally hovered behind the cameras; the two brothers sat side by side. Although not identical, they were recognisable as kin. Both were bespectacled, stout and of medium height. Wilfred was a shade taller, and with thinning hair; Winston was bald. Both had double-chins, in keeping with the good life, and a penchant for gourmet cuisine (often of their own making) and fine wines. Winston had been trying out a goatee beard. It gave him an intellectual air, which suited his credentials. Wilfred, in a sports jacket and tie, appeared as a seasoned reporter; Winston seemed academic, despite his safari suit. Both were self-educated. But their interests had diverged since they had travelled in Europe together in the late 1930s. Journalism had become Wilfred's preoccupation, to the exclusion of nearly all else.

Winston did not have any particular career and worked at some stage as a librarian, builder, politician (in Canberra, as a cabinet minister's secretary), and businessman. He was competent at all of them and made time for cultural outlets such as music and studying architecture. He called his unpublished diaries 'The Timid Adventurer', which he felt captured his life. It contrasted with that of his dashing younger brother, who, depending on the observer's perspective, had become Australia's most famous or infamous political son. No other politician, correspondent or observer from Australia commanded more attention on the world stage than Wilfred Burchett during the Vietnam war. He had also become the most influential journalist of the era: he was the only westerner speaking for 'the other side'; reporters had to go to him for source material on the thinking, attitudes, and positions of the key politicians, particularly Ho Chi Minh. Burchett had managed to gain positions of media power, and, from 1965 on, his articles and comments appeared in papers and magazines west and east. He acted as a consultant to the CBS network in the US, which was pushing harder than any other network for US withdrawal from the Vietnam war. Because of this Burchett had a great influence on anti-Vietnam war protesters in the US.

He could veto some journalists, such as Australians Denis Warner and Frank Robertson, and encourage others, such as Harrison Salisbury, of *The New York Times,* to report the war favourably for Hanoi. Often he would brief western reporters from all sections of the media en route to, or in, Hanoi. His procommunist views and influence during the Vietnam war also made him a figure of controversy in his own country. This ensured his media reception would be more of a confrontation than a conference.

Some of the journalists were rude and attempted to bully Burchett. The questions tested his resolute calm and politeness.

Many queries were presumptive statements. One sweaty, mop-headed scribe asked what Burchett had to say about the allegation that he had been a traitor during the Korean war. Galbally, prowling around on the outskirts of the media, looked ready to pounce as Burchett answered. 'That's preposterous! There's not a shred of evidence. No one has ever charged me with anything!'

It was a defiant response.

Reporters began to shout questions. 'You're not really an independent journalist, are you, Mr Burchett?' one called. 'You've always been writing propaganda for some communist regime!'

Galbally went as white as his hair but tripped on a TV cable as he was about to intervene. Burchett, however, was equal to the occasion.

'I am the most independent journalist in this room! I report the facts wherever I go!'

It was a debatable riposte, but it made some of them pause.

Another reporter asked about allegations that Burchett had interrogated Australian and American prisoners of war in Korea. He looked astonished but dismissed it as 'absurd'. Before he could recover, someone in the middle of the pack yelled something about his refusing to help wounded Australian POWs, just before the end of the Korean war.

'That's ridiculous!' Burchett replied. 'I helped those men. I brought them all beer and fruit!' Burchett recalled the incident well, and it seemed his answer had been accepted when a photographer, Eric Donnelly, broke in.

'You liar!' he yelled. 'I was one of those POWs! You never brought us anything!'

'I most certainly did,' Burchett replied, as he twisted in his chair. 'You must have missed out.'

That was enough for Galbally. He stepped towards Donnelly. 'How dare you speak to Mr Burchett like that!' he admonished. 'Show some respect, or you'll be in trouble. I mean it.'

The conference cooled down, and Burchett was able to field the rest of the questions with ease. Although he was surprised by the press hostility in Brisbane, he thought he had shrugged off the probes. Others watching on television were more sceptical of his performance.

The Australian Democratic Labor Party Senator Jack Kane, sixty-two, strode down the parliamentary corridor, answering questions from a persistent young female reporter as he patted his brushed-back hair. His replies were either grunts, or spoken with such rapidity that his words collided in an often unintelligible, throaty mumble. This and his blunt, laconic manner caused his many opponents to underestimate him. His friends, such as Senator Vincent Gair, whom he was visiting at the Australian federal parliamentary building in Canberra, never did.

Kane got rid of the reporter by ducking into Gair's office. The roly-poly little man in horn-rimmed glasses was watching Burchett live on television in a second news conference – at Sydney airport en route from Brisbane to Melbourne – which was more respectful than the aggressive quizzing in Brisbane. The interviewers were all political correspondents who wanted to pump him about Hanoi's attitudes to the Vietnam war. They had no wish to antagonise him. Gair raised a hand from its Buddha-like position on his stomach, half turned to welcome Kane, and in his nasally, grinding voice registered his disgust at the media's handling of Burchett.

'Commie bastard!' Kane grumbled, as he often did. Born the son of a Lithgow, NSW mine-worker, Kane (like Gair) had strong, working-class, Irish-Catholic roots. He had been thrown out of work for several months in the Depression in 1929 before he found work in the mines and as a vegetable hawker. Kane had been a good union man, and as such learned all he wanted to know about how communists operated. He first observed them in the Minority Militant Movement, which created communist cell operations through trained cadres in the mine unions. They tried to get him to join, but Kane's instinctive hate for their stealth, and his adherence to the Catholic Church's attitudes, led him to reject the overtures. The Militant Movement gained in strength after World War II, and he felt compelled to fight it.

Kane fell into politics during the Australian coal strike in the late 1940s. Because of his knowledge of the mining communities, he became a speaker for the Labor Party in support of Prime Minister Chifley's action against communists, who had caused the strike. He became a NSW Labor Party official in the early 1950s. Kane's experience was invaluable when the right-wing Catholic movement formed its own cell and cadre operations to counter communist power in the unions.

Kane was a force behind the splitting of the Democratic Labor Party from the Labor Party in the mid-1950s, which had the desired effect of keeping the extreme left out of state and federal government. The DLP set out to capture the votes of disaffected Labor voters, especially those with Catholic, working-class origins, who directed their preferences to the conservative Liberal and Country Party Coalition. The strategy worked for the next two decades and gave Kane his own kind of political power.

Gair groaned at what he saw as Burchett's easy ride with the press. Kane explained that since Burchett had issued a writ against Denis Warner, a journalist who had attacked Burchett in newspaper articles, the matter was sub judice. Gair wanted to stop Burchett getting a passport. In Gair's eyes, he was a Kremlin stooge.

Winston Burchett woke to the ring of the phone in his East Melbourne home. He looked at his watch. It was just after 3 am, and his first thought was that it was Wilfred's wife Vessa ringing from Paris. But the muffled, rasping voice on the other end of the line was local, male and menacing. 'We're gunnu blow Wilfred Burchett to bits,' he said and then hung up. Mary, his wife, asked who it was. Another death threat, he explained and decided not to wake his brother. Instead, he said, they had better employ a bodyguard for Wilfred, as Galbally had suggested. There had been death threats in the mail, with the usual paper cut-out messages, and the odd call, which had been the most frightening.

The brothers took the threats stoically and rationalised that, with all the attention that Wilfred was getting, someone was bound to attack him. With up to thirty TV, radio and newspaper interviews in the first couple of days, everyone in the country was aware that Burchett was back in Melbourne.

He had become a romantic figure, a symbol of anti-American forces in the Vietnam conflict. Burchett encouraged the attention. It was part of the way he operated. Yet even someone with his experience felt the pressures of media probes, death threats, and bodyguards. He grew restless. When

Winston suggested that they drive into the Gippsland bush to escape the city's claustrophobia, Burchett jumped at the idea. Apart from the pressures, he had been disappointed with Melbourne, which, after two decades, he found characterless.

The brothers left at dawn. Burchett was enchanted again by the vivid colours of the bush and the first red and yellow splashes of an early autumn.

Burchett talked lovingly about bush life, claiming that he never was a city person, despite living with his wife and three children in a smart Paris apartment. When Winston asked him if he would ever return to Australia to live, Burchett side-stepped the question by saying that he would at least like to have that option. He was also looking ahead and wanted his children, Peter, George and Anna, to have the right to live in Australia.

The further they drove into the bush, the more nostalgic they became. Winston remembered the time he was running a library in Ballarat in the late 1920s. He had then been conscious that his younger brother had been forced to leave school early, so he sent him six beautifully bound large volumes of the *New Popular Educator*. Burchett brightened at the memory of them. He was doing tough work on a dairy farm for one pound a week at the time he received them. He recalled absorbing outlines on philosophy, political systems, history, science, languages and journalism. He was entranced by politics and read everything from Kant and Berkeley to Marx, Engels and Lenin.

He was enthralled by the Russian Revolution, and became obsessed with learning languages – Russian, Italian, Spanish, German and French. He had little formal education and often remarked that his radicalism had developed because he had by-passed 'the system'. The books that Winston had sent him were a turning point.

Burchett turned on the car radio to hear a parliamentary broadcast. He had been forewarned that his supporters in the Labor Party would be putting pressure on the Gorton government over the elusive passport. Burchett grabbed a pad from the back seat and began making notes as the Prime Minister, John Gorton, said, 'So we feel it is sufficient to say we do not believe Mr Burchett should be provided with a passport'.

Burchett was angry, but listened as the Speaker said that the

Deputy Leader of the Opposition, Jim Cairns, had the floor.

'Is it not true that Mr Burchett asked for a court of inquiry to investigate the reasons for the denial of his passport?' Cairns asked. Gorton replied that a court of inquiry was not necessary to decide whether Burchett lived behind enemy lines during two wars. He was shouted down.

Burchett was frustrated by Gorton's response but remarked to Winston that Cairns had at least drawn the government into the open: Burchett had been ostracised because he had 'lived behind enemy lines'. On that basis, Burchett noted, every western foreign correspondent should have had his or her passport confiscated.

The Leader of the Opposition, Gough Whitlam, weighed in. 'I ask the Attorney General a question,' he said. 'Is it thought that Mr Burchett has broken any law of the Commonwealth? Alternatively, now that he is in Australia, is any investigation being undertaken to ascertain whether he has broken any law of the Commonwealth?'

Burchett punched the air. The Attorney-General, Tom Hughes, would not reply to the question but commented that he did not propose to bring any charges against Burchett. This brought 'oohs' and 'ahs' of mock surprise from the Opposition benches. The brothers were delighted. The Gorton government was backing down.

3. Krotkov Goes Public

The Burchett passport controversy became an international issue as famous names on the left, including Bertrand Russell, Simone de Beauvoir, James Cameron, Graham Greene, Melina Mercouri, Jane Fonda, Arthur Miller, Jean-Paul Sartre and Norman Mailer, signed a petition supporting his request for the document. The affair thrust him further into world headlines at a time when he already had a high profile.

By 1970, America's right-wing forces began to search for ways to hold the tide of opinion against US involvement in the Vietnam war as it threatened to weaken the US government's resolve to fight on against the North Vietnamese. Every anti-communist weapon had to be used, and a formidable one emerged with the defection to the West of KGB agent Yuri Krotkov. He was asked to give evidence to a US Senate sub-committee.

When Krotkov, slender and tall, with a shock of dark brown

hair greying at the temples, entered the conference room in the Old Senate Office Building, Washington DC, there was silence. The fifty-year-old defector was urbane, yet he could not hide his nerves. He was about to spill his espionage experiences to the world.

He feared he would more than ever be a marked man; the restrictions on his CIA-protected existence would be doubled. Krotkov sat at a long table flanked by his lawyer and Ed Hunter, an adviser and former CIA agent. He faced the committee led by the presiding senator, Strom Thurmond, and chief counsel, Senator J.G. Sourwine.

Krotkov was one of the most important agents ever to defect to the West. He had already gone through an exhaustive grilling by British Intelligence before being passed on to the CIA. His evidence had been checked and counter-checked. Krotkov had been stamped ready for public consumption.

According to the espionage expert John Barron, and author of *KGB: The Secret Work of Soviet Secret Agents,* his great specialty had been setting up sexual bait for foreign ambassadors so that they could be compromised into betraying their countries. Since World War II he had tried to lure scores of foreign representatives and journalists into traps – including diplomats from America, Australia, England, Canada, France, India, Mexico, Pakistan and Yugoslavia.

Krotkov always considered himself a KGB part-timer. He was a battling playwright, film script-writer and novelist, who always yearned for the freedom to express himself on paper.

Because of his easy charm and good looks, Krotkov was asked by the KGB to find attractive women whom it could use to seduce and blackmail foreigners. He found budding Russian actresses from his connections with Soviet theatre and cinema to whom he was able offer better roles, money, fine western clothes, and a high life they would never have known in Soviet society unless they reached the top of their profession. An extra for the suave young Krotkov was a chance to seduce these young women himself, all in the interests of the state. He became a state police pimp and this activity subsidised him as a playwright.

Krotkov's espionage work was so successful that his advance was rapid. He made pimping a more valuable business than any Madame Claude. Where the Soviet espionage forces had been known for their brilliant recruiting of western agents from the 1930s on ideological grounds, Krotkov added a new dimension to the KGB's reputation as the best spy outfit in the world.

Krotkov's slide into the murky world of the Soviet Secret Police began in 1936 when his father, an artist, painted a portrait of Lavrenti Beria, who was then head of the Communist Party in Georgia. It was a brilliant, if flattering likeness of Stalin's murderous henchman. Beria loved it so much that when Stalin promoted him to head of State Security, copies of the portrait were hung in every state police office throughout the Soviet Union. Beria asked Krotkov's father to paint many of his cronies in Security, and even suggested that Stalin sit for a portrait. Stalin refused because he preferred enlarged photos that could be air-brushed to make him look attractive.

Krotkov arrived in Moscow to study literature, and at once took advantage of his parents' connections in Security. During the war, the KGB's predecessor, the MGB, got him a job as a staff journalist at the Tass news agency, and later as a news producer at Radio Moscow, where he also wrote drama scripts. His journalism brought him in contact with foreign correspondents, who were impressed by his cultured style and fair ability in several languages.

After World War II, he became a secret agent but with far more than the usual freedoms because of his parents' links to Beria. He was posted to Berlin in 1947 and quickly became the person most western media and press people sought for information about Russia. It was here that he met Wilfred Burchett.

The senators on the small committee facing Krotkov were well aware of his clandestine influence in the diplomatic world, and they were ready for him.

The chief counsel, J.G. Sourwine, began a long, sometimes banal, often fascinating, investigation. The senate sub-committee was alert to Krotkov's evidence about the French Ambassador to the Soviet Union in the late 1950s and early 1960s, Maurice Dejean. Sourwine asked Krotkov to spell out how he compromised the ambassador using 'swallows', or state prostitutes. The senators had trouble keeping straight faces, such were the erotic details of the case. At one point, Krotkov was asked if the ambassador fell into the so-called honey trap easily. Before replying, he put a hand over his microphone and quietly consulted the rotund Ed Hunter. The French ambassador was a cultured, intelligent man, Krotkov remarked, and the KGB had to work hard by putting the best looking young women in Russia in front of him.

'Eventually he was cornered,' Krotkov remarked deadpan, in his slight Russian accent. 'After all, the ambassador was French...'

On the third day, the hearing got to the business end of Krotkov's vital testimony, when Sourwine told him to put on the record all he knew about Wilfred Burchett. Krotkov whispered an aside to Hunter and his lawyer and sighed.

'Okay, I'll do that,' he said. He seemed reluctant, and the tension returned to his face. 'I met him in Germany in 1947 when I went there by order of the KGB to "sell myself" to the British Intelligence Service. I was deputy to the Chief of the Bureau of Information of the Soviet Military Government in Berlin.'

Still anxious, Krotkov lit a cigarette.

'Burchett tried to sell himself to the Soviet side. He probably took me for an intermediary, if not an outright buyer.'

'Are you saying that Burchett was offering to act as an agent?'

'He gave us accurate and valuable information,' Krotkov said, nodding, 'however, the KGB, at the beginning, didn't want me to get involved with him. They had some information about him that wasn't positive from their point of view. The KGB told me that he probably even talked Russian.'

Sourwine frowned, and Krotkov added: 'They said he had been in Russia, in Siberia, and that he worked for the Soviet Intourist Agency – the travel agency – which he joined in London in 1937 for a time. Later on, however, the KGB bosses changed their minds because of how he behaved.'

Sourwine wanted an example.

'He warned us to be careful of a Mr Gray, who worked for the American Secret Service. Burchett also told us about a member of the British Admiralty who flew to Berlin specifically to ask Burchett about his visit to Peenemunde, the

German rocket installation, where Vee 2 rockets were made.'
(Burchett had been adamant that he had seen the installation
blown up. The man from the Admiralty quizzed Burchett
about it, because the west had been sceptical that the Russians
would destroy it.)

Krotkov went on about Burchett's Christian name: whether
it was Peter – the name he answered to for years – or Wilfred
because of a mix-up in *Daily Express* by-lines during the war.

Krotkov began to relax once more. He took off his jacket
and loosened his tie.

'Burchett invited me to a party in Berlin,' Krotkov said, 'and
introduced me to his father who had come from Australia – a
very nice old gentleman with snow-white hair. He was a very
active man, who in conversation openly declared his communist ideas.'

He explained how he lost contact with Burchett but heard
about his books, articles and exploits in Korea, Vietnam
and China.

'So when did you see Burchett again?' Sourwine asked.

'In 1956,' Krotkov said. 'I got a call from him in Moscow.
I checked with my KGB bosses and was told to meet him. I
went to his hotel, the Savoy. He had dinner at the Poplavok restaurant in Khimki Harbour. He told me he was a member of the
Australian Communist Party, a fact he had to keep secret,
however, since his assignments were of an illegal nature.
Burchett told me he had worked in Korea, where his expenses
were paid by the Chinese Communist Party. He was very close
to Chou En Lai, the premier of the Chinese People's Republic.
His job, in part, was to collect information from foreign correspondents. At the time of our meeting in 1956, all his
expenses were met by the Vietnamese Communist Party, by Ho
Chi Minh. And he mentioned that he was close to Ho Chi Minh.
Burchett told me that he visited him many times.'

The committee members exchanged glances. Sourwine
asked Krotkov to elaborate.

'Ho gave him a house, a car, and a secretary in Hanoi. He was
equipped very beautifully by the Vietnamese Communist
Party. He told me he went as Ho's personal secret envoy to the
communist groups in the Pathet-Lao. He gave hints that he
wanted to be in Moscow on the same terms as he had been in
China and Vietnam. He wanted money from the Soviet

Communist Party. To show how valuable a person he was, he also spoke of his relationship with Margeurite Higgins, an American correspondent. He said he was in very close intimate relations with her. He said she even wanted to marry him. She eventually married an American Air Force General. Burchett said we could use this possibility. But he added that he might be arrested in the States.'

Krotkov reached for a glass of water. After sipping it, he spoke of Burchett's efforts to ingratiate himself with the KGB in Moscow by gathering vital intelligence in troublespots in Eastern Europe.

'Next time we met in Moscow, Burchett gave me some confidential information about the situation in Eastern Europe, which he considered alarming. There was considerable unrest in Poland and Hungary. He gave valuable intelligence. It proved remarkably valid, because shortly after our talk, Poznan rose in revolt, and the Hungarian Revolution broke out. I asked Burchett to have dinner with me at the Kolass restaurant. The KGB ordered me to have two other KGB men there. I was asked by the KGB to tell Burchett he could move to Moscow, and that he would receive the necessary finance.'

Krotkov mentioned some hitches in Burchett's move. There was a change in KGB bosses, and the new ones said they didn't need Burchett.

'Burchett said he would go and see a representative of the Australian Communist Party,' Krotkov said, 'Representatives were in Moscow because it was the time of the Soviet Communist Party Congress. After his meeting with them – I don't know how it happened, he did it himself – everything was all right, and the KGB gave him a good flat, and, well, I guess, the necessary money.'

Thurmond called for an afternoon break. Krotkov put on his coat.

'Later I learned from Kartsev, his eventual KGB control,' he added as he stood, 'that they together organised some important operations. They called to London. They expected that someone would come from London to Moscow. Burchett and Kartsev discussed how to meet him.'

As the committee began to leave the hearing room, Ed Hunter took Krotkov aside.

'Who was this "someone" coming to Moscow?' Hunter

asked, 'an espionage agent or what?'

'That is what I don't know exactly,' Krotkov shrugged. 'I only heard some words from Kartsev.'

'It would have been too late for the two British spies, Burgess and Maclean,' Hunter said. 'They came to Moscow in 1951. When was this approximately?'

'Early 1960s.'

'Blake or Philby, perhaps,' Hunter said, referring to other British agents. 'Then again it may have been something more political. I think he helped get Harold Macmillan to visit Moscow in 1959.' Hunter added, 'You should put a little more about this on the record.'

Six months after Burchett returned to his Paris base, his three children were issued with passports by the Australian Embassy. Burchett saw this as a sop to Australian public opinion, and another rebuff in his fifteen-year battle to get an Australian passport. Without it he could not operate nearly as freely as he would have liked: only his powerful friends in the French left allowed him access to France. And he had the irksome task of renewing a temporary visitor's permit every three months. A passport would allow him to obtain a residence permit that was valid for one year.

Burchett's reasons for being in Paris were dwindling as the peace talks between the North Vietnamese and the Americans bogged down. No passport was a further irritation. He wanted to be able to move abroad, especially to the US. His cumbersome North Vietnamese Laissez Passez document and a Cuban passport, organised for him by Castro because of 'services rendered' to Cuba, did not endear him to US Immigration.

Vince Gair stood up in the front bench of the DLP ranks in the Senate and rocked on his heels. After clearing his throat, he began, 'Is the government aware that a defector from the Soviet Secret Police has given testimony to a United States Senate committee that an Australian, Wilfred Burchett, had been signed up by the KGB...'.

His words sent the chamber into uproar. Gair had to repeat himself and shout above the heckling: '...signed up by the

KGB – after having worked as a paid agent for the Chinese and North Vietnamese governments!'

Burchett's Labor supporters chorused, 'Witch-hunt, witch-hunt.' 'A slander on our greatest journalist,' one Labor Senator yelled. To which a Liberal replied: 'Our greatest *red* journo for sure!'

The Speaker had trouble restoring order before the acting Minister for Foreign Affairs was able to reply that the government was aware that Krotkov's testimony referred to Burchett. Several Labor senators attempted to howl down Gair by saying that the testimony of a 'KGB agent and pimp' should not be on the Senate record. After several interjections, Gair managed to have it read.

The DLP had been delighted to receive a transcript of the US Senate sub-committee hearing. Gair, Kane and the rest of the DLP hierarchy felt that they had found 'a smoking gun'. They were determined to ruin Burchett with it.

Australia's papers steered clear of reporting Gair's reading of the Krotkov testimony to the Senate. Writs had already been served on Denis Warner and the Melbourne *Herald* for an article that Warner had written on Burchett, and further reporting on him was subjudice.

Peter Samuel of *The Australian*, however, picked up on the Krotkov testimony and wrote an article for the DLP magazine *Focus*. It was headed 'The Burchett Revelations', and it said, in part: 'Readers of the nation's newspapers could be pardoned for suspecting a conspiracy of silence on Senator Gair's questions on the evidence of a defector from the Soviet KGB concerning an Australian journalist, Wilfred Burchett.'

Samuel went on to mention the key points of Krotkov's testimony and, apart from mentioning Burchett, named the Australian Communist Party delegates who happened to be in Moscow when Burchett met Krotkov, whom he said were Alec Robertson and Ted Hill. Samuel finished with the most contentious comment in the article when he claimed that Burchett 'proposed the blackmail of an American Air Force General with whose wife (Maggie Higgins) he had a "very close intimate relationship" '.

A milkman in Greenwich, North Sydney, who delivered to

the Robertsons, Alec and Mavis, asked her if her husband was a communist who had visited Russia. 'Yes, he was a communist,' she replied, and, yes, he had been in Russia. But Mavis was adamant that her husband was not the man referred to in the *Focus* article.

4. Mistaken Identity

Alec Robertson was stunned by the *Focus* article linking him to the KGB. A communist journalist all his working life, he was now editor of *Tribune,* the Australian Communist Party's newspaper. Robertson had also been a good friend of Wilfred Burchett since his 1950 visit, when Robertson had been a member of the National Executive of the Australian Peace Council. But the *Focus* article's assertion that he had helped Burchett join the KGB in 1958 was a link that Robertson could not ignore. His friends at the *Tribune*, and other communists, urged him to sue the DLP. Their views fortified his instincts, but he needed well-informed opinions before he rushed to court. Action would be costly, and he was not rich. Robertson was also concerned about the word of a communist standing up in court, particularly as his political ideology would be at issue. The right man to consult was Clive Evatt, one of Australia's cleverest and most flamboyant QCs, whose personal politics brought him close to Robertson. In a conservative profession, his shoulder length white hair and beguiling, cheeky humour added to a court-room act that had put him in demand at the bar.

Evatt had held several posts as a NSW Cabinet Minister between 1939 and 1959, when he lost his parliamentary seat. Evatt had always claimed that he was a 'Marxist-Leninist at heart', and his lengthy presidency of the Australian-Russian Society confirmed this, and led to his political downfall in April 1954, when he was forced to resign from the Cabinet. Evatt was a victim of the ideological clash that split the Labor movement across the country. It also ended the chances of his brother, Dr Herbert Evatt, becoming Prime Minister. Clive Evatt bitterly resented people like Kane and the DLP for their part in the Evatt family's political fortunes.

When Robertson drove to the Evatt family's retreat in the Blue Mountains, west of Sydney, he was surprised by the barrister's immediate support for a defamation action. What's more, he was willing to act for him. He promised Robertson that he would win him a handsome settlement and advised him to get a solicitor to sue the DLP for $100,000. Roy Turner was the solicitor he had in mind. And Robertson agreed.

Turner was the head of one of Sydney's most successful law firms, which specialised in several areas, including defamation and union work. He had clout. Turner had been a close friend of Robertson's since the time they served in the Australian Air Force in World War II. Both had fought against the Japanese in New Guinea. Turner, a redhead in his early fifties, invited Robertson to lunch in Pitt Street, not far from the NSW Parliament, to discuss the possible action. Despite his gregariousness, Turner was able to switch to an air of confidentiality. He punctuated his points with humorous and telling aphorisms, and quoted from the Bible, Shakespeare or Lenin with ease at every opportunity.

They ordered their food and wine. Robertson's shallow breathing made him cough and wheeze, and there was no hiding his chronic asthma. Turner was far more circumspect than the ebullient Evatt about suing, even before he had read the *Focus* article. Robertson took a copy from a battered briefcase, and Turner took a few moments to read it. He thought it a low piece of red-baiting journalism, and possibly defamatory. The problem arose in trying to convince an unsympathetic jury. Turner pointed out that the plaintiff invariably ended up on trial. He cited the case of Oscar Wilde, who sued the Marquis of Queensberry for defamation when he left a note at their exclusive London club that said Wilde had been 'posing as a sodomite'. Wilde's private life was exposed in court. He lost the case.

In the mind of the average all-male Sydney jury, Turner remarked, there was only one thing worse than being homosexual and that was being a communist.

'You end up in the box defending your life,' Turner said. 'The onus is on the defendant's counsel to show that you have no reputation to be defamed in the first place. You're a well-known communist. What's the reaction going to be from a conservative judge and jury, and a hostile press?'

Robertson became more adamant. He leaned forward, lowered his voice and read him the relevant passage he considered was damaging: 'Burchett wanted to be an accredited journalist in Moscow but needed to be maintained by the Soviet Party. He asked for an introduction to people who could put him on the KGB payroll. The KGB hesitated a while. Finally the deal was clinched by some visiting Australian Communist Party delegates...'

Robertson paused and looked up at Turner. 'Understood to be Alec Robertson, and none other than Ted Hill.'

Robertson claimed that he was not in Moscow in 1957. It was not him. Peter Samuel had mistaken Alec for Eddie Robertson from South Australia, who had been in the Communist Party and had spent a year in Moscow in the late 1950s after visiting China. Eddie Robertson died in 1962.

That gave Turner pause. He reached across the table and squeezed Robertson's forearm. Could he prove that he wasn't in Moscow at that time? Could he show it was a case of mistaken identity? Robertson was sure he could. He still had his passport, and he had evidence from his employer at the *Tribune*. He was also able to prove that he had been at an Australian Communist Party Congress in Adelaide when Burchett was supposed to have been asking him for help in Moscow. Turner squinted. There was only one sure thing in this kind of litigation and that was mistaken identity. Turner promised to take on the case.

Robertson ordered champagne. To hell with his writing

that afternoon, and his asthma. With two of the best legal people in the land battling for him, his chances had to be excellent.

Evatt had said that the DLP and whoever was responsible for the magazine would be sued. He told Robertson that Jack Kane was the editor. Robertson wondered if they would try to settle out of court. Turner was doubtful, even if he presented a watertight case. He thought Kane was the most underestimated politician in the country. He would fight and take it to court.

5. The Suit Fits

Clive Evatt was at his oratorical, flowing best in *Robertson* v. *Kane*. He had a case, a man, and a political cause to fight, and he put all his decades of experience into it. There was not a twitch from the four-man jury, the judge, or Kane's table during Evatt's opening address:

'So gentlemen of the jury, I put it to you: here we have a fine Australian, a man who fought in the Airforce at considerable risk to life and limb during the Second World War, for his country. For you and for me. *(Pause.)* The plaintiff is a respected professional journalist with a reputation for excellent reporting and accuracy. Is there any wonder that this heinous and defamatory reference has caused this man much suffering? And as the suit says, gentlemen, physical suffering too. For this courageous man has been a chronic asthma sufferer since fighting for his country, nearly thirty years ago. I ask you, gentlemen of the jury, consider how you would feel to be linked so viciously to the KGB, the Soviet Secret Police

– a hated, murderous, clandestine foreign force.'

Evatt produced an article from the October 1971 issue of *Focus* (the edition before the Burchett article), which described the KGB as 'dedicated to subversion and espionage overseas', 'latest in a long line of secret police organisations'. The *Focus* article also noted that the KGB was responsible for arbitrary arrests and trumped-up trials of such people as the writers Sinyavsky and Daniel. Evatt quoted from it, saying, 'Soviet Secret Police provide the palace guards for the ruling group in the Kremlin. They run the political prisons…the most notorious secret police'.

Evatt paused to sip a glass of water. With his back to the jury, he winked at Robertson. Kane exchanged glances with his barristers, Douglas Milne, QC, and John Traill. Evatt addressed the jury again:

'Now, gentlemen, the article in question refers to the wrong person. I repeat, the wrong person! An "Alec Robertson" of the Communist Party was the target of the article. The defendant did not mean just any Alec Robertson, but the one here today, so rightly seeking damages!'

The judge called for a lunch recess just as Evatt was in full swing. In Milne's chambers, Kane told his counsel to make an offer to settle. With Evatt in that form, Kane knew he had no chance. Better to cut the losses than to take another barrage after the break. After some further concessions, a jubilant Robertson in Evatt's chambers took the old barrister's advice and accepted a fair 'package' offer.

Robertson wrote to Burchett in Paris: 'Kane tossed the towel in a couple of hours after my case opened against him. They had been making a series of offers of private settlements for weeks, beginning at a miserable $2,000, all of which were rejected out of hand. On the morning of the case, 12 June (1972), they rang Clive Evatt in Chambers and offered $7,500, which was to include costs of court, so that meant their real offer was $5,000. This was also rejected.

'In court, with the four man jury waiting outside, there was an argument about a subpoena of DLP documents, and also, more significantly, an application by Kane for further adjournment because in the preceeding few days he had had some "unfavourable" publicity in the press over alleged free electoral advertising for the DLP in Frank Packer's media. This was rejected by the judge. Then Clive did his opening address and had nearly finished it when lunch came. During lunch, Kane's side rang us in Clive's Chambers, renewing the earlier offer. Rejected again, they approached us just before the resumption and offered a retraction in court by Kane, a verdict recorded for me, and an "undisclosed" settlement of costs, plus a $10,000 payment by them.'

Robertson went on to encourage Burchett to sue and advised him that his position could be improved by coming back to Australia. Burchett wrote to Winston about Robertson's success, and it was clear that he was toying with the idea of taking legal action. But he was still cautious. He received a call from Evatt, who said he should sue Kane because it would be an 'open and shut case'. Burchett was tempted, but was cautioned by his wife, who saw herself as his editor and critic; she was against court action in Australia. Despite the fact that the Australian government had given the children passports as a sop to the pressure Burchett applied in 1970, she felt the Australian court system could not be trusted.

A few months before the Australian federal election of December 1972, Evatt visited Burchett in Paris. The weather was fine, and, as Vessa, herself a journalist, was in Sofia on business, they decided to take a coffee in Boulevard Montparnasse not far from Burchett's apartment. They chose a cafe called Le Select where they could catch the late afternoon sun and watch the passing parade. Evatt, in his early seventies and slowing down a little, was enjoying himself. He had come to persuade Burchett to return to Australia to sue Kane, but he was in no hurry. He was too old to rush things.

Burchett pointed out the cafe opposite, La Coupole, a haunt of Jean-Paul Sartre. Burchett occasionally went there, but Sartre had been frequenting the elegant cafe for forty-five years. Burchett remarked that Yuri Krotkov had accused Sartre and the American economist and writer Kenneth Galbraith of being KGB agents. Evatt corrected him. Krotkov had actually said that these two had been used unwittingly by the KGB, because they were sympathetic to socialist aspirations.

There was a distinction here because Krotkov had been specific when he accused Burchett of being a KGB agent. It would be Evatt's aim in court to demonstrate that Burchett was no more a KGB agent than Sartre or Galbraith. Once that was established, Evatt said he would demonstrate to the court that none of these celebrated free-thinkers had ever been used by anyone, let alone the KGB.

While Burchett pondered this, Evatt said he was long an admirer of Sartre and Simone de Beauvoir. Burchett said he had known them since the 1950s, and that he and Vessa liked them both, particularly de Beauvoir. Sartre often quizzed him about the Vietnam war, he said, and wanted him to write something 'deep and philosophical' about it. This amused Burchett. He was a reporter and didn't have the time, he said, to 'sit around Paris cafes getting existential', although he was an atheist. He half-jokingly asked Evatt what philosophers did for a living because his son Peter was studying to be one, and it was costing a lot of money.

Evatt didn't have an answer and instead expressed concern that he might be wasting Burchett's precious writing time. Burchett assured him that he wanted the meeting. Besides, he had done his 5,000 word quota for the day. He usually started the day about four (today he had begun at two so he could spend more time with his guest) by taking notes on various radio broadcasts in Europe. He would then write until ten or eleven in the morning. The papers would be read, and followed by lunch, then afternoon appointments.

A late, two hour siesta would equip him for the rest of the evening. Burchett was usually in bed by ten. It was this discipline that led to his producing thirty books, scores of documentary films and innumerable articles over thirty years. The productivity and dedication stunned Evatt, but Burchett shrugged it off as a 'compulsion, like boozing'. He raised a glass of cool Chablis in salute and recited one of his favorite lines from Hemingway: 'Wine for pleasure, beer for thirst, whisky for work.' Evatt commented that Burchett would have to consume a great deal of whisky to match his word production.

Burchett drove his guest in his late model Volvo to the apartment, took his nap, and later cooked a superb *canard à l'orange,* helped by several bottles of a fine vintage Bordeaux. After the meal they discussed business. Cognac glass in one hand, and pointing with the other, Evatt suggested that Kane should be sued for a million dollars. Burchett made light of the figure, but Evatt persisted. He could not lose, he said. Gough Whitlam was going to put the federal Labor Party into power for the first time in twenty-three years. All the polls were saying it. Evatt claimed that NSW, the State with the largest number of federal parliamentary seats, was going to back Whitlam. Burchett asked about Victoria, his home state. It had never supported Labor federally. Evatt said that he had learned it authoritatively that the Melbourne *Age,* Victoria's most influential paper, would back Labor. Burchett didn't believe it. The conservative, Sydney-based Fairfax group owned the *Age.* Surely it wouldn't let it swing left? Evatt suggested Burchett was out of touch. *The Age's* editor, Graham Perkin, liked Whitlam and thought that the Liberal Prime Minister, Billy McMahon, would make a good haberdasher.

Burchett was excited by the prospect of a Labor victory. If *The Age* did support Whitlam, the party could take Victoria, giving it the two biggest states and certain victory.

Evatt got to the point. The climate would be right for Burchett's litigation against the DLP and Jack Kane. Burchett was excited but still wary. Nevertheless, when he remarked that suits were expensive, Evatt was encouraged. Turner and he were willing to offer their services free, if, by the remotest possibility, the case were lost. Furthermore, there were plenty of people in both the Labor Party and the Communist Party who were ready to back Burchett. He was a cause celebre!

Burchett noted that Evatt seemed keen to 'get Kane', and he knew why. Kane had been the nemesis of the left for twenty years. By forming the DLP as a breakaway group from Labor, Kane and Co. had stopped Clive's brother, Herbert (Doc) Evatt, from becoming Prime Minister. Defeating Kane in a big court case would settle old scores, Evatt felt. It would also herald a new small 'l' liberal, progressive era in Australian politics. Pressing his hard-sell, Evatt predicted that a loss for Kane would ensure that the DLP was destroyed as a political force, especially if it had to part with a million dollars.

Burchett was attracted by the prospect. He poured more cognac, and Evatt spoke of his domino theory. The first move would be successful litigation against Kane and the DLP. Then Denis Warner and the Melbourne *Herald* would be taken to court to contest Burchett's writ. Evatt thought that they would probably settle out of court for another million. When they were dealt with, the idea would be to pursue Rupert Murdoch and the Packers who, according to Evatt, had all defamed Burchett over the past two decades.

Burchett was pleased but adamant that his first priority was to clear his name. Evatt had inspired him, but he still would not commit himself to litigation.

Burchett's hopes lifted when Evatt's prediction of a Labor victory at the polls on 2 December 1972 came true. Less than forty-eight hours later, he received a phone call from Australia's Ambassador to France, Alan Renouf.

'I have instructions from the new Prime Minister's office,' he said. 'You are to be issued with a passport immediately.'

Burchett could hardly contain his excitement as Renouf added cheerfully, 'I am personally happy to bring you the good news. Congratulations and good luck.'

Burchett's mind turned to the chat with Evatt three months earlier. This was the signal that the time was right for legal action.

The next day he went to the Australian Embassy to pick up the slim blue booklet with the golden kangaroo and emu embossed on the cover. An official apologised for stamping it 'Not Valid For North Vietnam'. Burchett told him that he would have refused the passport with such an ignominious mark had the Liberals still been in power. But he was confident that Whitlam would change Australia's relationship with the north. Perhaps it would have been better if it had been stamped, 'Not Valid For South Vietnam', he said. Many Australian and Vietnamese lives would have been saved, and Australia's standing in Asia would have improved.

Burchett fondled the document and waved it to photographers as he walked out of the Embassy. It was finally his after seventeen years. No more pleading with mates in the press to intercede with Australian consular officials in foreign capitals. No more petitions or confrontations. No more problems about moving between ports, east and west, particularly his country of birth. His first act would be to change his status in France to obtain a yearly residential permit.

By denying Burchett a passport, successive Australian prime ministers from Robert Menzies to William McMahon had made Burchett's life as difficult as possible for seventeen years. They had succeeded in taking him out of circulation as an international journalist until the Vietnam war dominated world news in the mid-1960s. By then, Burchett was unstoppable, and, despite not having a passport, he was still able to see people such as the US Secretary of State, Henry Kissinger.

This visit by Burchett was seen as sacrilege by some. John Ashbrook of Ohio, who challenged Richard Nixon as presidential candidate in the 1972 Republican primaries, told Congress on 17 December 1971: 'Wilfred Burchett, deprived of a passport by his native Australia because of his aid to the enemy during the Korean War...has just been secretly welcomed into the White House offices for consultation. This constitutes unparalleled desecration of the White House...an obscene act...No agent of the President, indeed no President, has the right to desecrate the White House in this manner. Burchett was travelling on a Red Cuban passport. He also travels on North Vietnamese and Cambodian passports. Such incriminating documentation focuses attention on his virtual outlaw status in Australia and is an obstacle to his clandestine operations.'

Burchett had Whitlam to thank for wiping out these attacks. The new prime minister agreed with many of Burchett's views on international affairs, notably on South-East Asia. But in restoring Burchett's passport, he demonstrated the split in Australian opinion. The left, represented by the Labor Party, admired Burchett and his writings. The right, represented by the Liberal/Country Party coalition, saw him as a traitor for his propaganda on behalf of communist countries.

Burchett hoped that the return of his passport was symbolic of a new era in Australian foreign policy. Two weeks after receiving his new passport, he wrote in *Nation Review*: 'For too long the image most Asians have had of us is that of mercenaries jumping into every occasion to suppress Asian independence movements at someone else's bidding, and in defence of someone else's interests.

'Once the Vietnam war is ended, left of centre neutralist governments will emerge in South Vietnam, Cambodia and Laos, and probably a centrist-neutralist government in

Thailand. These countries will form with their neighbours a vast neutral belt almost everywhere south of the Himalayas from the Pacific Ocean to the Persian Gulf.'

He finished the article with a reminder to the Whitlam government, especially the Minister for Foreign Affairs, Dr Jim Cairns, that he was ready to help: 'If my passport and type-writer can serve to promote close and friendly relations with our Asian neighbours, then my forced exile in some of those countries will be seen to have had its positive side.'

Burchett returned to Australia in February 1973 for a much publicised lecture tour. His lectures drew him closer to the Whitlam government's policies. He told audiences in several cities that Australia's foreign policy could not be independent while big sectors of the economy were controlled by other powers, namely the UK, the US and Japan. These three owned about ten billion dollars of investment in Australia.

'Those super-patriots who did their best to stop me coming back to be heard here are precisely the ones who have been most active in selling off the country's natural resources,' he said. Burchett spoke of his vision of a vast, politically neutral zone from the Suez to the Pacific, and generally of the themes the Whitlam government was playing that would appeal to a new, stirring nationalism. He also raised the spectre of foreign military bases on Australian soil, which he had railed against on his visit in 1950. Then he had warned about being involved with the US and had urged a neutral path for Australia. This time, he referred publicly to the bases of 'foreign powers', a reference that may have eluded some of his audiences. In private, with close friends, he spoke of his concern for the US bases at Pine Gap near Alice Springs, Nurrungar in South Australia, and the North West Shelf. Burchett showed a remark-able interest in the bases and told a journalist friend that he did not believe the bases were simply space research centres as the Australian government claimed. Burchett said his own re-search had shown that the bases were being used by the Americans to spy on the rest of the world. He worried that this could make Australia a nuclear target and urged contacts in the Whitlam government to have the bases shut down. Burchett noticed a far more sympathetic response to his pronounce-ments about foreign matters than before. This fitted what Evatt, Robertson and other communists had been advising him. The timing was right for litigation against the nation's right-wing establishment and media. Alec Robertson introduced Burchett to Roy Turner, and a one million dollar defamation writ was served on Jack Kane.

Kane guessed what the long white envelope from Turner's office contained before he opened it, but it did little to soften the blow dealt by the frightening legal jargon in the writ. By Statement of Claim No. 193 of 1973, Burchett was suing Kane for a million dollars. The writ complained about the *Focus* article published sixteen months earlier, including the photograph in it, which had the caption, 'Wilfred Burchett...very experienced in espionage'. Burchett claimed that as a result of the article he had been 'brought into public hatred, ridicule and contempt'. He had also been 'injured in his credit, reputation and circumstances, and in his profession', and had 'suffered great pain of body and mind'. Kane hurried to his solicitor John O'Neill, the short, robust head of the Sydney law firm Murphy and Maloney, who allayed his fears. Over coffee and cigars in his smart Pitt Street offices, O'Neill pointed out that Kane was in a far better position with the Burchett writ than the one served on him by Robertson.

Despite O'Neill's suggestion that it might be a bluff, Kane's political antennae told him that Burchett would go through with it. The two men drafted a counter-strategy. Kane, now a senator, would use the Senate to start an official inquiry into Burchett's activities. He would contact Denis Warner, who had warded off a similar writ from Burchett by digging up damaging information on him, and he would again engage his friend John Traill, the barrister who had helped in representing him in the Robertson case. Kane and O'Neill regarded him as the best and most sympathetic counsel available. O'Neill told Kane he could claim the *Focus* article was a fair report of Parliament. It could be defended under 'qualified privilege' if the subject matter was published for discussion 'in the public interest', and if it was 'fair comment'. O'Neill, however, felt that this might not be strong enough. Kane would have a better chance of winning if he could present evidence of the truth of the statements in the article. That would give him a defence based on truth and public benefit. But, to prepare this, Kane would need to have Krotkov to give evidence under oath. Otherwise, it would not stand up in an Australian court.

While Burchett romped the country basking in his triumph over his political enemies, Kane rushed to head off the writ. He was stunned by a series of events that made him think there was a conspiracy against him. Kane began pushing for a Senate inquiry and found that a debate into whether it should be held would be supported by the DLP, the Independents and many Liberals. Together this group had a slim majority over the Labor Party in the Senate.

The night of the debate, DLP leader Vince Gair asked Kane to be his representative at a Government House reception. Kane agreed to go because he thought he had secured sufficient numbers to ensure an inquiry. At the reception, Kane bumped into Lionel Murphy, the federal Attorney-General and Labor's Senate leader. Murphy was unusually friendly to Kane as they engaged in small talk for several minutes. Kane became suspicious. Murphy and he were ideological enemies, and the Labor leader had never been friendly to him before. An hour later, Kane received an urgent message from Gair asking him to attend the late-night Senate session. He was losing the debate. Murphy had quietly changed the minds of enough Independent and Liberal senators to win. By the time Kane arrived at the chamber, it was all over. There would not be any official probe into Burchett's career.

Soon after that defeat, Kane asked his solicitors to subpoena ASIO (Australian Intelligence) files on Burchett. By coincidence, Murphy had just ordered Commonwealth Police to raid ASIO's offices and secure files, reported to be on Croatian political extremists, which had been withheld from the Attorney-General's Department. Only days after this unprecedented event, ASIO informed Kane's solicitors that it had only one item available to him in its Burchett file. At the same time, Burchett made newspaper headlines with a lecture tour that criticised ASIO.

'ASIO's first loyalty appeared to be providing information to a certain foreign power,' he told Adelaide audiences, which was again a thinly veiled reference to the US. Commenting on Murphy's raid, Burchett said, 'It seems that was the only way he could get the information,' and added, 'I don't think there is a need for anything like ASIO, if there are no wars. I am against all secret agent groups.'

Understandably, Kane's advisers wondered if Murphy could have taken Burchett's file in the raid in order to deprive Kane of vital evidence. O'Neill, whom Kane listened to most closely, didn't think so, but admitted that the string of events was amazingly coincidental. They prompted Kane to redouble his efforts to build a strong defence. He rang Denis Warner, one of Burchett's main antagonists for over twenty years.

Warner, like Burchett, was a prolific writer of books and articles, who had opted to be a roving foreign journalist. But while Burchett was obsessively anti-American, Warner believed in a strong US–Australian alliance. His most successful book was *The Last Confucian,* which was a warning to the US about the problems of getting involved in a war in Vietnam. Since 1957, Warner had covered all major events in South-East Asia, including the Vietnam war, the Indonesian confrontation with Malaya, and the conclusion of the Sukarno regime in Indonesia. He was in that small league of correspondents who were prepared to take risks to get a story.

Warner was sympathetic to Kane's predicament, because of Burchett's writ against him too. Kane wanted to know how he had kept Burchett from taking him to court. Warner explained that, four years ago, he and the Melbourne *Herald* had called on all their best contacts in Washington DC. Warner's 'defence', however, had not been without its problems. The Australian Department of Foreign Affairs, run then by William McMahon, had objected to Warner's and the *Herald*'s legal representative, Bernie Teague, acting like a 'state within a state' in their plan to approach the American government for help. Warner, showing a tough streak, got through to Prime Minister John Gorton and complained about the department's block.

Gorton over-ruled McMahon. Warner and Teague were able to reach people such as Henry Kissinger's deputy, Colonel Alexander Haig. He was helpful in ensuring that important official files were opened to them, including those from the National Security Council, the CIA, Defence and State Departments. Warner told Kane that when Burchett learnt of their research in the US he decided to put the writ on hold. Yet the court action could be executed at any time. The threat hung over Warner like a black cloud, and that caused him to pledge as much help as possible to Kane. If Kane was to lose a legal battle with Burchett, Warner knew he would be in a vulnerable position.

In the year before the trial, the *Burchett* v. *Kane* battle shaped up as a classic ideological fight. On the hard left were Burchett, Evatt, communists and others. On the hard right were Kane, the DLP and its Catholic supporters in the Melbourne-based NCC – the National Civic Council. The NCC had taken over from the Movement, which had been formed in 1945 to fight communism. Its founder was Bartholemew Augustine ('Bob') Santamaria, who, in 1945, had been approached by Labor Party leaders to help them fight communist penetration and control of key unions. A communist cell had been formed in each union's branch. The cell would gather secretly before each union meeting, plan its programme of action and select candidates for office. Santamaria offered to give Kane as much help as he needed, including access to the NCC's files, which included a dossier on Burchett. Not surprisingly, Kane's counsel, John Traill, a bald and bespectacled forty-one-year-old, came from the Catholic, NCC, anti-communist ranks. Traill's intellect was matched by his 100 kilogram frame. He had joined the Jesuits after doing law, but did not have the inclination for the isolated, rigid conditions and lack of intellectual stimulation in the first year. He dropped out to do a Masters of Law degree at Sydney University. Traill worked for a time with Santamaria's NCC development of small rural co-operative settlements for Catholic farmers. While building his career as a barrister, he worked in his spare time for the Catholic Church's conservative causes, such as countering abortion and euthanasia through the Human Life Research Foundation.

Traill was more than pleased to have a chance of tackling Burchett. He saw a victory in such a highly publicised case as a chance to rise in legal ranks. Kane thought highly of Traill's skills but felt he would be no match for Evatt in court, which made it even more important for Kane to build a strong defence.

Traill was told to go anywhere in the world to gather

evidence against Burchett. The defence counsel's strategy was two-pronged: he had to show that Burchett had had a long-standing connection with the KGB, as a political agent, and demonstrate that he was a traitor. In tandem, Traill would try to link Burchett to various communist governments.

If the KGB link could not be buttoned down, the objective was to make Burchett look so disreputable in the eyes of the court that he would have no reputation to 'defame'. Traill began his research, and soon, like Kane, he saw his mission as a crusade.

By mid-1974, Roy Turner had become concerned about rumours of Traill's travels. The word was that Traill had managed to pick up some sensational witnesses who could be most damaging to Burchett. Fortuitously, Turner had arranged a meeting with Traill at his home in Gordon, North Sydney, because they had legitimate matters to discuss about a NSW Law Society committee – examining computers and the law – on which they both served. Turner arrived early for the meeting and was given tea by Traill's wife, Margo. Her husband had been delayed on his drive home, and in the innocuous discussion between Turner and Margo while they waited for Traill, the solicitor learned more about Traill's activity. Turner remarked on some Chinese cane furniture, which Margo said had recently come from Taiwan. A painting had been bought in London. Two recent-edition American books on US politics sitting on a glass-topped coffee table indicated that Traill's travels had taken him to Washington DC.

Turner learnt enough at that visit, without a word about the *Burchett* v. *Kane* litigation, to recreate roughly Traill's itinerary over the last twelve months. Further research by some of his staff allowed Turner to calculate Traill's exact schedule, and even some of the people he had seen. They included several former American prisoners of war from Korea.

Turner phoned Clive Evatt, and they discussed Burchett's having been accused of interrogating POWs from the US, UK and Australia during the Korean war. At first, Evatt was sceptical. It was all very well visiting five continents to meet people, but how many of them would make an appearance at the trial? Would Kane be prepared to pay the costs for bringing several witnesses from the US? And what could they contribute if they did come? Burchett, after all, had always denied interrogating POWs. He said that he had only questioned them for newspaper and radio interviews.

Turner was able to answer the question of cost, at least in part. O'Neill was demanding a guarantee from Burchett against costs, and Winston Burchett had been asked to put up a bond of about $10,000 for his brother. It meant that Kane was either engaging in a monumental bluff or was serious about his defence. This gave Evatt pause, and he said he would make his own inquiries.

Turner also later discussed the problem at length with Alec Robertson, who had heard through colleagues that Kane had followed up Traill's visits in the US. More rumours suggested that he had been successful in his bid to lure witnesses across the Pacific. It sounded ominous for Burchett, and Robertson decided to write a letter to him in Paris.

During 1974, the euphoric atmosphere in which Labor was swept back to power began to change. The Whitlam government was forced to hold an early election, which it won. But Opposition party and conservative forces, aided by US intelligence efforts of the NSA – National Security Agency – and the CIA, began to discredit the government over its spending in efforts to buy back control of Australia's vast natural resources, which had fallen into foreign hands since World War II. The Whitlam government was being portrayed as a group of fiscally ignorant, profligate mismanagers. Much of the gloss of the new Labor era was diminishing.

Turner began to worry that the timing for the Burchett case was already late, and his instincts were confirmed when Clive Evatt decided not to act for Burchett. Ill-health was given as the reason, but Turner knew that the wily old barrister had agonised over defending a client who would be accused of interrogating Australian POWs. Evatt had graduated from Australia's Royal Military College, Duntroon, in 1921, before going on to study law at Sydney University. He was proud of his Duntroon days, during which he had won the King's Medal. The efforts of Traill and Kane in gathering witnesses had created a conflict for Evatt. He pulled out, and junior counsel

Harvey Cooper was brought in. Another blow for the Burchett camp was the death of Alec Robertson from an asthma attack.

Turner, who said that the Catholic Church could be dragged into the squabble, thought it was time for a face-saving compromise. He rang Traill and suggested that the case be called off, and that costs be split between the two parties: it would avoid a long and bitter court struggle. Traill thought that the offer was worth considering and promised to speak to Kane after mass the next day. Kane listened to the argument, but was not impressed. 'I guess it's just the Irish in me, John,' Kane said with a fierce grin, 'I want to go through with it. I want to get that commie bastard!'

PART
TWO

*Traitor
or Hero?*

6. The Trial Begins

The trial, *Burchett* v. *Kane*, began in the brick, nineteenth-century courtroom in Sydney's NSW Supreme Court on 20 October 1974. The atmosphere was humid, and one humming fan was inadequate for cooling the packed room. Most of the all-male jury looked over forty, and ten wore spectacles. They sat motionless at the start. The audience was an odd mix of unkempt, long-haired types and those with more of a business executive look.

Mr Justice Robert Lindsay Taylor sat impatiently in his crimson robes beneath a royal coat of arms. He liked to lean forward, elbow on the bench, with his chin cupped in a large hand.

Taylor was the son of a well-to-do sheep farmer who wanted his intelligent son off the land. He had a superior air, which prompted a Burchett lawyer to remark that he had 'a turd for a tie-pin'. Yet there was also a sense of the pragmatic and the incorruptible about Taylor, right down to his laceless boots. He was nicknamed 'Bully' for his cavalier style in dealing with incompetent performances by barristers. Put on a direct, substantial show, and you had a chance with Bully, who once told a member of the Sydney legal profession that he had neither the wit nor the competence to be a barrister of the Supreme Court. That pleasantry was delivered in the middle of the counsel's defence of a man charged with murder.

In short, Taylor would not, in the words of a profane Sydney barrister, 'tolerate them talking their usual bullshit'. This put big John Traill for Kane at a distinct disadvantage because, unless he could make a breakthrough with a witness or fresh evidence, it would seem from the beginning that he was trying to demonstrate the unprovable: that Burchett had been in the pay of the Chinese and North Vietnamese governments, and the KGB. Payrolls with such organisations simply did not exist. On day one, Traill's style also seemed to lack directness. He appeared to move his massive bulk as he thought – ponderously. Some vital information had not reached Traill's chambers when the case started, but he seemed to know where he was going.

If Traill was the tortoise, his rival, Harvey L. Cooper, was the hare. He had no grand design but was a sharp, if not at times brilliant, tactician who liked to make quick, telling points. Cooper, the forty-year-old son of a Jewish tailor who emigrated from England in the early 1930s, was short with a black, Groucho Marx-style moustache. He chain-smoked out of court and had the habit of drumming his stubby fingers on his desk. Although a coil of nervous energy, he delivered his lines with precision and logic, which might please Taylor. Cooper had nothing like the guile and experience of Evatt; he would never be the witty court jester. Perhaps Cooper's only performance came when he stacked his desk near the jury with many of Burchett's books. Their titles could easily be read by the twelve stolid-looking men. Cooper took every opportunity to pick one up and leaf through it, as though every paragraph contained pearls of Burchett's wisdom.

Cooper had won round one in the beginning of the trial when, in April 1974, he and Traill visited Washington DC to take depositions in a mini-court from Yuri Krotkov. The former KGB agent had decided not to appear in the case in Australia. He could not be guaranteed safety from his old employers in Moscow. He was now a settled writer-in-residence at

Oberlin College, Ohio. Why jeopardise all that to accuse Burchett once more?

With evidence given under cross-examination and in accordance with Australian court rules, Cooper cornered Krotkov and restricted his testimony. The subsequent transcript was a slightly watered-down version of the original US Senate Hearing evidence. More vitally, the weighty 180 pages of questions and responses, peppered with Cooper's stifling objections, would have little impact on the Australian court compared to the smash hit for the defence of Krotkov in person. Instead of an urbane, impressive Russian spy, there was a plethora of confusing words that needed study and comprehension of everything that had gone before, not to mention a substantial knowledge of the inner workings of Soviet, Chinese and other communist spy organisations.

With only a lumpy manuscript to fend off, Cooper raced into the trial several points ahead of the defence. He paraded journalists willing to vouch for Burchett's status. First, there was Guy Morrison, features editor of the *Sydney Morning Herald*. This respected professional spoke well of Burchett's reporting at the peace talks during the Korean and Vietnam wars. Cooper had created the impression of a man interested in peace, not war. Traill cross-examined and established that Morrison's esteem for Burchett was based on 'two or three meetings'. He had only read part of one of Burchett's books on Vietnam.

Alan Ashbolt, ABC radio's director of special projects, was next in the stand. He went further and put him in the top class of what he called 'hard-nosed international reporters', along with Edgar Snow, who went into China's interior to seek out the Red Army in the 1930s, and Herbert Matthews, who interviewed Castro for *The New York Times* in 1958 when he was a Cuban guerilla leader. Ashbolt, like Morrison, recalled Burchett's expertise on the Sino–Soviet split in 1959–60. After Cooper asked him to make a few observations, Traill seemed to work him laboriously in no direction at all and could not get him to say that Burchett favoured Russia in the Sino–Soviet split, or that he was a writer of 'sensational' reports. Traill was looking for the opening that would allow him to link Burchett to the KGB and communist governments early in his career, but Cooper, and Burchett's character witnesses, were making it difficult. As yet, facts about Burchett's possible early links to communists were not forthcoming, despite Traill's prodigious research.

During the days leading up to the trial, and in the first two days of the case, Traill spent many hours out of court concentrating on Burchett's activities in the years 1937 to 1946. Traill started with the hypothesis that Burchett was a 'sleeper' Russian agent from 1937 when he joined the Soviet travel agency, Intourist. He saw Burchett as having a career similar to that of British double-agent Kim Philby, who was recruited by the Soviets in the 1930s while at Cambridge University. Both spent much of their careers in journalism, which was a useful cover for espionage. Philby roamed Europe all through the 1930s as a student and journalist. He had witnessed some of the key moments of the 1930s – Berlin in 1933, Vienna in 1934, the Spanish war, and the retreat from France. In the 1950s and early 1960s, when he was suspected of being a KGB agent, he worked for the London *Observer* and *The Economist* as Middle East correspondent based in Beirut. Burchett also roamed Europe, first as a tourist in the late 1930s, and later as a journalist. Each made his name as a war correspondent, and did stints with the London *Times*. Philby was a covert operator for the Russians, while Burchett, according to Traill's hypothesis, performed more of an overt role. He always protested his independence. Where Philby used establishment manners and techniques to serve 'the other side', Burchett was the out-front, open-necked Aussie version of the same creature. He served the communist cause by an outpouring of books, articles and films. But did Burchett act as an agent of influence, paid by the Russians and other communist governments? Did he perform as a political agent called on whenever English-speaking troops were engaged in war against communist forces? Could he have gone further and provided communist forces with military information in the field? And was it possible that this engaging, very public journalist had been a spy?

Traill had consumed all the published material on Philby and Burchett, in addition to private files, and had found some remarkable similarities. Burchett was born a year earlier than Philby, in 1911. Both spoke languages, including German,

French, Spanish and some Russian. Both were very fond of women, and most popular with them. Each also had a penchant for excessive drinking, although Burchett held his alcohol better. He was rarely, if ever, seen wildly drunk, whereas Philby made alcoholic oblivion a favourite refuge from his double life.

Traill also found that even their family relationships and conversion to communism had a familiar resonance. Both fathers dominated their sons' early thinking and intellectual development. Philby's father, H. St. John B. Philby, was a notable Arabist and explorer, who chartered vast new areas of Arabia. Burchett's family was among the first to settle Victoria's rugged bush. A rebellious attitude to established ideas was instilled into both Burchett and Philby, who were taught that virtue in life came from making one's own choices and being faithful to them.

Introduction to communism came at about the same time. While Philby was first attracted to Marxism at Cambridge in 1931, when he met a former miner, Harry Dawes, Burchett was roughing it in Australia's outback. As an itinerant worker in the Depression he met a communist organiser – another ex-miner – known as 'Greyhead', who had an enormous influence on him.

Later, Philby joined the British Foreign Office, whereas Burchett tried for recruitment to Australian military intelligence and failed.

In court, Traill made his first attempt to expose a Burchett–Philby connection by referring to their first wives. He pointed out that both married German–Jewish refugees. Philby's wife, Litzi Friedman, was a communist agent. Burchett's first wife, Erna Hammer, was pro-communist. Traill's ploy did not, however, prove to be successful. The judge was aware that it had become fashionable for chivalrous young Englishmen to marry refugees so that they could be saved from fascism. Burchett and Philby were not exceptional. W. H. Auden, for example, had married Thomas Mann's daughter.

All references in this attempt to link Philby and Burchett were stricken from the record. First round in the question of the KGB connection had gone to Burchett.

7. The Anti-Fascist Connection

Traill's investigation of Burchett's life between 1937 and 1946 involved interviewing scores of people, from intelligence agents to journalists, who had been with him in several countries. The most comprehensive information came from an agent with the UK's MI6, which was essentially an espionage and intelligence gathering service operating mainly outside the UK.

Traill met the agent at MI6 offices in the Ministry of Defence, Whitehall, London in mid-1973, and again in Washington DC when they had some convivial lunches. The MI6 man, helped by files that stretched back to 1937, enabled Traill to prepare a succinct account of those early years, beginning in April 1937 when Burchett and his brother Winston arrived by ship at the French port of Marseilles.

The reception window at the London King's Street office of the

British Communist Party slid open only a few centimetres. 'I'm an Australian comrade,' Burchett began. He was interrupted by the female receptionist.

'Colonial department around the corner,' she said, and slid the window shut. Burchett wandered to the indicated door, but that was shut. He had wanted the party to help him join the International Brigade to fight in Spain against the fascists but had had little co-operation from English communists.

He and Winston had come to Europe seeking adventure, but such rebuffs seemed in keeping with their experiences since leaving Tahiti, where they had had an erotic stopover before sailing on to Marseilles in the spring of 1937. They were jeered and heckled in that rough port city for wearing maroon berets, which they did not realise were worn by Spanish fascists. In Paris, the callow Aussies, both in their twenties and on their first trip to Europe, were conned by dirty postcard sellers and confused by bidets, which they assumed were for washing feet. Their most gullible moment came on the Champs Elysées. Winston noted in his diary that a tout for a bordello lured them to a 'special free show of the Follies girls in a sumptuously decorated apartment'. They were offered expensive champagne and scantily-clad girls. 'My heart sank while my pulse leaped,' Winston wrote, 'I knew we were trapped.'

Winston planned to stay in Europe only a few months before making his way slowly home overland through Asia. Wilfred had other ideas. He wanted to experience more of the excitement and turbulence of life in Europe as war clouds gathered. His visit to the British Communist Party offices was his first attempt to fight for the International Brigade. After that he approached Spanish Republicans in a Trafalgar Square rally. His name and address were taken. A few days later he was visited by two men claiming to be representatives of the International Brigade. They asked searching questions about his life, background and ideals. The visitors asked why he was learning Russian, and seemed fascinated by his attitudes to the Soviet Union. They were also interested in his travelling on a Commonwealth passport. The probing was necessary, they said, because the International Brigade had been infiltrated by spies and agents, especially Nazis. After another meeting he was told that he would not be recommended for the Brigade but was asked if he would be interested in doing other work for the communist cause.

The men told him to keep their discussions secret, and they suggested that he forget about his dreams of fighting against Franco's troops. For the time being he should satisfy his idealism by fraternising with other communists, such as those in the Society for Cultural Relations with Russia. He was advised to take further Russian lessons and to brush up on his German. He would be contacted when something suitable was found.

Burchett had been having Russian language lessons from a friend in Melbourne, Dr Patkin, who had given him written introductions to comrades in Paris and London. Inspired by his mysterious callers, he took up Russian again, and German and French, at the Linguistics Club in Kingsway. But the brothers were short of funds and were soon involved in a get-rich scheme devised by a communist lawyer from Sydney, Bob Burns, whom they had met on the boat to Marseilles. He was also en route to the Spanish war and never quite made it.

Burns had a plan to exploit what he and the Burchetts saw as the twin forces of reaction: capitalism and the Catholic Church. The three men created the CPC – the Catholic Publishing Company – for a few shillings after a search of Somerset House revealed that no company by that name existed. Another ten shillings a month obtained them a smart business address in Chancery Lane.

The plan was to publish Catholic calendars for each London parish. They would feature the latest portrait of the Pope, along with a list of Catholic feast and holy days, and detailed information of the parish. The calendars would be distributed free, and, they hoped, with the co-operation of parish churches. The CPC would make its money from advertisements sold around the pictures and text. The strategy was to work a parish, spend three months in Europe on the proceeds, then return to England to plunder another.

The Burchetts left relatives, with whom they had been staying outside London, and rented a bed-sit in the attic of a four-storey apartment at 152 Camberwell Grove, for eleven shillings and ninepence a week. The country lads, who had experienced the rigours of Australia's outback, now had a taste of low living in one of the world's most crowded cities.

The bed-sit had a kitchenette, one sagging single bed, and a battered Victorian sofa. Biting, foul-smelling bugs emerged nightly from behind disintegrating wallpaper to sample their blood. This forced them out often, and they usually dined at a cafe in Mile End Row, where ten pence bought a large plate of lamb's fry, bacon and mash, a big, stodgy Bakewell tart, and a cup of tea.

On the CPC's opening day's operations, on Wednesday 16 June 1937, Burchett proved the salesman of the three by chatting up an elderly music teacher about Chopin and Beethoven. She was conned into buying a guinea-and-a-half's space. She even gave him two complimentary tickets for a recital by a Russian pianist that night at Wigmore Hall. Winston and Burns fared badly, however, and the venture was soon a flop.

It was Burchett's first and last entry into self-employment. Winston would do better in future, more worthwhile ventures. (So well, in fact, that he would eventually be treated with disdain by some communists.)

After the CPC minor fiasco, Winston cut his losses and did some freelance journalism for the *Age*. He even scored a scoop interview with his hero, H.G. Wells, which was published on 19 February of the following year.

Burchett was forced to scour the jobs columns of the London papers, but found nothing in carpentry, the only trade in which he was trained. He did find work with the travel agents Thomas Cook and Sons, however, who hired him because he spoke passable French and his Australian background was useful because of the tens of thousands of Australian tourists coming to London for the 1937 coronation festivities of King George VI.

Burchett was restless in a white-collar job. He preferred something more in keeping with his romantic and revolutionary spirit. He worked hard on his Russian and attended all the Soviet functions he could. The break he wanted came when communist contacts with the Society for Cultural Relations with Russia (of which Philby had been a member until he became a fully-fledged Russian spy) invited him and Winston to attend a weekend conference at Welwyn Garden City, Hertfordshire. The brothers took a chartered coach to a conference house in Digwell Park, a rambling and old building, with large assembly and dining rooms and scores of bedrooms. The house was surrounded by large grounds and sporting facilities. The Burchetts were glad to be away from their bed-sit squalor for a couple of nights.

The fifty or so guests included the Soviet Ambassador, Ivan Maisky, and other members of the Soviet embassy and trade delegation. During the conference, an Englishman spoke about the Moscow trials. Disturbing information was filtering west about purges and destruction of the old revolutionary vanguard in Russia. The speaker claimed that the news was largely incorrect and indicated that it was important for Stalin to keep strict Soviet Communist Party discipline in these trying times. In private discussions on the weekend, the Russians blamed Fleet Street for gross exaggeration and distortion. Perhaps power struggles were going on, it was conceded, but the Soviet system was intact and growing in strength.

A Viennese journalist named Peter Smolka lectured on the subject of his latest book, *40,000 Against the Arctic*, which covered the Soviet conquest of the polar regions. (Smolka and Philby were close friends. In 1934 they set up a small news agency, London Continental News Ltd, to collect and distribute information for Fleet Street from Central and Eastern Europe.) Smolka was also a KGB agent. The London Zoo's Dr Vevers discussed Soviet achievements in zoology, and Victor Gollancz, publisher of the Left Book Club, gave impressions of his recent visit to Russia. Gollancz told the audience, 'For the first time, I felt what it was like to move in a society completely free from anti-semitism.'

Burchett practised his Russian on anyone who would listen, even Ivan Maisky. On the second day, Burchett was asked by another member of the Embassy if he would like to be involved in the opening in London of Intourist, the Soviet travel agency. The pay would not be great, but there might be free trips to the Soviet Union, including Siberia, a thought that excited Burchett. He wasted no time in resigning from his boring job at Thomas Cook, and joined Intourist in October 1937, where he remained for the next year.

Burchett's stay in this tightly controlled and secretive organisation came to an abrupt end in October 1938, when the Soviet Trade Commission was raided by police after a tip-off that all its staff, Russian and British, were Soviet spies, or being trained to be spies. Suspicion fell on all Soviet operations in London, including the fledgling Intourist. The Russians retaliated by stopping the issue of visas in London for travel to the USSR. Intourist closed, and Burchett was out of a job. He next got work with the Palestine-Orient Lloyd travel company, which specialised in handling emigrant traffic from Germany. At the same time, Burchett met dark, slim and beautiful Erna Hammer at the Linguistics Club. Erna, a Jewish German refugee from Hitler, was cultured and intelligent, and she and Burchett had similar tastes in theatre, music, art and literature. Another strong bond was their anti-fascist political outlook. Burchett learned much about the Nazi regime from Erna, whose family and friends had suffered. All their property had been confiscated before Erna left for England. She had relatives who had been persecuted and thrown in concentration camps. Her experiences confirmed for Burchett the rightness of the communist cause in its resistance to German fascism, which was largely being ignored in England. The leading papers were not even reporting the Jewish persecution. Some were even pro-Hitler.

In September 1938, Burchett and Erna married at the Hampstead Heath registry office. Two daughters from a previous marriage of Erna's were adopted so that they could be secure in England.

In November 1938, Von Roth, the Nazi Ambassador to France, was assassinated by a Polish Jew, and Hitler retaliated with a series of anti-Jewish pogroms in Germany. One of the first victims was Herbert S., who had a chain of clothes stores in Germany and Holland. He and thousands of other Jews in Berlin were rounded up and taken to Buchenwald concentration camp near Weimar. The Nazis had secretly built Buchenwald as an extermination camp in 1937 for all 'undesirables' such as communists, anti-Nazis, political detainees, religious fanatics, homosexuals, criminals and Jews. Many prisoners were to be sterilised, castrated, or the subjects of other hideous medical experiments.

In the first few days that Herbert S. was interned, he was given a preview of the horrors awaiting him. He was in a food line outside a mess hall, when a prisoner a few metres in front of him was abused by a guard for having moved his head to look behind him. The prisoner protested, and guards dragged him from the line to a tree, where he was hanged in full view of the other inmates. That was enough for Herbert S. who resolved to get out. By luck, he discovered that he knew the camp commandant from school days in Berlin. The commandant told him that the only 'legitimate' way out of Buchenwald was if he had a visa to another country, and this was only acceptable if he had a new German passport. There was a catch. He would have to sign a certificate giving all his wealth and assets to the Nazis before a passport would be issued. Herbert S. had no second thoughts about giving away his wealth. He was convinced that he would die in Buchenwald if he did not act.

Herbert S. arranged for a consular letter to be sent to him from a country willing to accept him. He tried the Palestine-Orient Lloyd shipping line run by a fellow German Jew in London. It had offices in Berlin that he had used to apply for a trip to London so that he could marry Marie, his non-Jewish fiancée. Such 'mixed' marriages were forbidden by Nazi law in Germany. Herbert S. smuggled a message out of Buchenwald to Lloyd's Berlin office, where a telex was sent to London. The next day, the Berlin office was closed by Hitler's Brown Shirts. They smashed the front windows and nailed planks across them. Scribbled on the planks in white paint were the words, 'Schmutzige Juden' – Dirty Jews.

Wilfred Burchett had been with P-O Lloyd only a few weeks when he became enmeshed in the risky business of helping clients escape Germany. He made his first trip to Berlin in November, 1938, and returned with a plan that would help some of Lloyd's Jewish clients get out. His boss approved of Burchett's scheme for Lloyds to obtain and pay for visas for these people as long as there was some hope of being reimbursed later. Few countries were willing to take refugees, and Burchett had difficulty in raising interest in London in supplying visas, but he was pleased by the reaction in Australia.

All the Burchett family gave support. Winston, who had arrived home, quickly answered his brother's cables and letters. The Immigration Department, although working overtime with refugee applications, was, however, slow about issuing the vital documents. On the eve of his wedding, Winston received an urgent cable from Burchett about Herbert S., who was in a dangerous position in Buchenwald. He was suspected of attempting to arrange the transfer of possessions to the Dutch branch of his clothes shop business.

Winston took an all-night train to Canberra and forced his way into the head of the Immigration Department's office to explain the life or death matter. The department agreed to cable the visa permit numbers to London immediately. Winston took the train home to Melbourne in time for his wedding and wondered if he had saved the life of Herbert S.

In London, Burchett was working overtime doing the rounds of Central and Latin American consulates attempting to acquire visas, which often had no real validity. The clients could use them to flee Germany but never enter the countries that had issued them. Some demanded exorbitant sums for sending the one paragraph letter to their Berlin consulate counterparts, and Burchett was forced to return to Germany to collect payments from P-O Lloyd clients.

Burchett discussed his work with several communists, including those who had helped engineer his job at Intourist. They suggested that his travels to many parts of Germany – including Hamburg, Breslau, Frankfurt-am-Main, Vienna and Keonisburg in East Prussia – would be useful to the anti-fascist cause. Burchett thought it might be adventurous to observe certain military activity such as troop placement and movements, and the building of strategic roads. He carried an Australian passport and was not subject to visa restrictions in Germany. With war possible, many foreigners, including the English, were finding movement in Germany difficult. Burchett also spoke German and his contacts agreed that any intelligence gathering would be valuable in the fight against Nazism. Burchett briefed himself thoroughly on such things as the Nazi chain of command and uniforms. (When he returned to Melbourne the following year, he was able to write knowledgeably about this and the observations he made in Germany. In this way he became, retrospectively, a journalist, for there were few Australians with such experiences.)

Burchett also prepared codes for his note-taking in case he was searched. His cover while carrying out his P-O Lloyd work would be to act as the diligent tourist. In his youthful naivety and enthusiasm, he had not thought too deeply about the risks.

On his next trip to Vienna and Berlin late in 1938, he noted the increase in strutting, grey-clad Wehrmacht officers, and the SS, in their shining, black uniforms. Burchett wrote that they looked 'elegant' as they saluted each other, 'like automatons'. He was bemused by some of the state 'advertising', such as signs at Vienna airport telling people to avoid 'laziness' and work hard for the führer. At railway stations signs and placards campaigned for a return to German control of former colonies lost after World War I.

Burchett took copious notes everywhere he went in tracking down P-O Lloyd clients and their contacts. He observed military camps and paid special attention to the construction of autobahns. He took a bus on one that ran east from Berlin's ring road to the Polish border. Three more, open but still under construction, ran west. Burchett guessed that they could be intended as jumping-off points for the invasion of the low countries. Closer inspection showed that the autobahns were being reinforced so that they could take heavy tanks and move truckloads of troops fast. Burchett concluded that they were really strategic military highways and an integral part of the German Wehrmacht's Blitzkrieg tactics.

Burchett's meetings with clients were always furtive. All kinds of artifacts and valuables were thrust at him as payment for visas, but he had to reject many of them because of the difficulty in smuggling large items through customs. He usually accepted jewels, however, which he could hide. At first he was not worried about carrying contraband, for foreigners seemed to be getting less attention than locals, especially coming into the country, where his Australian nationality appeared of little significance. His false sense of security was shaken one night at Berlin's Haus des Vaterlands restaurant, where he met and had coffee with a young woman friend of Herbert S. He told her that she should apply to the Australian Embassy for his visa, which had arrived from Australia by way of London. In return, the woman passed Burchett a small cloth bag stuffed with diamond rings and other expensive jewellery. He pocketed it and invited the woman to dine with him. She was hesitant as she looked around the restaurant. The sight of two SS officers at a corner bar put her off. The woman thanked Burchett for his help and kind offer and left. He dined alone. In the middle of the meal, Hitler's rasping voice came over the loudspeakers. Other diners stopped eating, but Burchett kept munching. The others stared at him. The two SS men strode to his table. One brought a fist down on the table and brusquely reminded him that the führer was speaking. Burchett pleaded ignorance and continued his meal. His passport was demanded, and his papers inspected.

Burchett was suddenly very conscious of the bag of jewels in his coat pocket. One of the SS observed loudly that Burchett was a 'bloody foreigner'. They marched away. Burchett realised that he had made a careless error. If the SS had searched him, he would have been in trouble, because the discovery of the jewels would have led them to his luggage in his hotel room where much more jewellery was hidden. He resolved to be less foolhardy and returned to his London flat at 81a Belsize Lane. He wrote to his family on 9 December 1938: 'You will see that I am back from the land of darkness. I have seen enough misery and frightfulness to last me to the end of my days. You know that even before I left Australia I had a pretty fair idea of what was going on in Germany. Since then I have good cause to know that all we read was an understatement of what was actually happening here. To go there and talk with the people who are the victims makes me think that all I read was absolutely nothing. I was in Germany altogether for eighteen days, and travelled to Frankfurt-am-Main, across to Breslau in Silesia and up to Keonigsberg in East Prussia. And of course, I was in Berlin a good deal of the time. Everywhere the same tale was told, except that in the lesser known towns the persecution was even more brutal than in the capitals, if there can be a degree of cruelty in such a pogrom. I spoke with many men who had been in the concentration camps, but who are mostly frightened to say a word, as they have to sign a paper saying that they will not divulge anything that happened in the camps under the pain of instant death.

'In Breslau they collected about sixty religious Jews and made them prepare to set the synagogue on fire. When everything was ready, they got an old man and commanded him to apply the match. He refused, and they killed him instantly, in front of the others, and made someone else fire it.

The George Cross winner,
Derek Kinne, a star witness
for the defence

In step, father and son.
George Burchett, a sprightly
seventy-five with son
Wilfred in Berlin, 1947

Burchett's parents, George and Mary, and his first wife, Erna
Hammer, in Melbourne, 1941

The mystery Mercedes. Burchett's parents and son Rainer in 1947 in Berlin. The car attracted ASIO attention when it arrived in Melbourne in 1951

Now you see them, now you don't. North Vietnamese communist defectors Bui Cong Tuong and To Ming Trung, who testified against Burchett. After the trial and their return to Saigon, the communists took over South Vietnam, and the two witnesses were never heard of again

The morning after. Alan Winnington passes out while Burchett drinks on after a celebration during those long cold days in Panmunjom, Korea, 1951-52

Shooting the Breeze at Panmunjom. Alan Winnington, left and in profile, chats with Tibor Meray, facing camera, and other journalists. In the background, two Korean communist soldiers guard the path to the communist tents. The UN forces had similar quarters

The exile reads all about it. Burchett reads about his exploits on his daring return in early 1970. The second headline, 'Bomb After Phone Threat', refers to a threat to bomb Winston Burchett's East Melbourne home, where Burchett stayed during the visit

The air ace, Walker 'Bud' Mahurin, one of the most highly decorated men in American military history, and a witness for the defence. With him is his wife Joan

The counsel for the defence, John Traill

'In Vienna, they made a group of people walk up the staircase of the Jewish Kultus Gemeinde, up to the second storey, and then jump out of the window into the street. Some were killed, others broke arms, legs, etc. No one was allowed to assist them as they lay in the streets. They tore people's ears off, and they tore their nostrils. Every imaginable cruelty was perpetrated.

'Well, I got a few people out of the camps, and others will get out with consular letters, etc. I am very proud of Poowong [from where the Burchett family organised help for refugees], and in the Jewish community in London, the name of Poowong stands very high.

'I am very busy all the time, and in Germany I flew everywhere, and finally back to London – only five hours instead of twenty-four. I like flying very much and have no sensation of sickness like I do on the sea. As soon as I come back from Berlin, Erna and I will take the first boat to Australia. I got a new passport today. There is nothing to show now that I have ever been in Germany before, which is very good. In Erna's passport there is absolutely nothing to show that she was formerly German, so that I think that we are both quite safe. When I came back on Monday, I smuggled out a good lot of jewellery for different people. I had it well hidden and the Gestapo had no suspicions at all. I look like such an innocent Australian tourist. I think that you can't publish the fact that I have been in Germany as it might be bad for me...'

About the time this letter was written, Herbert S. took a train from Berlin to the Dutch border. His luggage was given a perfunctory search, but his identity card and Australian visa were scrutinised by Gestapo officials stationed at the border specifically to apprehend Jews. He was finally let through. After a joyful reunion with his fiancée, the couple sailed to England and were married in London. Days later they set sail for their new home in Australia. In March 1939, they were met at the Melbourne docks by Winston and Mary Burchett, who remained their life-long friends.

Meanwhile, Burchett's escapades came to a halt in Berlin. He was tailed through the Kurfurstendamn shopping area and on a bus to Unter Den Linden. Burchett became nervous, because he was again carrying jewellery. With the shadow always close, he spent an hour wandering the Deutsche

Museum at Kaiser-Wilhelmplatz, where he made small talk with one of the museum caretakers, whom he had begun to know in the four months he had been making the Berlin run. Burchett was then followed back to his hotel. He hurried to his room, where he found that his luggage had been searched. This was it. He had to leave the country.

Two hours later Burchett slipped out through the hotel's rear entrance and caught a taxi for the railway station, although he had told the desk clerk that he wanted a ride to the airport. Burchett made sure all his jewels were stowed in false compartments in his luggage because of a body search he would have to undergo at customs. An inspector gave his overcoat shoulder pads a prod, unrolled his socks, and motioned him on.

The train ride to the German–Dutch border was jittery for Burchett as he prepared for another inspection. He began to worry that the Gestapo, whom he guessed had been following him around Berlin, had cabled frontier guards to apprehend him.

Burchett was stunned by the number of uniformed armed guards at the frontier to greet the train. Nazi officials made their way down the carriages inspecting passports and, much to his horror, searching luggage. Burchett tried to act nonchalantly, but this time he didn't impress an official who ordered him to open his luggage. Experienced hands were run around the insides. Burchett prepared himself for the worst as the official suddenly seemed distracted. Burchett began gabbling in his best German but was ignored. The official began examining books, and his face clouded as he read some of the titles. He referred to a list, which Burchett presumed was of banned literature. His books were mostly Nazi propaganda, which Burchett had been studying to understand the fascist mentality. His relief was short-lived. The official wanted to know about two small notepads. They contained his special codes. He explained that they were for studying German. The official continued to flick over pages, then handed the pads back and moved on. Burchett slumped in his seat and pondered the two near misses. He had made his last trip to Hitler's Germany.

When the train moved over the border, Burchett took his case to a toilet and transferred the jewellery to his clothes pockets, in preparation for the far less harrowing English customs at Dover, which he would reach after a rough, four-hour ferry ride from the Hook of Holland. He was never so pleased to see those white cliffs and was jaunty as he handed over his passport to the dour-faced customs man, who had no special love for foreigners, even colonials. The man asked for more identification. Burchett fumbled in his overcoat pocket. A gold bracelet clattered to the concrete floor. The customs man bent over to retrieve it. Burchett was asked to turn out all his pockets. No amount of explanation could help him avoid being taken aside and interrogated by police. He and his luggage were thoroughly searched. His precious notepads and some of the books that had so intrigued the Nazis were confiscated, along with all the jewellery. And he was quizzed for two hours over his contraband. Detailed notes were taken about him, his work, and his travels. The police refused to believe his story about P-O Lloyd clients and paying for visas. He was released after promising to report to Scotland Yard in London the following day. To his amazement, the matter was dropped. For posterity, British military intelligence files marked Burchett down as a smuggler.

Traill was encouraged by his discoveries of Burchett's pre-war activities in Europe. He wanted to know more about his possible early links to the KGB's forerunner organisation, which had been actively recruiting in the UK in the late 1930s. The KGB had been most interested in controlling agents with Commonwealth passports. Furthermore, Intourist UK mainly employed agents, many of them involved in espionage. Even at the time of the trial, Traill learned, it was a Soviet intelligence cover operation that tended to employ locals, some of whom were trained as spies. (The same applied to the Soviet Embassy, its trade delegations, and other operations such as NAFTA, the Moscow-owned and operated retail petrol chain, which had 150 stations throughout the UK.)

Every hour of the trial Traill was becoming more aware of how weak his case looked without documentation to back the *Focus* article. There simply was no list of KGB staff. There would be no hidden payroll. Agents were paid in hard cash, almost exclusively in American dollars, stuffed in envelopes. It would be enough to keep an agent living well on an assignment but always on the run. He could never retire on communist pay-outs.

Traill was left with little alternative but to attempt to indict Burchett by showing links with the KGB and other communist organisations over thirty years. He recalled his MI6 contact's words about agents of influence, whom he suggested were used in the KGB's most insidious operations. Through them the Soviet Union tried to develop its own disguised voices in foreign governmental, political, journalistic, business, trade union, artistic and academic circles. Such agents could transmit intelligence, but their overriding aim was to alter opinion and policy in the Soviet Union's interests. According to the MI6 contact, no KGB activity abroad had higher priority than its efforts to manipulate the thought and action of other nations by insinuating its people to positions of power. He cited the incident of September 1971, when MI6 and MI5 smashed a massive KGB operation to suborn politicians, scientists, businessmen and civil servants. About 105 KGB and other Russian agents were thrown out of Britain.

After analysing all the material on the 1937–39 period, Traill put a priority on knowing more about the two men who interrogated Burchett after his attempt to join the International Brigade. If he could prove that they were Russian agents, it would at least indicate an early Burchett connection with the Soviet secret police.

8. The Plaintiff's Best Witness

Harvey Cooper was delighted to represent Burchett right from the first meeting. He found him engaging and warm and when Cooper had Burchett home for dinner during the trial, he got on with the children, who were in awe of this amazing witness to history. They were studying the subject, and Burchett was able to give them first-hand insights, which they could cite and use as references in essays. He even produced secret communiqués in French about his involvement in the Paris peace talks, which confirmed that he was a key negotiator.

More importantly for Cooper, his client seemed honest and unshakeable in his protestations of innocence. No ifs or buts. He was neither a KGB agent nor an agent of any other communist government. Cooper did not probe why someone like Krotkov would create such a fantastic story about his connections to Burchett. And Burchett dismissed the allegations as part of a right-wing, ASIO/CIA-instigated plot to discredit him because of his role in the Vietnam and Korean wars.

Burchett admitted that he knew Krotkov from Berlin days in 1947. But so did everyone else in the press corps there. The Russian was, after all, the press attaché with the Soviet military. Their later meetings in Moscow from 1956 were nothing more than two old acquaintances getting together. Burchett said it was natural for them to meet, because he was using all his contacts in Moscow to set himself up as an independent journalist in the Soviet Union.

In one way, this simple line of defence made Cooper's business easier. He could sit out the accusations and stick to the truth, as Burchett portrayed it. Yet trouble would come when and if more complex allegations arose. Without careful preparation to cover surprises from Traill, Burchett would be vulnerable, and instead of making the running, he would look more like the defendant. Kane would be transformed into the plaintiff, and, as Turner had warned, Burchett would be on trial.

This became apparent early in the trial as the defence paraded hostile military witnesses before the court, including POWs from Australia, the US and the UK. The evidence had to have an effect when people such as Brigadier Phillip Greville took the stand. The jury would remember him as an educated patriot still serving in the Australian Army. Greville had been a POW in Korea, where he was tortured. Traill led him adroitly into showing that Burchett was 'on the other side', writing communist propaganda that dominated the literature allowed into the POW camps in Korea. The defence could not present direct evidence that Burchett was a KGB or Chinese agent. There was only circumstantial evidence of links. So in court Traill worked hard instead to build an emotional base against Burchett.

Traill asked Greville what Burchett's reputation was during the Korean war.

'He has been in two wars that Australians have been associated with (Korea and Vietnam), and has done traitorous acts,' the Brigadier remarked, 'and as far as we are concerned he is a traitor.'

Cooper tried to isolate this as an army view, which was not representative of Australians in general. But when other Australian POWs from Korea called Burchett a traitor and a 'collaborator' with the enemy, damage to Burchett's reputation had been done. Traill had subtly orchestrated the concept of traitor; it would stay with the jury, if repeated often enough. It did not link Burchett to the KGB, but the accusation would tamper with Burchett's reputation. Cooper noted the definition of a traitor in an Oxford dictionary: 'One who betrays any person that trusts him, or in any duty entrusted to him; a betrayer. In early use often, and still traditionally applied to Judas Iscariot. Specifically: One who is false to his allegiance to his sovereign or to the government of his country; one regarded guilty of treason or of any crime so regarded.'

So far the defence had made the running on this issue in its bid to lower Burchett's reputation. The trial had tacitly become one on treason as much as, if not more than, whether or not Burchett was a KGB man. If Cooper was to take them up on this key point, the defence had a strategy based on showing that Burchett was far worse than Britain's Lord Haw Haw – William Joyce – who was convicted of treachery for broadcasting on German radio in a manner that would cause 'alarm and despondency' among British servicemen and hanged at the end of World War II.

Traill was ready with quotes from Rebecca West, who wrote a book, *The Meaning of Treason,* which examined the activities and lives of British traitors such as Joyce. She claimed that sooner or later all traitors eventually sought the sanctuary of their own countrymen: 'They had forsaken the familiar medium; they had trusted themselves to the mercies of those who had no reason to care for them; knowing their custodian's indifference, they had lived for long in fear; and they were aware that they had thrown away their claim on those who might naturally have felt affection for them.'

And another from Dr Evatt, which appeared in his book, *Rum Rebellion:* 'Treason can never prosper – there's a reason: If treason prospers, none dare call it treason...'

With the expert aid of Greville and Warner, Traill aimed to show the court that Burchett had made inaccurate reports of the peace conference, which were read by POWs in either special bulletins or English language editions of *Shanghai News, People's China, China Review* and *China Pictorial.* Then Traill planned to link Burchett to the torture involved in forcing POWs to confess falsely to war crimes.

Cooper and Burchett considered tackling the issue head

on but decided against it because it might have raised further doubts in the jury's mind. Instead, Cooper decided to put Burchett on the stand. They both knew he was his own best witness.

Burchett's presence in the witness box sharpened the atmosphere in the courtroom. His supporters became silent as they stared at their hero, as did his antagonists. He wore a crumpled dark suit, white shirt and blue, white-striped tie. Burchett's medium frame was a little overweight. Despite his undershod chin and jaw and thinning hair, he managed a rugged look because of a prominent nose and ears. His double-chin, spectacles and tendency to frown formed a dignified, world weary expression. Burchett's intelligent eyes concentrated on Cooper, his counsel, and seemed oblivious of the tension. His accent was something of a mystery. It didn't have the nasal, tight-lipped tones of a self-educated man, which he had once been, yet it was different, too, from an educated Australian's modulation. Rather it had a mid-Atlantic, sonorous strength, and he didn't sound as if he could be easily rattled. His speaking style was impressive, and he looked at ease as he waved a large hand to emphasise a point. But at times he laughed nervously, as if to indicate what a ridiculous situation he found himself in.

Cooper established Burchett's background with a few brush strokes, playing up his tough beginnings just enough to engender sympathy, and drawing out his heroic work in Germany to focus interest, and possibly support, from the jury.

Traill was alerted as Cooper asked to whom he offered his services when he returned to Australia in 1939. Burchett explained that he became a retrospective foreign correspondent by writing articles for the *Sunday Telegraph,* the Melbourne *Age*, and others, which discussed the Nazis and Japanese, about whom he seemed remarkably prescient.

'I established myself in journalism to go to New Caledonia and collect material for some articles,' Burchett said, 'and while I was there I got a telegram from the Department of Information asking me to return as an expert.'

Traill thought that Burchett's period back in Australia again may have fitted his hypothesis that he was a communist agent.

Burchett had been most keen to join the intelligence services, and he and Erna anticipated this employment. In a letter, dated 11 July 1940, in German from Poowong to a friend in Sweden, Erna wrote:

'Our financial position is more than bad. We had large debts when we started life here. If I don't get this position [teaching as a child psychologist] I shall have to look for some other work, meaning in a munitions factory...

'We will work with the Intelligence Service, that is, as soon as we have moved into town. He [Wilfred] has gone to Melbourne today to look for a flat. For this kind of work he will, of course, have to live in the city and so as a matter of course we would have to live separately if I get work in a school.'

Erna was half right. Her husband was rejected by External Affairs (the Foreign Office), and by military intelligence. In the end the Department of Information hired him for the tedious job of translating enemy overseas broadcasts from Berlin, Rome and Tokyo.

Burchett visited New Caledonia in late 1940 while still in his translating job and did research on his first book, *Pacific Treasure Island*. A fellow-translator recalled that Burchett stole documents from the Vichy administration and sent information on its plans in the Pacific back to Melbourne.

In his attempts to uncover any possible communist intelligence links, Traill examined Burchett's decision to visit Burma and China in 1942, which would have been consistent with the Soviet Union's spying activities in the region. The Russians had set up strong espionage networks to monitor the Japanese–China war and had been obsessed with the Japanese since the Russo–Japanese war of 1904–05. But Traill realised that it was unlikely that Burchett would have had a Russian 'control' in Australia or South-East Asia. If he had been doing communist intelligence work, it would have been under directives from the Australian Communist Party, which followed Moscow's instructions during World War II. Traill had no proof, however, that Burchett had been a secret member of the party.

Later, Cooper angled his questions so that Burchett could discuss his visit to China in 1942 and to allow him to slip in a few points early about germ warfare, which Burchett said he had first discovered as a journalist in that period. He claimed that the Japanese had developed killer-disease germs and dropped them on the Chinese. This was important in the argument about Burchett's further claim that the US had taken over the Japanese germ warfare unit after World War II, in order to drop germ bombs on China and Korea during the Korean war.

Traill felt compelled to counter Burchett's impressive opening with evidence from his arch-rival Denis Warner who had known Burchett since a meeting during 1944 in Saipan in the Central Pacific. As usual, Traill prepared his witness at the Sydney apartment of the Herald & Weekly Times, where Warner and his wife were staying for the trial. Warner recalled his rivalry with Burchett and cited examples which could be used to denigrate Burchett if they were allowed by Judge Taylor.

Warner remembered an incident in Honolulu after the American Guam operation late in the Pacific war. A party was thrown for him and Burchett by the manager of Radio Corporation of America (RCA), through which they filed their dispatches. There were about twenty correspondents and local women at the evening barbecue party held in the grounds of the RCA manager's bungalow. When the food was being cooked, Burchett disappeared with the voluptuous hostess. About twenty minutes later, Warner noticed the host, a cripple with a club foot, moving to the bungalow. There the host caught Burchett and his wife in bed. There was a shouting match, and when Warner and others walked to the bungalow, the host was yelling at his wife. Burchett was sitting on a chair putting on his shoes. Warner was embarrassed and annoyed, because the journalists relied on the RCA manager to get their dispatches to their newspaper outlets.

Another bit of by-play between the two occurred during the Battle of the Philippine Sea. Warner was on board an American aircraft carrier when Burchett joined it from a destroyer. They shared a cabin on the carrier for about two weeks, and there were several other correspondents aboard. Because of Warner's friendship with the carrier's Admiral Brogan, he provided a plane to fly out the correspondents' copy. Burchett volunteered to fly out with the plane to take the copy to Pelelui, including Warner's long dispatch on the Battle of the Philippine Sea.

A month later, in Honolulu, Warner learned that his dispatch to the Melbourne *Herald* – one of Warner's usual outlets – had not been transmitted and published. But one by Burchett had.

Warner evened the score at their next meeting, at Saipan, when both men were scheduled to take the Super Fortress air raid on Tokyo. Burchett told Warner that he thought the trip was too dangerous, that he would not be going. Burchett thought he would get a story to the London *Daily Express* more quickly if he stayed at Saipan. Warner gave the impression that he did not write for a London paper, which indicated there would be no competition over the story.

Warner flew on the raid and later filed a dramatic first dispatch to the London *Daily Mail*. Warner scooped Burchett; it was one all in their forty-year war.

Traill liked these stories but could not see how they could be worked into Warner's responses, unless it was under the banner of a question on Burchett's reputation at the time.

While they worked on the demolition of Burchett's character, Burchett and Cooper were trying frantically to find detonators to use against Warner's reputation. Burchett claimed that he was suspicious that Warner might have links to ASIO or the CIA, or both, and Cooper and Burchett spent many hours in the Sydney Public Library scrambling through old newspapers in search of damning evidence. But they found nothing.

In court the next day, Traill asked questions that would erode Burchett's image, but responses from Warner were cut short by spirited objections from Cooper, which were upheld by Taylor.

Warner, a strongly built man with lugubrious, aquiline features, proved to be the most articulate witness so far for the defence, but the credibility of his testimony was lowered by a bizarre incident during his early depositions. In creating Warner as an important witness, Traill had run through his background, which included service with the Australian 9th Cavalry Division in the Syrian Campaign of World War II, and action with a commando platoon in the Western Desert and at the battle of El Alamein. At one point the jury foreman interjected. 'Is the witness sure he was attached to the 9th Division in the Syrian campaign?'

Warner was certain of his facts. He explained them more

fully. Taylor asked who his commanding officer was. Warner answered, 'Colonel Bassett. The second in command was Major Mumps,' and explained the circumstances of his action in the Middle East. The jury foreman stubbornly maintained his scepticism.

During a court adjournment military books were checked, and experts contacted. Warner was correct. Then the judge, either through a misunderstanding or a slip of the tongue, told the court that the 9th had not been in the Syrian campaign. There was no point in Traill or Warner contradicting Taylor, who could be crusty. The error had been compounded and Warner's testimony damaged in the eyes of the jury.

The incident forced Traill and Warner to be wary. In early testimony, this star defence witness's testimony sounded almost as if he was pro-Burchett. Traill asked him what Burchett's reputation was like among war correspondents working together in the Pacific in 1944.

'He was a very good *Daily Express* reporter,' Warner said. 'He was imaginative. Most of us were more concerned with covering the day-to-day activities of forces in action, whereas the *Express* seemed to require a bigger story on occasions.'

Warner said that Burchett usually preferred to operate from an aircraft carrier instead of going ashore with the troops to cover island invasions. A dive-bomber man's eyewitness account that would arrive in London within a day or so of the beginning of a battle was worth ten stories filed from the beachhead and delivered two weeks later.

'He was regarded with a good deal of esteem as a fine correspondent,' Warner said.

'When did you last speak with the plaintiff?' Traill asked.

'11 June 1945. I remember the date very well, because I was being married on the following day. He attended a party that I gave with my wife-to-be in Melbourne on that day. I was unaware that he was in town. He heard of the party and came, but he would have been invited had I known he was there.'

The question and answer session between Traill and Warner began to exasperate the judge.

'Mr Traill,' Taylor said, 'this witness has been in the box for nearly an hour, and apart from a very exhaustive account of his past life, what has anything that he has said got to do with this case?'

Traill fumbled an unconvincing answer, and the hearing was adjourned for the day. The experience dampened the Kane camp's spirits as he, Traill and the Warners met for a post-mortem at the Herald apartment. Traill wanted to keep Warner in the stand for hours yet but would have to change his approach to avoid the judge's ire. Traill had to focus on more pertinent points, so he and Warner worked into the early hours of the next morning shaping a counter-attack.

But Burchett was not about to sit back because of the early successes. He seconded an English journalist, Russell Spurr, to help search for damaging material on Warner. If it could be raised in court the following day, the defence's case could be further tainted. A second, more comprehensive delve into Warner's writing confirmed nothing more than that he was a pro-American correspondent during the Vietnam war. Burchett was irritated, for it was his strategy to accuse Warner of an espionage connection to diffuse the accusations against *him*. He became obsessed with the link, but abandoned the research for another day after Spurr, he and Cooper again raided the Sydney Public Library for several hours immediately the trial proceedings were completed for the day. For all that, Burchett was happy with the trial's progress. He drank with Spurr, who would later be called as a supporting witness, and then joined Mavis Robertson, and several other communist friends, for dinner. They ended up at Mavis's apartment in North Sydney, where the party continued. Burchett as usual consumed more alcohol than anyone, yet never seemed more than merry. He was even lucid enough to discuss the case and expressed the desire to be allowed to give more testimony on his journalistic career, in the hope that they could keep the initiative away from the defence. Burchett was keen to let the jury know of his greatest scoop from Hiroshima.

Coincidentally, information came to Traill that night from his MI6 intelligence contact in London that threw new light on Burchett's writing triumph. Traill could now construct events in Burchett's career from 1945 to 1946 in the hope of weaving more threads that showed the plaintiff as a KGB 'sleeper' agent.

9. The Secret Scoop

General Kenny, the US Air Force commander on the island of Tinian in the Pacific during World War II, had just finished breakfast in his hut when his assistant said an Australian journalist wanted to see him. It was Burchett. Kenny invited him in for coffee and learned of Burchett's attachment to a US troop transport ship, USS *Millett*, which was part of a vanguard occupation unit of Marines. Kenny was surprised by Burchett's request to see the bombs on the island. The weapons were part of the arsenal about to be dropped on Nagasaki and Hiroshima, a top secret operation only days away. Bombers were about to receive their orders to make the only two nuclear raids in history.

Kenny asked how he knew about the bombs, and Burchett said rumours were rife among American forces that a new monster weapon was about to be used to end the war with Japan.

Kenny asked about his writing outlets. Burchett told him and mentioned a few names of people in the higher echelons of the US Central Pacific fleet. He was bursting to speak of the weapons, because of their awesome power and the impact they were about to have on the war. Kenny told Burchett he would not be allowed to write anything, so what was the point? Burchett said he was curious to know about them anyway. He put it down to natural journalistic instinct. If he couldn't write anything, and if the war was about to end, would there be any harm in his curiosity being satisfied? Kenny was reluctant, but after some deliberation and another half hour's chat over more coffee, he relented.

Accompanied by two other officers, Kenny took Burchett to an unimposing shed guarded by twenty marines not far from a military aircraft runway. Inside, Kenny pointed to a large fibre sheet that hid the weapons. Burchett wanted to look at them. Kenny refused but could not resist boasting about them. He spoke of the devastation they could cause. Burchett then asked two questions that implied he had a certain expertise: what was the bomb's all-up weight, and what was its production rate? These were the two most important military secrets in the west at the time. The all-up weight was that of the complete weapon when loaded into an aircraft, which determined the type of plane used to deliver it, and how many one plane could carry. It was vital intelligence for another reason. The Nazis had been developing the V2 rocket at Peenemunde in North Germany, and the Russians now had control of the site. If the bomb was not too heavy to be fitted into a missile, it could supersede the bomber and put the Russians ahead in the arms race between the post-war super-powers.

Kenny was in full verbal flight extolling the weapon's devastating virtues, when Burchett put his queries to him. The general replied that the all-up weight was four tonnes, and the production rate was six bombs a month, with eight in store. Burchett had one of the great scoops of the war, but he did not break it with his press outlets. He was determined to find out more about the weapons, and see the results once they had been used.

The next day Kenny called together some selected correspondents, including Burchett. They were given some of the details that Burchett had gained and were sworn to secrecy.

In reviewing Burchett's activities from 1938 to 1945, when he reached the high-point of his reporting career at Hiroshima, Traill gained a healthy respect and admiration for Burchett, which he confided only to his wife Margo during the trial. Yet he was totally opposed to him and again encouraged by the circumstantial evidence. The defence, he was becoming convinced, was on the right path about Burchett's long KGB affiliation.

Traill wanted to follow up on Burchett's scoop of extracting vital bomb data from General Kenny, and he noted that all pro-Soviet agents in relevant positions of influence and espionage in the immediate post-war period had focused on hastening Russian bomb development. Dr Klaus Emil Fuchs had been busy spying on the Manhattan Project to create the US atomic bomb. In August 1945, after the Hiroshima bomb, a British scientist, Dr Allan Nunn May, handed over samples of uranium and information about the theory of atomic energy to the Soviets. Later Philby, Burgess and Maclean would steal many US secrets about atomic bomb designs.

Traill wondered if Burchett had transmitted the very important data that Kenny had given him. Moscow would have considered it invaluable. Traill also wanted to ascertain if Burchett had been doing the KGB's bidding at Hiroshima, knowing well that any report would damage the US's image worldwide and, again, possibly allow Stalin more time to develop the USSR's nuclear weapons programme. *Daily Express* journalists and executives had told Traill that Lord Beaverbrook, the *Express*'s tough and eccentric owner, had directed that the paper break the Hiroshima story first and with detail which would certainly upset the Americans.

Traill was further tantalised by information from an award-winning Australian journalist, Frank Robertson. He had won the Overseas Press Club of America's special award for the first report from Tokyo following the Japanese surrender – a trophy personally presented by President Truman. Robertson, like many journalists of his day, held firm left-wing views, especially before World War II broke out. He and Burchett were friends and colleagues during the Pacific war but, apart from the occasional chat, had not spoken about their ideological leanings. So Robertson, in 1945, was stunned to receive a letter from Burchett in London, which in essence suggested that Robertson should divorce his wife, Jean, because she would not fit in with the plans that Burchett had for him. Robertson described Jean as 'intelligent, but not political'. At the time, Robertson believed that Burchett was a communist and assumed that the letter indicated that Burchett wanted to arrange clandestine Australian Communist Party work for him.

Traill thought that Burchett may have been intent on helping to set up a network of Moscow-controlled agents of influence throughout South-East Asia, but Burchett never followed up on the strange communication.

After World War II, Robertson's political views became more conservative, and he wrote for the London *Daily Telegraph, The Observer* and *The Christian Science Monitor.* During the Vietnam war, Robertson became aware that Burchett harboured some hostility towards him. Burchett was recognised as having an unofficial veto over western media and newspaper people wishing to visit Hanoi after the Americans had bombed the city in 1969, and Robertson believed that Burchett vetoed him for his writing and post-World War II political viewpoints.

In isolation, the Burchett letter to Robertson was no more than another straw in the wind, but in the context of the rest of Burchett's circumstances until the end of 1945, it was encouraging for Traill. The defence, however, was still a long way from making the jury comprehend, let alone accept, its convictions.

10. Berlin's Espionage Market

When Burchett was on the stand again, Cooper questioned him about his 1945 to 1949 period in Berlin where he was for the most part the *Daily Express* correspondent. He wanted to defuse the Krotkov testimony, and it seemed to be an easy enough task. As it turned out, the reconstruction in and out of court by both counsels of events in those heady Berlin days was similar. The disputed point was whether or not Burchett was trying to 'sell' himself to Krotkov. Was Burchett's enormous enthusiasm for the Soviet cause being misinterpreted by his opponents? Or was he doing everything he could to ingratiate himself with the KGB agent so that he could obtain a more lucrative and permanent status?

In the autumn of 1947, Krotkov, then a senior information officer with the Soviet military in Berlin, took Burchett, his father George, and two other correspondents from the London

News Chronicle and Reuters to the island of Peenemunde in the North Sea where the most mysterious and massive structures of the Nazi war machine stood. They were the only people invited to see the destruction of some of the buildings that had once been guarded by electrically charged barbed-wire defences and 4,000 SS officers.

Hitler cleared this pine-clad island of its inhabitants in 1935 and transformed it into a huge research station for the production of 'V' weapons. He spent 100 million dollars on the project, which produced flying bombs for attacking England late in the war. The RAF's retaliatory low-run bombing cut the production rate well below Hitler's 100,000-a-year target and saved London from total destruction.

When the Russians were first to reach Peenemunde, they claimed that the key German scientists had fled with their research. The Allies suspected that the scientists had been taken back to the Soviet Union. If this were true, the best scientific brains in missile development would be put to work on the Russian nuclear weapons programme in a concentrated effort to produce ballistic missile systems – delivery vehicles for the atomic bomb – which were still not fully developed by the Soviet Union.

Rumours spread in Northern Europe that the Russians were testing missiles from Peenemunde. The Soviet military's information section, run by Krotkov, invited these guests to see the destruction of the assembly plant, workshops, wind tunnels, and launch pads to prove that the Russians had not taken the scientists. Western intelligence suspected that reports from these observers helped deflect attention from the possibility that the German scientists were already hard at work on the Soviet programme.

George Burchett wrote a report on the visit that was published on 30 June 1948 by the Good Companion and Christian Social Order Study Group in Australia:

'Our guide and interpreter was a young blue-eyed Georgian [Yuri Krotkov] from Stalin's birth-place. He was a delightful character – an artist – his great loves, music and the ballet. He had conducted Mrs Churchill's party on their tour of Russia. He shortened the motor journey for us by singing excerpts from operas and Russian folk songs interspersed with interesting stories of his experiences piloting important visitors through his country.

'On reaching Peenemunde we were faced with a scene of destruction, which, even after the six months spent in the ruins of Berlin, seemed terrific. Part of the destruction must be credited to the work of the RAF, and the Russians were loud in their praise of their excellent job. The rest of the demolition was the work of the Russians.

'The truth about Peenemunde is that as a military or scientific installation it no longer exists...

'We watched some of the demolition taking place. One long wind tunnel was due to be destroyed, and as the Russians knew we were interested in taking back some documentary evidence of the work, they agreed to blow up a one-third portion of a wind tunnel which was already primed for destruction. We settled ourselves in a concrete lookout from which the Germans had previously observed the firing of the V2's, and watched the top of the wind tunnel disappear in a cloud of smoke...

'My son took back to Berlin forty photographs which were immediately developed. The RAF Berlin heard of our visit, and one of the officers called at our flat next morning. He was so impressed with what he saw that he rang London and in a few hours one of the chiefs of the War Office arrived bringing the plans of Peenemunde, by the aid of which the RAF had carried out the raids.'

This was a contentious point. In court Burchett said: 'An officer of the Admiralty came to me and asked certain specific points which were of interest to them. I said I could not help on the basis of what I had seen, but I would try and find out for him...I went back to see Krotkov [for the details].'

Krotkov, however, had a different version. Burchett came to see him to tell him the British reaction to what he had seen at Peenemunde. According to Krotkov, Burchett often passed on intelligence material to him in an effort to gain the KGB's confidence.

Burchett had a useful advantage when dealing with Krotkov's depositions. He had had time to study them and to prepare his responses. This gave his answers an air of certainty, mixed with appropriate indignation if the situation demanded it. He looked in command during this part of the cross-examination. Each time the defence raised the question of espionage plotting, Burchett had a reasonable explanation. It was beginning to exasperate the unflappable Traill, and he rued his not being able to put Krotkov on the stand.

The Berlin period, which involved Marguerite (Maggie) Higgins, the attractive war correspondent who built her reputation as a courageous reporter in Europe during World War II, began to emerge as important in the trial. She and Burchett had an affair in Berlin, and it seemed for a while that they might marry. (In 1947, Burchett divorced his first wife Erna.) Maggie was fascinated by Burchett's commitment to the Stalinist cause, which was opposed to her right-wing American views. She admired his romantic ideals and found him 'honest, warm and charming'. Maggie also thought that he was proud of his reporting record but modest when he had a lot to shout about. Burchett told friends that she had wanted to have a child with him, but in court remarked that she had 'turned down' his marriage proposal. Their affair made Burchett the envy of most male correspondents in Berlin. Maggie was highly respected among her peers, but a woman who was capable of using her sex appeal to get information. Berlin colleagues said that she would use Burchett to uncover facts from his extraordinary contacts on the Soviet side; in return, he would expect her to provide information from her connections in the US military. According to Higgins, no correspondent in Europe had a better command of military matters, ranging from equipment to strategy, than Burchett. His attention to minute detail in, say, aircraft comparisons between the two super-powers, was exceptional.

He used his prodigious memory to retain and recall facts when required for a quick dispatch. Maggie, who later married a US air-force general, often remarked on Burchett's obsession with the bomb, which had come from his experiences in Hiroshima. He felt peace and the bomb was the most important issue of the twentieth century, he told her, and he would do anything for the cause of peace, even give up his career in journalism.

Their affair was harmonious, and they only argued over ideology. Burchett was pro-Stalin and pro-communist in private and intent on writing about developments in the new Eastern bloc communist countries. He tried to convince her that communism was the way of the future and that capitalism was in its death throes as predicted by first Marx and then Lenin. Maggie would counter by inviting him to visit the US and see what a great nation it really was. But he would always switch the discussion. This rigidity was the only trait in Burchett's character that disquieted her. It was not that he raved and ranted. It was not his style. Instead he would switch off. He was supporting the right side. History would be the judge. Arguments were futile, although debate about which side was honest and right about any single issue were rife.

Maggie always claimed that Burchett was one of the few people in her life who, through his actions and utterances, made her examine her own beliefs and values. Yet she claimed that she never waivered in her support for her country, although Burchett's ideological rectitude and passions forced her to define and defend what the US stood for. She confided to friends that she learned much more about the way his mind worked than did any male correspondents whom he seemed reluctant to open up to in those Berlin days. Maggie felt certain that all her American colleagues were oblivious of his deeper attitudes, as were his other contacts in the west. His job as the number two ranking reporter in Berlin for the conservative *Daily Express* was a quaint cover for such a radical thinker. And it was this radicalism that had a lot to do with their affair never developing into a lasting relationship. Both had fixed paths. Although Maggie would follow any future conflicts that involved the US anywhere around the globe, she wanted to make a home in America. Burchett said that he would never live there on principle. Burchett had tried to 're-educate' her but was appalled by her tough and unwilting pro-American views, based on patriotism. They had often discussed the concept of 'my country right or wrong', and Burchett showed his distaste for nationalism, which he said was a mask for jingoism. Although he was proud of his nationality and rustic, pioneering Australian roots, he saw himself as an internationalist who believed in a humanist ideology. In short, he had a greater faith in communism, which encompassed atheism, than anything else. In that immediate post-war period, with super-power clashes looming and communism spreading over one-third of the world, he had undoubting answers to everything. His conviction, Maggie thought, was unshakeable.

Burchett threw a party in his Berlin apartment in 1947 for his father's seventy-fifth birthday. More than forty guests attended, including Krotkov, and two other Russians, a young German pianist, Maggie Higgins and a score of other correspondents – among them Roland Pullen of the Melbourne *Herald*. Snowy-haired George, sprightly and alert, delivered a long speech that turned into an anti-US, pro-Stalinist harangue. The old man impressed Krotkov with his grasp of international affairs from a communist perspective, and he was sure this was part of Burchett's effort to find a way in with the KGB. Later, in private, Burchett warned Krotkov about an American military officer – Bob Gray – whom he suspected of being an intelligence operative. Krotkov had mentioned Burchett's information on Gray as another example of Burchett's efforts to show the KGB that he was a valuable source.

In court, Burchett handled this with aplomb. Why shouldn't he warn the Russians that Gray was not what he appeared? Acting or not, his performance was convincing.

11. Man of Peace

Burchett relaxed during the weekend break of the ten-day trial by dining at Sydney's Spanish Club. He even took time out to see a beautiful and talented artist, Hueston Kennedy, who insisted on painting his portrait in a rushed, one-day sitting, in which she painted six fingers on one hand. Hueston liked to paint famous figures of Australia's left. Her most recent effort had been Clive Evatt, not Burchett's favourite person at the time, although he avoided mentioning his disappointment about Evatt's withdrawal from the trial.

Hueston gave Burchett a Scotch and asked him to talk about his life. This was not a difficult request, because it had been flashing past him in recent days. He spoke about his early childhood, his tramping around Australia's outback, and his love of the bush. There was no hint of edginess or concern, and he didn't mention the trial. Hueston found him relaxed and friendly. He had no special charisma, style or presence, yet she found there was 'something distinctive' about him, which she captured on canvas at perhaps the most critical moment in a most turbulent, full life.

By contrast, Kane's defence team was working overtime in preparation for the run home in the trial. Although Traill's strategy was not in disarray, it lacked penetration. The aim now was to concentrate on Burchett's many communist links, notably in the Korean war, and hope that bit by bit the KGB connection would look more plausible.

The defence's hopes rose with the appearance of three star witnesses from the US. First there was greying, handsome Colonel Bud Mahurin, the dashing air-ace from World War II and Korea. He was one of the most decorated men in the military history of the US, with medals including the American Distinguished Service Cross, the Distinguished Flying Cross with seven clusters, the Air Medal with nine clusters, the British DFC, and the French and Belgian Croix De Guerre. In the crude vernacular of war, Mahurin had scored 36 'kills' in the air and was fortunate enough to have survived two 'kills' against him, when he was shot down over Germany and in North Korea. In Germany, he was able to flee to France, and he was never captured. In Korea, he was put in a POW camp, where he spent eighteen months in solitary confinement. There, the paths of Mahurin and Burchett crossed. The American was at the trial on a revenge mission.

Burchett personified much of the reason for misadventures that befell Mahurin in Korea and afterwards in the US when the government turned its back on one of its most courageous sons. He had capitulated after long torture by the Chinese and confessed to war crimes, such as dropping germ bombs on China and Korea, which he and the US government claimed afterwards had never happened. Mahurin had maintained a bitterness over two decades, and now he wanted to settle a score with an old enemy.

He and his dark, lean wife Joan had been put up at the Wentworth Hotel. They would add a touch of glamour to the courtroom drabness, and Joan would wear a different, and impeccable, outfit each day. Although she understood her husband's coming ordeal at the trial, she was determined not to present a long face. She was there to give Bud support and to enjoy herself.

'I watch all the courtroom dramas on TV at home,' the former 'Miss Hollywood' told a Melbourne *Herald* reporter, David Elias. 'Perry Mason is my favourite.'

Where Mahurin was ebullient, the second key witness to settle in, Paul Kniss, another American pilot shot down in Korea, was less so, yet no less substantial. He still flew, but now for a US commercial airline. Kniss's motive for making the long trip over the Pacific to appear in the case was less emotional, and not revenge as such. He had put his Korean POW experiences behind him, and he did not hate Burchett. Nevertheless, he wanted to see what he saw as justice done.

Neither of the Americans, despite their determination, was likely to have anything like the impact on the courtroom of former Northumberland fusilier Derek Kinne. He had migrated from England to the US after the Korean war, where he, too, had been a POW. In what the defence hoped would be a trial coup, Traill had stumbled across Kinne's name in his autobiography, *The Wooden Boxes*, which chronicled his heroics in Korea. Traill then tracked down his address and wrote to him in Tuscon, Arizona, where he was running a picture-framing business. There was no reply for some time. But not long before the trial, Kinne sent Kane a sensational tape of his encounter with Burchett in Korea. He was coming to Sydney. Kinne had won the George Cross for his courage as a POW, and therefore provided more substance and credibility for the defence. But he was mercurial and unpredictable. He had developed an obsession for revenge against Burchett that bordered on instability.

Cooper and Traill worked through the weekend. Cooper concentrated on going over the 180-page Krotkov testimony and prepared a defensive stand for Burchett against the anticipated barrage on the Korean war. He relaxed, read part of the Frederick Forsyth thriller, *The Day of the Jackal,* and invited Burchett to his home for dinner on Sunday night.

Cooper was taking his lead from Burchett's attitude. Burchett seemed unconcerned and confident that they would muddle through the next five days, and win. He knew the Krotkov deposition backwards and, like Cooper, expected Traill to target him with it in the final days, for that was still the only direct reference by any witness to Burchett working for the KGB. He also seemed to have no qualms about the witnesses from Korea. Burchett didn't remember anyone called Colonel Mahurin. He couldn't recall Derek Kinne, although he had recollections about Kniss. Burchett's word was good enough for Cooper. If any accusations came from them, Burchett would need to defend them stoically. Unless Traill had documented evidence to back any accusations about Burchett's Korean war activities, he would simply deny them.

Traill was invited to go sailing but declined in favour of doing some heavy homework. He expressed concern that the case might be slipping away but was spurred on by new revelations about Burchett, and writings by him, which did not endear him to Traill. Traill admitted – as did Denis Warner – thinking that some of Burchett's books on South-East Asian politics were informative. But Traill was disgusted by the book, *People's Democracies,* which dealt with the post-war development in Hungary, Yugoslavia, Greece and Bulgaria. He considered it the worst piece of mendacious communist propaganda he had read. Perhaps he could have forgiven a twenty-year-old Marxist undergraduate for such a work, but not a man approaching forty with several years as a top war correspondent behind him.

From 1948, Burchett was writing as a stringer for both the *Daily Express,* for whom he would do lighter, more sensational articles, and the more sober London *Times,* which was still the most influential paper coming out of Fleet Street. The *Daily Express* editors had not been pleased with the pro-communist slant and emphasis his articles were taking from Berlin, and there had been several long-distance arguments on this. Burchett had insisted that the *Express* should be running more of his stories on happenings behind the Iron Curtain; the paper was either spiking him or running only a few paragraphs, and the editors kept telling him that political events in East Germany and Bulgaria were of no interest to the British in Glasgow, Leeds, or London. Relations became strained when Burchett filed a story after a quick trip to Paris early in 1948. He had heard a rumour that some French generals were planning a coup, and he checked the story with the London *Evening Standard's* correspondent in Paris, Sam White. They both agreed it was false, and that the story should not be run.

For some unaccountable reason, Burchett filed an elaborate story that was splashed across the front page. The *Express* was the only paper to carry it. His editors were surprised. They may have disagreed with his politics, but they had never found him inaccurate. Burchett could not run on credit from his legendary war reports for ever.

Burchett had become frustrated with writing from Berlin and wanted to tour Eastern Europe for the *Express*. The editors did not share his enthusiasm for developments in Stalin's satellites, and in order to make the trips he had to forfeit his status as a staff correspondent. Burchett followed the vicious Stalinist line in the show trials of 1948–49 in Eastern Europe. In these, those opposed to Kremlin control were put on trial on trumped-up charges and often executed after making forced confessions to phoney accusations. The trials were similar to those Stalin used to destroy opponents in Russia a decade earlier, where he annihilated those old Bolsheviks and revolutionaries who were Trotsky's or Lenin's original supporters in the Russian Revolution.

Traill was angered by Burchett's description in *People's Democracies* of Cardinal Jozsef Mindszenty, the Prince Primate of Hungary. The communists put him on trial in a 'people's court' and charged him with espionage and illegal foreign currency dealings. Mindszenty acted the Christian martyr against the communists, and Burchett depicted him as a power-mongering throwback from the Middle Ages who stood in the path of progress.

Burchett ridiculed suggestions that Mindszenty had been tortured and drugged into false confessions and noted that being questioned at length was hardly torture. But Burchett seemed to have ignored the evidence of methods used by Stalin's secret police to extract information. They could kill and leave no useful propaganda element and were therefore less effective.

But communists had for decades perfected psychological techniques for changing a victim's attitudes. The memoirs of Eugen Loebel and Artur London, both communist casualties of purges in Czechoslovakia, let the world know what a harmless phrase such as 'interrogated in depth' could mean. Days, weeks, even years of isolation would be followed by victims being hammered with queries for fifty hours by shifts of interrogators. Food would be kept to a minimum to weaken resistance. Sleep would be interrupted at any time. Prisoners might be asked to jump to attention every few minutes, or sit in awkward positions for hours on end. It took little imagination to comprehend the effect on the most resistant mind of the trusted method of dragging someone from their bed in the middle of the night, placing a bulletless revolver at the person's head, and squeezing the trigger.

Burchett was either ignorant of Russian Police Chief Beria's methods from the late 1930s on, or he chose to ignore them. Having studied Burchett's career and affiliations, such as his links with the Society for Cultural Relations with Russia in London, Traill found it difficult to believe that Burchett was unaware of these techniques. Traill's conclusion was that Burchett was a Stalinist stooge from at least 1948 to 1953. Traill thought that more evidence of this was Burchett's uncritical analysis of the communist takeover in Hungary in 1947–48. Before the takeover, 90 per cent of the population supported either the rural-based smallholders' party or the Social Democratic Party. Inside two years these organisations had been obliterated.

Burchett's cavalier attitude to Tito and Yugoslavia also reduced his credibility as an independent observer. Tito was written off in absurd clichés as being in league with western spies because he refused to submit to Stalin's pressures on Yugoslavia to remain under Kremlin control.

Another thread incensed Traill. Burchett's background and life showed an anti-Catholic Church streak. His father had run a bigoted Anti-Papist group in Poowong in 1920. Burchett had created the Catholic Publishing Company in London to exploit the church. He had attacked Mindszenty. Even though the Vatican had also tacitly dismissed Mindszenty as an anti-semitic extremist, Traill felt Burchett's abuse was victimisation directed more at the church than at the individual, who just happened to be a juicy communist target.

After attending mass near his Gordon home on Sunday, Traill met Kane and Terry Tobin, a young legal assistant who had travelled overseas with Kane in search of witnesses. (They had tracked down Mindszenty in Los Angeles in an attempt to get him as a witness, but he could not remember ever meeting Burchett.) Traill wanted to discuss Burchett's apparent hardening as a communist supporter during his stay in Berlin, and the three focused on 1949, which seemed to have been a turning point in Burchett's life. Burchett had moved to Budapest, where he had a smart apartment overlooking the Danube and a beautiful Hungarian girlfriend, and all his professional energies appeared to be going into the peace cause. The communist nations – Cominform – met for the third time in Budapest in November of 1949 and put out a press release saying that it was of the utmost importance to unite all genuine supporters on the broadest possible 'fight for peace' platform. The reason for this decision was to counter the 'imperialist' powers, which were 'pursuing a policy of aggression and preparation for a new war'. Reading between the lines, the peace movement was being used in an all-out effort to pressure the US into slowing its atomic weapons programme, just at the time the Russians were exploding their atom bombs. In China, Mao's long-marching communists had taken over, and a conference of Asian and Australian trade unions set up a liaison bureau in Peking to act as an offshoot of the Cominform. Both the Budapest and Peking meetings strengthened the world peace movement.

Burchett was at the Budapest meeting. According to his father in the biography, *He Chose Truth,* that Cominform conference caused him to 'throw all his energies into the fight for peace'.

The year 1949 was one of transition and commitment for Burchett. It seemed complete when he dumped his Hungarian girlfriend and married Vessa Ossikovska in a Sofia registry office at Christmas. There were two witnesses, an eighty-year-old poet, Mladen Issaev, and Svetozar Zlatarir, the son of a Bulgarian communist scientist. Burchett and Vessa had first met in the summer of 1948 in Sofia, when Vessa, in her job as a government press officer, had been his guide. She was wary at first of this gregarious Aussie reporter, whose professional reputation as a top western journalist working for the prestigious *Times* had preceded him. But Burchett charmed Vessa and impressed her with his linguistics and communist views.

Vessa spoke five languages, including Russian, and had two PhDs in Arts and Literature in Italy (at Padua University) and Bulgaria, and Burchett admired her communist pedigree and record. Vessa's mother had come from a wealthy land-owning family. Her father had been a prominently placed party member long before the communists took power, and Vessa, as a teenager, had lived some time in Italy, where she had worked with the anti-fascist movement. During the war, she had helped the communist-controlled Italian resistance. Burchett, urged on by his father, had always looked upon the right ideological marriage as essential to his life. George had approved of Erna, but was much more enamoured of Vessa.

After consultation with Tobin and Kane, Traill worked late into the night. He was shaping his attack on Burchett for his activities during the Korean war, concentrating on information about Burchett's activities leading up to Korea, from which he hoped to extract clues to Burchett's behaviour in dealing with POWs. Although Traill did not have access to ASIO files on Burchett, he had contacts inside ASIO who fed him some of the files that Kane had not been allowed to see. Under the thirty-year rule, the files that were of interest to Traill would not have been released to the public until the 1980s.

12. The Long Road to Korea

Melbourne, November 1950

The poster outside the Melbourne Town Hall exhorted readers to 'Unite For Peace' and advertised Burchett as the 'famous London *Times* and *Daily Express* war correspondent' from the World Peace Council. Others with respectable billing included Frank Hardy, author of *Power Without Glory,* the Reverend F.J. Hartley, one of the many churchmen who had allied themselves to the peace movement, and communist journalist Rupert Lockwood of the *Tribune.*

Inside the packed hall, Burchett, dressed in a double-breasted suit and carelessly knotted tie, harangued the several thousand listeners, including unionists, communists and members of the clergy, who had gathered to hear the arguments against the west's spread of atomic weapons. At thirty-nine, he looked lean and fit. His speaking style was unremarkable and not in his father's league. Burchett was still impressive, however, for someone whose forte was the written rather than the spoken word. He spent most of his solitary professional life behind a typewriter, poring over notepads, and it was a change to be making a hectic ten-day tour of Australia. He was following through on his promise to dedicate himself to the peace cause or, more precisely, the 'cause' outlined by the Cominform in Budapest a year earlier. The World Peace Council had sponsored his first trip back to Australia in the six years since the end of World War II. He concentrated on the evils of the atomic bomb.

'I was the first journalist to enter Hiroshima after the atomic bomb explosion,' Burchett said, pumping the air with his outsized hands for emphasis, 'and anyone who saw the frightful sights – the mangled bodies of countless thousands of men, women, and children, maimed and blinded babies – and *still* advocates using the bomb, should be certified insane!'

This brought applause, as it usually did, and was a hallmark of Burchett's oratory. He liked telling horror stories during this period, and he used them often in florid articles and in his books. From the bomb he moved to speaking of the 'East European peoples', who were 'really masters of their own countries'. They only wanted peace and no more bombs.

'Coming back into the western world,' Burchett told them, 'was like coming back into a madhouse.' He followed this with a ritual attack on the Menzies government, which was advocating making the Communist Party illegal, and then showered more praise on the way that communist governments were peacefully reconstructing their countries after the devastation of World War II. Burchett would hint at what he saw as the real enemy of 'true and peaceful democracy' – the evil empire of the US. By 1950 he had become even more firmly anti-American, which made him a contentious figure, not merely because of Australia's basic ideological link to the US. With the collapse of the British Empire by the 1940s, the US was the strongest ally Australia had. It had saved Australia from in-vasion by the Japanese in World War II in the Battle of the Coral Sea, giving the two countries a historical connection. Burchett was telling his audiences that there was another, post-colonial choice for Australia. Enthused with what he had seen in Hungary, Bulgaria, and East Germany, Burchett wanted Australia to follow suit and become an 'independent' communist state.

The fundamentally different choices emerging for Australia after the war had created the most divided period in the country's history. The local communist movement had been strengthened by its links to the anti-fascist front during the war and encouraged by the fact that several countries in the region, such as Indonesia, India and China, had shed their colonialist, imperialist skins. Recently, the Waterside Workers Union had refused to allow its members to load arms to be used by the Dutch in their suppression of Indonesia's independence movement. Just a year earlier, in 1949, the then Prime Minister of Australia, Ben Chifley, put troops into the coal mines to keep the power industry going during the communist-provoked miners' strike. Part of Australia's intelligentsia was attracted to radical political change. The mother country was 20,000 kilometres away, and psychologically much further since the war. The concept of 'starting anew', like so many near neighbours in the Asian Pacific region, was seductive.

The nation's conservative forces were reacting. Australia did not experience the witch-hunt of the proportions in the US, yet there were signs that it was on the way with the new Prime Minister, Robert Menzies, pushing his Communist Party Dissolution Bill.

Burchett, more than anyone else, was cleverly presenting a picture of emerging paradise in the communist states in Asia and Europe. He had reported from and lived there, and his words to this group of mainly converted supporters seemed reasonable, even inspiring. Not even the interjection of a couple of rowdy hecklers could throw his delivery.

'Tell us all you know, Burchett,' one stood up and yelled. 'It won't take long.'

The man was booed.

'I'll tell you what we both know,' Burchett snapped back. 'It won't take any longer.' His reply was a steal from Menzies's repertoire, but the audience appreciated it.

Seeing his mate defeated, the second heckler, a more robust, no-nonsense type, shouted, 'If the commies are so flamin' terrific, why don't you go and live in Russia?'

The thought was closer to Burchett's heart than the heckler would have realised. Living in the Soviet Union had been Burchett's long-held dream, something he told many of his friends and family he would do, when the right opportunity arose. But instead of risking press comment, Burchett just grinned as the two men where bustled out of the hall by bouncers.

At the back, a trim young man with a black moustache looked on. He took notes on a small pad but was not with the group of twenty or so reporters who were crouched or seated near the podium. He seemed concerned not to be seen, and with good reason, for he was part of the ASIO contingent following Burchett everywhere on the trip. ASIO and its military intelligence predecessor had been compiling a large dossier on Burchett and every member of the family since the earliest report on Anzac Day, 25 April 1934. It was from a memorial service sermon at the Poowong Methodist Church.

The report to the Intelligence Section General Staff of the 3rd Military District, Southern Command, noted: 'As local Methodist preacher, father [George Burchett] appealed to the congregation to show tolerence to that great country Russia ... (the informing agent) saw that Wilfred supported his father. [Burchett] later acted as superintendent to a boat load of Jewish refugees – Austrian and German – arriving about twelve months ago [mid 1939] and married one of them ...

'Ringleaders of communistic [*sic*] group in town [Poowong] distributed communistic literature ... There were two foreigners carrying on a poor business in town, one staying with the Burchetts ...

'Clive [Wilfred's eldest brother] Burchett's wife separated from him because of his extreme communistic beliefs ...'

The military officer accepting the report also recorded that the informant, Mr J.S. Johnston, of Hastings Road, Cranbourne, 'although apparently reliable, appears to be nursing an old grudge against the Burchetts'.

Since those early files were made, the information coming in on Burchett had stepped up, especially with the advent of ASIO in the late 1940s, which had developed out of the Defence Ministry. In ASIO and the military's eyes, Burchett was political public enemy number one. There was no proof of his Communist Party membership, although he was rumoured to be a secret member.

But it mattered little. Burchett was open enough about his politics. It took courage to be so public, yet Burchett seemed to enjoy the notoriety, and there was a touch of the showman about him. A stronger reason still for his overt activity was an over-riding certainty about the correctness of his beliefs. Some saw his attitude as romanticism, others as plain fanaticism. When he addressed workers at factory gates in Sydney, or crowds on the banks of Melbourne's Yarra River, there was a determination in his words born of prophecy. Burchett had seen revolution in many countries, and he was convinced it was coming soon to Australia and the US.

Burchett's speeches, writing, letters and personal conversations exhibited a stubborn conviction in 1951, which was to fade behind a more pragmatic manner a few years later, when he would become angry at being dubbed a communist. (He wanted to be known as an 'independent'. The thoughtless vitriol in his writing was replaced by a more acceptable, sanitised style that would allow conservative papers to run his articles. He was a late maturer in terms of his profession, but it paid off in terms of an increased readership, notably during the Vietnam war.)

That stirring meeting in the Melbourne Town Hall was the last of its kind he could address. Doors shut across the nation to the World Peace Council. Frustrated, its representatives called for another meeting at the Melbourne Town Hall. A big crowd attended, but all doors to the grey, heavy, colonial building were shut. Burly cops at the entrance told Burchett and Winston that nobody was getting in.

'Then I'll speak from here,' Burchett said, lifting a loud-hailer to his lips. A police sergeant told them to move on because they had formed an 'unlawful assembly'.

'Just what is the law concerning assembly here?' Winston asked.

'You may not assemble here,' the sergeant said, 'and you may not move forward around the hall in any kind of group!'

The Burchett brothers glanced at each other. In the confused silence, tension mounted. The sergeant motioned to some of his men to close ranks in front of the main doors. Others moved towards Burchett. Would he urge the several thousand crowd to disperse, or charge?

'It seems we can move backwards!' Burchett called, much to the enjoyment of the throng. He used the loud-hailer to inform those on the outer reaches. Then he and Winston began to walk backwards. The bizarre action caught on and left the sergeant and his men perplexed. Yet no move was made against the laughing, stumbling throng, for no law was being broken. Burchett continued to address them.

'The World Peace Council is a very progressive, forward-thinking group,' he called. 'Listen to us when we tell you not to move back into a past controlled by imperialists. Let our young nation move forward, free and independent!'

This brought cheers from the crowd, some of whom linked arms. Not far from the police, the ASIO man watched in detached amusement, and made notes. Anticipating the Burchetts' later movements, he strode off towards a nearby hotel for a beer.

Just before six o'clock closing, a dishevelled Burchett and his entourage staggered into the ladies' lounge. They flopped in chairs a few metres from the ASIO man, who pretended to read the Melbourne *Herald*. A clergyman in the Burchett group went to the bar and ordered beers. Burchett asked one of the party if she had managed to get something on prescription for him. He was handed a small bottle. He sampled the contents, and the woman, a Communist Party follower, insisted on knowing what it was. Burchett joked about it being a 'truth drug', and called it Aktedron. Then he explained it was Benzedrine, which he had first started using in Hungary, where he could get it over the counter at any pharmacy. He claimed it kept him awake during the Mindszenty trial, and that it sustained him during his busy schedule. He said that Benzedrine had also been used by Mindszenty, who had been the first to report it – in the London *Times*. Winston told the group that Burchett had written a play about Mindszenty called *The Changing Tide*, which would be staged at his house at Rosebud on the coming weekend. Everyone was invited to see it.

With the six o'clock rush for last orders in the pub ruining the acoustics, the ASIO man took a tram to his office on St Kilda Road, where staff were beginning to leave for the day. He took the lift to the fourth floor, and began to type up his report.

'By Burchett's personal appearance and remarks it would appear that he is a heavy drinker and possibly a drug addict,' the ASIO man began. He remembered to make a note to have Burchett's play on Mindszenty investigated.

The Changing Tide was performed in the garage of Winston's house at his Rosebud bungalow resort. Since his push from federal politics (in 1949 Winston felt he had to resign from his job as a private secretary to the Minister for Air and Civil Aviation, the Hon. A. S. Drakeford, because of rumours of communist connections), Winston had been running the resort, which was mainly patronised by union groups for holidays and seminars. About a dozen people watched the play, which was about Mindszenty and a Hungarian peasant girl, and demonstrated the Catholic Church's supposed collaboration with landowners in the exploitation of the Hungarian peasantry. One of the guests, who worked for the local post office, and intermittently informed the intelligence network of the activities of discussion groups run by Winston Burchett at the Rosebud bungalows, told ASIO about the play and its participants.

That night Burchett did not endear himself to Winston and Mary by using one of the bungalows for a menage à trois with two of his Communist Party admirers. Winston was disappointed with his brother's behaviour and the realisation that they had drifted apart. The halcyon days they shared as close mates in their youth had ended after their trip to Europe thirteen years earlier. Winston had become homesick, but Burchett had no such stirrings. He had married and taken on ties that would distance him from Australia. Although he did return from 1938 to 1941, he travelled abroad again during the war as a correspondent. Not even the birth in 1941 of a son, Rainer, to Erna, could restrict his wanderings, and Erna and her family settled back in England. Burchett had not been the most dedicated husband or father. Burchett's career came first, and he rarely saw his family before divorcing Erna in 1947. A string of exotic women in Asia and Europe fulfilled his superficial needs for relationships until he married the strong-willed Vessa, and his commitment to her lasted thirty-five years.

The morning after the play was presented, George Burchett visited the bungalows. He, Winston and Wilfred strolled the beach on a cloudy, late spring day. George felt closer to Wilfred, who was immersed in ideas about radical change, than his other two sons. Clive had been a good unionist and communist but not gifted or ambitious. Winston, who was Wilfred's intellectual match, had been more successful in the conventional sense, but he was not as dedicated to the cause. Winston was more pragmatic and less adventurous. He had irritated his father and brothers by telling them that he 'could not swallow any supposedly infallible doctrine, book or leader, be it Pope John, Stalin, Marx or Menzies'.

Winston had a cynical attitude to the revelations of omniscience by Stalin and Marx, which were trustingly accepted by George, Wilfred and Clive. He would often be one out arguing over the Stalinist doctrine that all scientific disciplines would be better following Marxist principles. Winston, for instance, would not buy the fashionable communist idea in the late 1940s that vegetables grown in the Soviet Union reached massive proportions when Marxist ideals governed their development. This is not to say that Winston was not pro-Stalinist, and forever pro-Soviet. It was simply that he was widely read and would not accept the more stupid claims of fervent communists.

George pledged to continue publishing Wilfred's works (his World Unity Publications had already put out *People's Democracies*) and, if he couldn't, he would urge communist publisher Joe Waters, who had brought out Burchett's *This Monstrous War*, and the party to help. Father and son spoke about China, and George urged Wilfred to go there and be first to inform the world of the country's changes since the communists had taken power. Wilfred said he was already thinking about it because a good Chinese contact, Chen JiaKang, who had been Chou En Lai's private secretary in Chungking during World War II, had met him at the World Peace Movement's Congress in Prague in the spring of 1949. Chen had urged Burchett to come to Peking where there would be plenty of work with the new regime. English-speaking professionals would be welcome. George said the Chinese would need him to counter American efforts to destroy the Chinese communists' image. He spoke of a two shilling booklet he had just published *Will America Dominate the World?*, which featured his usual anti-US diatribe. It was the latest in George's never-ending writing production line.

The old man had been a builder for the first fifty years of his life in the best Burchett family tradition. Before migrating to and pioneering southern Australia in the middle of the last century, the Burchetts had been farmers and house builders for hundreds of years in the Surrey-Kent counties of England. George had been the first to attempt to break the tradition and dabble in jobs that exercised his mind. He was a frustrated communicator, who took every opportunity to write freelance articles. His letters addressing big topics, such as the formation of the League of Nations, often appeared in the Melbourne *Age*. He formed local debating societies and discussion groups, which were both far-reaching in scope and controversial. It became fashionable for academics and the local intelligentsia in the late twenties and the thirties to visit Poowong, 110 kilometres east of Melbourne, to lecture to the Burchett-founded discussion groups, and police and military intelligence informants began to report them. Free-ranging thought, especially when it touched on such issues as Marxism, Leninism, and independence for India, was seen as a danger to the realm – the British Empire – of which Australia was a dominion.

George scribbled and spoke on, undaunted. He was an excellent public speaker, who debated in the old style, where the object was to score intellectual points and win, often with disregard for the truth. He was also a lay-preacher who preferred to open the congregration's mind to global topics such as war and peace rather than to rely on the scriptures. This caused the local Methodist Church to close its doors to him. But he was not worried. He had found his cause. George's hot gospelling was heard more now by emerging pro-communist groups and was scorching the pages of first anti-German, then anti-US booklets. The world communist movement could do no wrong. When he wasn't praising Stalin or Mao, he was railing against the US. His latest booklet (published 1950) attacked all major American institutions: 'The spectacle today [in the US] is of a panic-stricken people, whipped into a frenzy of war hysteria by propaganda which makes the Goebbel's machine in Nazi Germany look like child's play. The leaders have hauled down the democratic flags and turned the country into a police state.'

Much of George's invective had come from Wilfred's

writings or from their chats. He reassured his father continually that the Americans could not stop the advance of communism, even in the US. Once Menzies was toppled, Wilfred said with certainty, there would be nothing in Australia to stop it. George worried about the press backing Menzies's efforts to destroy legally the Communist Party. The Melbourne *Herald,* run by Keith Murdoch, was of particular concern.

'Mark my words,' Wilfred told his father, 'one day soon it will be the *People's Herald.*'

He was not concerned if Menzies dissolved the Party, because he thought it could be more effective underground. Wilfred predicted that inside a decade, or two at the most, there would be a communist revolution in the US and Australia.

13. China Syndromes

When Burchett arrived in Peking in the bitter cold of February 1951, it was the beginning of China's 'golden years' before Mao's murderous excesses, which would out-do even Stalin in forced and disastrous social engineering. Peking was vivid and hopeful. The clay-walled inner city enclaves – hutungs – formed a huge and colourful mosaic of ordinary Chinese endeavour. The minor merchants of everything, including even a specialist in second-hand wash-basins, advertised their wares. Kettle drums rattled, whistles were heard non-stop, and trumpets sounded. The only violence in the never-ending marketplace was when Moslem priests slit the throats of unsuspecting sheep. Hooded falcons sat on their owners' wrists so that they would not be distracted by the occasional rodent weaving past unsuspecting human feet. Men and women gossiped as they made or stitched footwear, and chopped food, which sent a variety of smells into the atmosphere. It was almost impossible to walk into a hutung without being tempted to buy something cheap and delectable to eat or drink.

Burchett and Vessa lived first in a hotel, then in a courtyard house in For Lang. They made use of Burchett's list of important contacts in the Chinese capital whom he had befriended in the early 1940s in China. They included Madame Kung Peng, who now headed the Information Department of the Foreign Ministry; her husband, Chiao Kuan Hua, now Assistant Minister of Foreign Affairs; the poet and journalist Yang Kang, now a writer for *Jen Min Jih Pao*, the communist party's daily paper. Through these decade-old connections, and introductions from the Australian Communist Party, Burchett was appointed an adviser to the Foreign Ministry, where he got to know British communist writer Alan Winnington of the UK *Daily Worker*, who had a similar appointment. Burchett also picked up work for the French communist evening paper, *Ce Soir*, and was promised possible outlets with the New China News Agency, and broadcasts over Peking radio. Conditions and prospects seemed good. The Chinese Communist Party was picking up all his expenses as he explained to his father in a letter (to which Traill was never privy):

'I don't have to worry about finances here. I am treated on the same basis as a local writer although you need not spread this news outside our own circle. In other words I am relieved of financial cares and given facilities to see what I want to see, travel where I want to travel, interview who I want to interview...Luxury needs are not catered for but basic needs are. Most government employees live on that basis. What I need, for example, comes to me, from food and writing paper and typewriter ribbons. I sign for it and it's a book entry somewhere. That's how all artists and writers operate here and I am treated as an honoured foreign guest writer.'

He and Vessa were soon mixing well with the foreigners in the city and became friends with Jean-Paul Sartre and Simone de Beauvoir and many other writers who had come to experience the biggest revolution of them all. The limitation that prevented real communication with the people, however, was the language. Burchett, a gifted linguist, made a gallant attempt to learn it, but failed in the short time he had. Only a few foreigners were able to master it.

On 23 March, Burchett was guest of honour at a rally in

Peking presided over by Kuo Mo-jo, president of the China Peace Committee. In the keynote speech, Burchett said: 'If Australia was spared the sufferings of a Japanese invasion, she did suffer from an American occupation. While Australian troops were bearing the brunt of the fighting in New Guinea, hundreds of thousands of American troops poured into Australian cities. They brought with them the gangsterism and corruption which are such a feature of American life. The Australian people are determined that they shall never again suffer from either Japanese aggression or American occupation. They are resolutely opposed to any form of re-militarization of Japan; of any granting of Pacific islands to Japan; of any establishment of American army or naval bases in Australia or New Guinea...

'The Australian people have long watched with utmost sympathy the struggle of the Chinese people for their liberation from foreign and internal oppression. The more progressive elements of the Australian people, the Australian workers, have shown their sympathy in the past in practical ways...The Australian peace fighters have been working under great difficulties. The peace delegates who defied the government's ban and attended the Warsaw Congress had their passports confiscated when they returned to Australia. The government passed a bill which made the Peace Council, the Communist Party, and other democratic organisations illegal. But the peace fight went on. Signatures for the Stockholm Appeal were collected, and 200,000 people signed, despite semi-official threats that the activity might be punished with five years' imprisonment. The peace movement has received the widest support among the Australian people, and the best measure of our success has been the failure of the campaign to recruit troops for Korea.'

Within weeks of arriving in China, Burchett began one of his doctrinaire, didactic 'before and after' books (this was how bad it was before the communist revolution, now see how great it is), which was published as *China's Feet Unbound* by his father's World Unity Publications.

The book's introduction, dated Peking, 15 July 1951, accused the US of waging germ warfare in Korea. The book, Burchett said, was 'written against the background of American bombs landing on Chinese soil, American tanks rumbling towards China's frontier, American germ warfare launched against China's neighbour'. In the body of the book he linked American germ warfare with Japanese germ warfare: 'Numerous boasts by top officers in the US War Department make it clear that the US is busily preparing for germ warfare based on the activities of the Japanese war criminals, with their active assistance.'

Burchett did not document these unsubstantiated charges, but he would have been fascinated to have had access to US military files, which disclosed specifics about US and UK preparation for mass production of germ bombs towards the end of World War II. Ironically, it was Burchett's nemesis Warner and his wife Peggy who first made public the information in their book, *The Sacred Warrior*, on the Japanese Kamikaze death squadrons:

'By 10 December 1943, work had been advanced to the point where the director of the (US) War Research Service requested that the Chemical Warfare Service should undertake developmental work on both botulinus toxin and anthrax spores. The Warfare Service established research facilities at Camp Detrick, Maryland. The field testing station was at Horn Island, Mississippi. The pilot plant produced botulinus toxin with relative safety and fair yields...Anthrax spores, it was discovered, could be spread either in the form of a dry powder, or in a "slurry". No satisfactory method of immunisation against anthrax spores had been developed, although research was developing.

'General Porter reported on 2 February 1944 that eight months would be required to construct a plant for production of [biological] agents from the time of receipt of a directive. An operating force of 250 people would be required, and he recommended that approval be granted for the immediate construction of the plant, which would produce anthrax spores, botulinus toxin and other agents. It was estimated that the unit would produce...one million four-pound bombs of anthrax spores, or 250,000 four-pound bombs filled with botulinus toxin...'

Nothing in Warner's research indicated whether or not the US had gone on with germ warfare development at Fort Detrick, and no germ bombs were used against the Japanese, although it was planned. Yet it raised questions about what happened to production. The US records spoke of anthrax and botulinus bombs being developed, while communist propaganda campaigns concentrated on claiming that the US had dropped bombs that led to cholera.

Burchett's startling charge in *China's Feet Unbound* about US germ warfare attacks preceded by three months a publication by the Institute of Law of the Soviet Academy of Sciences of a book on the trials of Japanese germ warfare bacteriologists at Khabarovski. They had been experimenting during World War II in preparation for launching attacks on Japan's enemies. The Soviet book was called *Bacteriological War – The Criminal Tool of Imperial Aggression*. Some of the same material in it appeared in Burchett's book.

Burchett accompanied the London *Daily Worker*'s Alan Winnington and six Chinese journalists on the long drive in an open Russian truck from Peking to Kaesong, Korea, in mid July 1951. The beautiful walled city of Kaesong set among low hills was to be the initial site for the Korean war peace talks, which Burchett and Winnington were to cover from the North Korean/Chinese side. They were destined to play a vital role in the propaganda part of a war that had its roots in a secret deal at the Yalta conference between the leaders of victorious nations of World War II – Churchill, Roosevelt and Stalin – in February 1945. It was agreed that American and Russian troops should enter Korea to accept the surrender of Japanese forces, the Americans to the south of the 38th parallel and the Russians to the north. It was at this line that the Cold War became 'hot'.

The Russian command set up a Soviet-style administration in the north and put in Kim Il Sung, who had been a major in the Soviet army. In the south, the Americans backed Syngman Rhee. After the failure of all discussions on Korea, in Moscow and at the UN, two separate states were set up. In South Korea, every pro-communist group was eliminated. Similarly, every non-communist group was rendered impotent in the north. Most of the American and Russian troops were withdrawn. Skirmishes began between whole divisions of troops along the 38th parallel.

On 25 June 1950, there was a successful large-scale attack

by the North Korean troops. In only weeks they occupied all but the extreme south-eastern corner of Korea, the 'Pusan Perimeter'. In the UN, the USSR boycotted the Security Council, and a resolution was passed on 27 June calling on UN members to support South Korea against North Korean aggression. The US responded swiftly, and sixteen nations contributed to the UN force. The Pusan Perimeter was held against a North Korean attack beginning on 1 September and on the 15th, the brilliantly executed landings at Inch'on took the North Korean army in the rear. By late October 1950, the UN troops occupied almost the whole of Korea. Then the Chinese got involved and sent a million troops into action, and they forced the UN troops back as rapidly as they had previously advanced.

During the spring of 1951, the line was stabilised along the 38th parallel. Truce talks began on 10 July, a few days before Burchett and Winnington arrived at Kaesong.

In effect, they were to act as publicists for the communists on the peace talks and later in the germ warfare campaign. The Chinese were shrewd in using these two English speakers to deal with the western press. Winning the information battle was important to both sides, and Burchett, particularly, was expected to be invaluable. He knew most of the western press, and they respected him because of his professional record in Asia, the Pacific and at Hiroshima, and his shock appearance from the communist side was, in itself, a PR coup for Moscow and Peking.

Burchett had to gain the confidence of as many western correspondents as possible, and he anticipated he would win some and lose some. His arrival at the peace talks villa compound, to meet the press with Winnington, caused a sensation. The first to greet Burchett was a fellow writer from his *Daily Express* days, Russell Spurr. As Burchett climbed from a jeep, Spurr asked how he had travelled from Peking.

'Now, I can't really tell you that,' Burchett said, with an enigmatic look, 'can I?'

Spurr was surprised by the remark but understood that this meant he had come by a military route that the Chinese would not want disclosed. It was a quick message that Burchett was with 'them'. It intrigued Spurr, who had been, and would remain, a close friend.

In the compound over the following months, Burchett

received a mixed reaction. Some of his old American colleagues snubbed him; others shook hands. One New Zealander who refused to shake hands was Lachie McDonald, a friend of Denis Warner's, who wrote for the *Daily Mail*.

'It's like that, is it?' Burchett remarked.

'Yes,' McDonald replied.

'You're just like Denis Warner,' Burchett snapped. He pointed a forefinger at McDonald and added, 'You tell Warner, I've been watching his stuff about me. Some day I'll get him!'

Burchett turned away to join Winnington and other communist writers.

Walter Simmons of the *Chicago Herald Tribune* called after him, 'You goddamn commie...!'

Burchett kept walking and did not respond. He never approached that group again. It included United Press International reporter Richard Applegate, who went out of his way to greet Burchett and Winnington each day, 'Hello, traitors.'

One of the American journalists who did not react unfavourably to Burchett's support for the communist side was Maggie Higgins, who had been reporting the war as a correspondent for the *Herald Tribune*. At one meeting during the peace talks, the two strolled and talked for four hours in full view of the rest of the press corps. At times they linked arms affectionately. Higgins took notes and wrote an interview with Burchett for the *Herald Tribune* about this curious Australian who had switched sides after making his reputation as a western reporter in World War II. Higgins alluded to Burchett's future in the article and, during the chat, attempted to probe deeply. But he would not be drawn beyond his belief of the 'rightness' of the communist cause. Higgins later told friends that she detected an uncertainty in Burchett about where he would go after Korea. Yet he seemed to have few fears about his future. She still felt that he could be won back to the west.

Their Berlin romance was not renewed. The press from the east and west were only to meet on neutral ground to cover the talks. They would disappear to their respective sides at night. Nevertheless, the two retained a passion for each other tempered by time and circumstance. Burchett was happily married to Vessa, and while having a reputation for amorous pursuits at every opportunity, he was dedicated to their marriage. Maggie was expecting to marry an American air force general, and although she and Burchett would both cover the Vietnam war, they were destined never to meet again.

Burchett's hostile reaction to Warner, as expressed to McDonald and others, was provoked by the first of his broadsides for the Melbourne *Herald* (5 October 1951). It covered Burchett's unusual freedom in moving 'behind the iron curtain'.

Unlike Burchett, Warner had reported the war itself. He had been editorial manager for Reuter and Associated Press in Japan and Korea. Then he began a six-year South-East Asian roving assignment for the *Herald*. When the paper was at its peak, Warner had arguably the most important foreign correspondent's job. If the Pacific war had not made his name, this did.

He went back to Korea at the end of June 1950 when the North Koreans first attacked. Warner was with American troops during their first engagement and remained in the country until 1950. In those few months, seventeen correspondents were killed. Among them was a colleague of Warner's from the London *Daily Telegraph*, for which he was also reporting. Another *Telegraph* man was wounded, and this left Warner as the paper's only correspondent in a competitive and dangerous environment.

Later in that year, when based in Singapore, Warner began to read Burchett's material in the *Radio Malaysia Digest* of Peking radio broadcasts. Typical of his writing at that time was his comment about US General Van Fleet's 'wringing his bloodstained hands [in Korea]'. This sort of vitriolic propaganda at first astonished Warner. Until then he had regarded Burchett as a good, objective western correspondent. Only a few years earlier he had reported the Pacific war courtesy of the US navy. Now he was against the US, Warner wanted to know much more.

Just before Burchett left Peking for Kaesong, he rushed to have his *China's Feet Unbound* published. At the same time, the communist news agency, Telepress, claimed in a report that General Matthew B. Ridgway, the UN Commander in Tokyo, had sent three Japanese bacteriological experts, including a General Shiro Ishii, to Korea to help the US armed forces prepare germ warfare against North Korea and China. The Russians had accused these men of producing weapons for human extermination.

The Telepress release was the first significant attack in the campaign. The allegations were quickly dismissed as propaganda by the US, but a few months later, in February 1952, the charges became specific as the well-planned orchestration unfolded internationally. On 18 February, Moscow Radio's Korean language broadcast accused the US of poisoning wells and spreading smallpox and typhus bacteria. Three days later, Peking Radio said that American aircraft, between 28 January and 17 February 1952, had spread large quantities of germs. Then on 26 February Pak Hen Yun, the North Korean Foreign Minister, accused the Americans of use of germ warfare in North Korea. Yun claimed that in the past month American planes had dropped 'bombs' laden with germ-carrying insects in large quantities on North Korean positions and behind the lines. Yun did not give details on what species the insects were but did say that they carried plague and cholera germs. Chou En Lai, China's Foreign Minister, followed by accusing the US of conducting bacteriological experiments on hundreds of thousands of Chinese and North Korean prisoners.

Days later, and for several months to follow, Peking sent a flood of documentary material to the World Peace Council's headquarters in Prague. The council's branches in many countries continued the campaign. Then the Russians, who seemed to be masterminding the international effort, delivered their trump card in the affair by involving Dr Zhukov Verezhnikov, who had been the key witness at the Kharbarovsk trials of the Japanese scientists. On 14 March, he addressed a rally in Moscow and again made the claim that the US had dropped germ bombs on the North Koreans. Verezhnikov then produced evidence – infected insects – which was said by many observers to be convincing.

Burchett led the follow-up campaign by journalists writing in the west with articles in *Ce Soir*, and the New China News Agency, and broadcasts over Peking radio. He was supported by Winnington, and Tibor Meray, who worked for Szabad Nep, the central newspaper organisation of the Hungarian Workers' Party in Budapest. Meray was briefed in Hungary by

Marton Horvath, director of Agitprop in the Central Committee of Hungary's Communist Party, and sent to Korea to cover the peace talks in Pyongyang. Before he even arrived, Meray was convinced that the Americans were dropping the germ bombs.

During the early, freezing days of March 1952, Meray and a Polish and a Korean journalist were shown evidence in North Korea that either verified one of the worst war crimes or was the greatest war-time hoax of the century. Chinese soldiers introduced to him reported that they had discovered unusual insects dropped in paper bags above rivers and streams. Biologists examined the insects and said that they were germ-bearing. In the intense cold of March, it was observed that many would die, but the cholera germs would live on and lie dormant until the snows melted and allowed them to enter the water supply. This would lead to an epidemic.

Meray was taken to a laboratory where he was shown insects labelled with the date and place of their discovery. Then he visited a village called Sonori, twenty-eight kilometres from Pyongyang on the frozen Tetenghan River, and was introduced to peasants who said that they had found eight heaps of flies. Fires lit by the locals had destroyed many of them, but Meray reported that he had seen some still living. Dressed in mask and protective clothing, he went to a house where a sixty-two-year-old man and two children had died of cholera. The man was said to have found three heaps of flies in his courtyard scattered with South Korean pamphlets.

The three journalists led by Meray accepted all the evidence without searching questions. No one bothered to ask how the pamphlets just happened to be in the same courtyard as the flies. Either the US pilots were remarkably accurate in their fly and junk mail dropping, or the evidence was planted.

Meray apparently was not interested in how some of these flies managed to survive in piles for many weeks in the freezing temperatures and out of their normal environment. No one could explain what sort of bombs these flies were being dropped in. There was evidence of the bombs' contents but not in their casing. Nevertheless, the presentation (or charade) continued.

At Dai-Dong in North Korea, Meray learned of a country girl who had found a straw package containing a certain kind of clam on a hillside. She took some of the clams home, so the story went, and she and her husband made a raw meal of them. Within twenty-four hours they were both dead. Cholera was said to be the cause of death. By coincidence the local home guard found more of these killer clams, and they were found to be infected with cholera. Meray and the others were convinced of the US's guilt.

Western journalists began to take a mild interest in the accusations, and several applied to see the evidence. All were turned down while Meray's unchallenged reports got worldwide publicity and shocked the US. Protests were heard from the Hungarian Academy of Science to the American Academy of Science, and a rally in Budapest on 19 March called for the UN to conduct a public trial – along the lines of the Stalinist show trials – of all the guilty men. Other rallies were held in Moscow, Prague and Sofia. The Chinese gave a sneak preview of the mass hysteria that would come with the Red Guards, when, under Communist Party directives, they rallied and demanded an end to germ warfare. The population was mobilised into a mass killing spree of flies, mosquitoes, fleas and rats to destroy everything that might be a carrier of the germs. The Chinese government recorded that in the first year of the clean-up the lights went out for 120 million rats, and 0.5 million kilograms of flies, mosquitoes and fleas. Tonnes of insects, rats, clams and chicken feathers were exhibited in Peking as 'proof' of US misdemeanours.

When western journalists were not allowed to view the evidence, the US Secretary of State, Dean Acheson, offered to submit the charges against his country to a neutral International Red Cross investigation. The president of the Red Cross wrote to Acheson, North Korea's leader Kim Il Sung and to General Peng Teh-huai, commander of the Chinese People's Volunteers, agreeing to carry out the investigation if both sides found it acceptable. The U.S. offered to co-operate. But the communists wouldn't bite. Whether their allegations were true or false, they were on the best anti-American propaganda ploy ever devised. If it would distract the world and help gain concessions from the Americans in the peace talks, the campaign would be played for all it was worth.

14. Fear in Korea

O fficials had to keep people away from courtroom number seventeen at the start of the second week of the trial. The regulars in the public gallery got there early enough to make sure that they didn't miss a word, all except one long-haired man who often fell asleep, snoring loudly. One woman knitted, another sewed a white polka-dot dress for her daughter. One hirsute man would occasionally take out a big blue comb and stroke his large beard.

Proceedings were laboured at times, but they were never dull as the two sides became combative over Burchett's activities more than twenty years earlier in Korea.

Traill put Tom Hollis in the witness box. He was a burly Australian barman at a Sydney RSL Club and a former Korean War POW. Hollis had joined the Australian volunteer forces as a private to fight the North Koreans and Chinese in Korea. He became a member of the 3rd Batallion there on 26 December 1950. Less than a month later, he was taken prisoner by the Chinese. Traill attempted to show the hardship experienced as a POW, but Cooper objected successfully, and so Traill was limited.

Hollis said that he had been marched to several prison camps in his first year in captivity until he was put in Camp 5 on the Yalu River, North Korea, in late 1951. He explained that there were several communist newspapers available in the camp, and that he was familiar with Burchett and his attitudes from them. The former POW joined the others, who had called Burchett a collaborator with the Chinese.

'The Chinese wouldn't let anyone into the camps who was going to write an article against them,' Hollis said. 'It's commonsense.' He spoke of Burchett at Camp 5. Hollis and three other Australian POWs, Don Buck, Bob Parker and Keith Gwyther, were taken to a hut to be interviewed by Burchett. There was a heated discussion, and Hollis accused Burchett of being a 'bloody traitor to his country'. Buck asked Burchett if he was a communist, and he said 'No'. He said he was a communist 'sympathiser'.

According to Hollis, Burchett offered them a trade-off of better food and treatment, such as making sure their mail reached Australia, if they co-operated in his interviews. But they rejected the offer, and there was a shouting match before Burchett left.

The next witness, Bob Parker, went over the same ground but added that he argued with Burchett over whether or not the Chinese were treating them well. The former POWs both complained that they had lost weight and told Burchett that he had no idea of the poor conditions they had experienced.

Cooper's cross-examination concentrated on showing that the POWs were hostile to Burchett and tried to imply that their testimony was unreliable. He also showed that Burchett had not been party to any 'brainwashing'; nor had he intimidated the Australian POWs.

The jury had been most attentive, and Traill calculated that the defence had gained some ground. He had Warner on the stand to capitalise on this by explaining the communist build-up of the germ warfare propaganda campaign. He said that on 17 May 1952, Peking radio announced that Burchett had been invited to be part of a 'joint interrogation group of specialists and news correspondents', which investigated whether US pilots had dropped germ bombs on North Korea and China.

Warner told the court of the anti-American tone of all Burchett's writing. The judge intervened and asked what Burchett's reputation was during the Korean war.

'He was regarded by many journalists and many others as a traitor,' Warner said, 'and he was frequently called this.' Warner took the opportunity to say what he thought about Cooper's interventions.

At the end of the day's court proceedings, Burchett was angry at Warner's attack. He, Spurr and Cooper made a third and last attempt to uncover something incriminating on Warner based on further information from Gregory Clark, a journalist working for *The Australian* newspaper in Toyko, who was due to give evidence at the trial. Clark, a former employee of Australia's Department of Foreign Affairs, claimed he would receive memos from ASIO requesting that a 'friendly' journalist visiting, for instance, Taiwan, should be given every co-operation. Warner was one of those who would turn up in Taiwan. Burchett took this as meaning that Warner's links to ASIO went beyond those maintained between a roving foreign correspondent and his country's intelligence service. Clark added that there was nothing unusual in any journalist drawing on ASIO for information. Burchett's obsession with any link between Warner and espionage activity was groundless.

Eric Donnelly, the photographer, was the next witness called by Traill. He had been hostile to Burchett at the press conference in 1970, when he contradicted Burchett's claim that he had given beer and fruit to Australian POWs. Now under oath, Donnelly spoke of Burchett's reputation as a dangerous man and a liar. Cooper, who was kept on his toes objecting, again managed to curtail a damaging deposition by getting Donnelly to say that he supported the Australian Journalists Association's efforts to get Burchett a passport.

The first of the defence's three star witnesses, Derek Kinne, entered the witness box looking tense. The rest of the defence had been apprehensive about him, for he tended to have a volatile, mercurial personality; people found him friendly one day, and then difficult and morose the next. It was anyone's guess how he would perform in the pressure-cooker tension of the courtroom. Jack Kane had confidence in him and remarked that he thought Kinne was the bravest man he had ever met.

Traill began by eliciting that he held the George Cross, and that he had been in the Royal Northumberland Fusiliers with the British forces in Korea. Kinne spoke of being captured in South Korea and taken to POW camp number one at Chong Son in North Korea, in an accent that was a mix of British working class and middle America. In an electric moment, Traill asked him if he knew who Burchett was in this court action. Kinne stared hard at Burchett and said, 'I do'.

'You see him in court?' Traill asked.

Kinne pointed an accusing finger at Burchett and said: 'He is right there.'

Burchett sat impassively, staring back as the eyes in the public gallery flicked from Kinne to Burchett.

Traill moved on to a vital confrontation between Burchett and Kinne when Burchett visited the camp to address the POWs. The Chinese told the POWs – about 1,400 Americans and British – that Burchett was coming, and most of the men knew who he was from the literature – communist newspapers – in the camp. The strain showed on Kinne's face, and he mumbled.

After a few responses, Traill asked him to speak up. The witness looked ready to explode, and he did, in a blast of words that shook the courtroom. He was not as articulate as some of his predecessors, but the impact was enormous. No one in the courtroom could doubt the man's sincerity.

'So where did you see him [Burchett]?' Traill asked.

'On the football pitch, sir,' Kinne said. 'In the prisoner-of-war camp.'

'On the football field?'

'Yes.'

'How many of you were there?'

'It was all the Americans and all the British, about 1,400 men. They put a table on the football pitch, and the football pitch was facing east and west. He came and stood in front of the table, and he faced us. There was one guy I remember particularly, carrying a noose, and he was swinging the noose, and he would say, "You will hang", and the chorus used to be, "You'll hang you bastard, you will hang", and he [Burchett] went into his damned spew...'

The woman knitting for her daughter stopped and the snoring man sat up to attention. Cooper objected to 'damned spew', and Judge Taylor, who had been drily witty and impatient at the defence's occasional dithering, leaned forward.

'What did he say, this man Burchett?' Taylor asked, for the first time reacting as if this case, and especially Kinne, was exceptional.

'He went on to say, sir,' Kinne began, the pain of the recall evident, 'that through the tireless efforts of the Chinese People's Volunteers, the peace talks [between the US and other UN forces on one side, and the Chinese and North Koreans on the other] were going on, and that the Americans had sabotaged the peace talks. He was getting booed down, and the Americans started to take off their belts and put a noose in them, and they would swing them. It became pretty well bedlam. So he got rather pissed off, and he said, "All right, you people, you think when the peace talks break down, and the Americans come this way, you will be liberated; but I've got news for you. You are going that-a-way." And he pointed to China...'

Kinne looked down at Burchett and said angrily, 'Don't look surprised! You remember!'

Burchett shook his head in bewilderment. Cooper was about to object, when Traill intervened so that Kinne would not be interrupted. Taylor seemed fascinated.

'Just tell us what was said, please,' Traill said.

'I was in the front row. He turned his back and began to tidy up his papers, and I...' Kinne paused and touched his forehead. 'Oh, there was a theme. He was always saying, "Our side" and "Your side". I went to the front, and I faced him.'

Until that moment, Kinne had been mainly responding to Traill, with glances at the judge. Now the witness turned towards Burchett, as if this was the correct way to re-enact the confrontation, and addressed him. 'I was facing west, and he was facing east, and I said to him, "Are you biased, you son-of-a-bitch? Are you biased?" He said, "No." I said, "Why do you refer to the Chinese and the North Koreans as 'Our side', and the Americans as 'Your side'?" I can't remember whether he said, "That's the side I correspond for" or "The side I work for"; and then I said to him, "Well, you can tell your side to get some dental treatment in here because men are having their teeth extracted with regular pliers; also thirty-nine men went up Boot Hill. I saw the dogs dragging the bodies out [of the graves of a cemetery], and we ate those dogs." And I said, "We are starving to death." I went up to the Chinese, and I told him...'

Taylor sat transfixed.

'Did Burchett say anything?' Taylor asked.

'No, sir. He kept his mouth shut.'

Judge Taylor spoke again, trying to regain his neutrality. 'Mr Kinne,' he said, 'I have no doubt you went through some very trying experiences in this camp, but would you try to keep calm here and not get distressed? It is quite natural you should be so, but it does not help to get on with the trial. To use an expression from your own country, "Play it cool".'

Taylor had forgotten that the witness was British not American.

Traill, without being assertive, was manipulating proceedings with a quiet subtlety. Kinne was under control despite the judge's mild protestations.

The sheen had gone off Cooper's performance. He had no idea that anything like Kinne's devastating deposition was coming. Burchett was ill at ease. He kept shaking his head and whispered twice to Cooper that he didn't know Kinne. He had never seen him before.

'He must have the wrong man,' he said in Cooper's ear. 'It must have been Alan Winnington.' Burchett's expression changed to one of indignant anger as Traill manoeuvred his man gently on. Any theatrics now from the normally sedate Traill would have broken Kinne's spell on the court.

'Can you tell us further conversation?' Traill asked, softly. Kinne was wound up.

'I told him that I had complained to the Chinese, and they took me away. They put me in a room for seventy-two hours and tied me up and told me that I was there to reflect, and I reflected. Burchett got mad, and he told me, "I could have you shot," so I ran around the table, and he started to move around the other way. I went around the table, and I said, "You son-of-a-bitch! If you are going to have me shot I will tell you something." I pointed to Boot Hill, and I told him that 600 men had died from malnutrition, and atrocities, and he said to me, "What can I do about it?" I said, "You son-of-a-bitch, you can tell them at Panmunjon [where the peace talks were being held]." And he said, "It would be a good thing if I had you shot!" I stood back because everybody started to get at him. Then I remembered the reason I went there, and I went back to him. And I said, "My brother was killed in Korea, and he is buried in North Korea. Could you help me to see his grave?" He crossed his arms and his legs, and he looked at me, and he said, "You ought not to have come. If you want to see his grave, you beg!" I said, "You bastard! I will see you in hell before I beg!" I went back to the camp. I went down to the river, and the Chinaman came...'

Cooper objected twice, but Taylor was the one to intervene.

'Did that conclude all you saw of Burchett that day?'

'Yes.'

'Did you have any further contact with Mr Burchett?' Traill asked.

'No, sir.'

Traill wanted a strong finish, but one that would be in keeping with the judge's line of thinking. Taylor had asked just about everyone what he thought Burchett's reputation was. So Traill shrewdly posed the same question, restricting Kinne to his feelings about the plaintiff in Korea. Kinne said: 'He was a traitor.'

It was a remark the court had heard many times, but somehow, Kinne's emotionalism gave the accusation more sting.

Traill asked: 'Since then, have you seen any written material of the plaintiff's?'

'Do you mean writings, books?'

'Or articles or things of that nature?'

'No.'

What Traill lacked in drive, he certainly did not lack in timing.

'Would you tell the court,' Traill said, 'what your knowledge of his reputation is at the present time.'

'He is a traitor,' Kinne repeated. 'He is a louse.'

Then he added the words that, under the circumstances, only he would have managed without a reprimand from Taylor: 'He should be shot!'

15. Anybody's Trial

Derek Kinne's testimony shook Burchett's team and over night left the trial wide open. It was as if a fine boxer had received a knockdown from his less talented opponent after coasting for several rounds. Well into the contest, neither side could be sure how the jury would score it. Cooper felt that he had stopped the jury from seriously considering that Burchett was a KGB agent, but he faced the fact that he had failed against enormous odds to prevent doubts creeping into the jury's mind. The jury was made up of ordinary Sydney men, who would have been influenced by Kinne. He had given force to the traitor accusation, which Cooper would have been happy to debate anywhere but in the courtroom. The odds were that most of these men would not have been convinced by any argument about Burchett believing more in ideals than in 'my country right or wrong'. Such an argument in court would have been stretched by the intellectual Traill, whom Cooper knew would have relished it. Even in front of a team of philosophers, Cooper would have been hard-put defending how far a citizen in a western democracy should be allowed to go in supporting principles or ideology. If protest is acceptable against a democratically elected government's decision to, say, go to war, should there be limits to this protest? Should the citizen be allowed to help the enemy and still be above prosecution? Was it acceptable that he be an open or clandestine agent of that enemy? Should he be permitted to involve himself in interrogation of his countrymen by the enemy, if he firmly believes in the ideology of the enemies of his country? Cooper and Burchett decided for the second time in the trial that such fundamental and controversial issues were better side-stepped altogether.

Burchett swore that he had never met Kinne and suggested again that he had been confused with Alan Winnington, who had been rumoured as being tougher with POWs than Burchett. Cooper had faith in Burchett and believed him. In any case, he told Burchett, there was only Kinne's word that the confrontation had occurred. That heartened Burchett, and he agreed that the best counter would be for him to defend himself in the witness box. Kinne's deposition could not be left unanswered.

Burchett still appeared his ebullient, cheerful self, but he seemed confused by Kinne's outburst. The gravity of what he found himself in had struck him. He was suddenly more aware of Roy Turner's warning about the plaintiff being on trial rather than the defendant.

He rang Vessa in Paris and, in a long conversation in French, put on a happy front. He was always boosted by her love and strength.

Vessa asked if he thought the court action had been a good idea. Burchett said that it had been but suggested that he reserve his full judgment until the verdict. He also said he had no regrets about anything raised in the trial, which puzzled his wife. A worried Vessa asked for details, but Burchett at first declined. When pressed, he mentioned 'some witnesses' that the defence was 'pulling out of the hat'. Burchett ended the conversation by telling her not to worry. He would win. Later at Mavis Robertson's apartment he joined some supporters who were at first quite subdued after the day's shattering experience in court. Yet, as the wine flowed, the troubles were submerged. Burchett drank heavily and fell asleep on his couch in the early hours. Tomorrow would be another day.

The defence team members thought that Kinne's performance had given them their first sense of hope in the proceedings. The general pessimism that had pervaded the Kane camp evaporated, and although the atmosphere in the Herald apartment was not euphoric, it took on a new vigour. Now that Kinne's characterisation of Burchett had presented a negative image of him to the court, Traill was determined to make it more vivid. He met Warner, who had spoken about North Vietnamese communist defectors he had met in Saigon. They knew a great deal about Burchett, Warner claimed, and they could possibly incriminate him further.

Warner had come across the defectors in Ben Tre province in the Mekong when travelling with a Vietnamese official from the Saigon government's psychological warfare section. The official was talking with one of the defectors, who had been a party secretary in charge of information and education in the province. The discussion went on until late in the night, and Warner fell asleep on the floor. The defector wanted to know who Warner was. When told he was an Australian, the defector said he knew only one other – Wilfred Burchett.

The official woke Warner. The three then talked for several hours about Burchett's visit to the Viet Cong group in the province with which the defector was linked. He claimed that Burchett came escorted by a large number of North Vietnamese troops and had a letter stating that he was a secret member of the central committee of the Australian Communist Party. Burchett was given the red-carpet treatment by the Viet Cong and even had access to a radio station, which was denied to all but the highest party officials.

Traill would have preferred something indicating a KGB link, but second best – a direct link to communist governments other than in the Soviet Union – had to do for the moment. He was still working on a breakthrough over testimony to back Krotkov, but so far it had not materialised. The lawyers estimated that they had three to five days left in the trial, and this limited the defence's capacity to fly in witnesses from abroad.

Could Warner track down those Vietnamese? He said that he would do his best, and Traill suggested that they could stall proceedings by at least half a day, and perhaps by one full day, by having Terry Tobin read Krotkov's testimony to the court. It was a legitimate exercise, but it would not endear the defence to Taylor. They could hold up the flow of the trial only once like that, and then the judge would get tough. And Traill feared putting the judge offside, for he had sensed a change in him during the Kinne performance. Although Taylor had been short, even scathing about Traill's approach at times, it was now possible that he would give him freer rein, because the defence might just have an argument against Burchett. Despite putting on a confident front, Traill was not optimistic of Kane's chances even after Kinne. His sort of devastating testimony had to be driven home to the judge and jury at every available chance. Traill did not think it possible, although he still had some faith in the coming performances of the Americans, Mahurin and Kniss. 'If only Warner could get those Vietnamese communists,' he told Kane, 'we could be in this with a real chance.'

Warner was preoccupied with capturing all that Derek Kinne had to say without the restrictions of the courtroom. Warner was looking ahead. If Kane lost the trial, he might appeal, and Warner thought it better to have as much preparation now as possible, because there would be no guarantee of gathering all the witnesses for any future re-trial. Warner also wanted as much evidence as possible on Burchett on the record for posterity, and for professional purposes. He took Kinne to a Channel 7 network TV studio and interviewed him in detail while he was still willing. With the cameras rolling, Kinne spoke excitedly of other experiences at Camp 5, soon after his confrontation with Burchett. He was summoned to the Chinese camp commander's office and reprimanded for having a hostile attitude to Comrade Burchett.

'They called him Birdshit,' Kinne said, laughing, 'because they couldn't pronounce "Burchett". They said that I was attempting to hang him, and that I created all this hostility on the football pitch. They lectured me. I said I wasn't to blame. They put my hands behind my back, handcuffed me, and took me to another room. They tied a rope around my wrists and put it over a roof beam. They pulled the rope down, tight, until just my toes were on the ground. Then they took a noose – another rope – and put it around my neck, placed it over the beam also and put the other end around one leg, which was pulled up. And they said, "Now you wanted to hang Comrade Birdshit. If you let your leg go, you hang yourself, and it's your fault." The Koreans said that they were my doctors, and that I was sick in the mind and that they were going to cure me. Well, I had a hernia. So they started to hit that. Then they started beating all over me with planks – something like a two-by-four – and rifle butts. They started slapping and kicking me. Then they said they were going to leave me to reflect. Well, I had had seventy-two hours reflection before this, and I didn't particularly like the idea. This time I was on my toes. So my leg kept going down. I started to throttle. I tried to put my leg up. It wasn't doing much good...'

Warner, an experienced television interviewer, seemed stunned by Kinne's explanation.

'The rope started to throttle you?'

'Yeah,' Kinne said. 'One rope was around my neck, and the other was around my foot. My foot was behind me, so if I let my foot down, I strangled myself. I got panicky. Thought I might as well do it all at once. So I pulled my leg down real fast, figuring, you know, that I'd strangle myself. But the Korean guards must have been looking through a crack in the wall. They came running in. They took me down. It was panic stations. They took me into the room again, and they said, "Confess! Confess!" I said, "Okay. I confess." They undid me, and after a while my blood circulation came back. I asked for a cigarette. They said I had to confess everything. I started to write out *Goldilocks and the Three Bears*. I wouldn't let them look at it until I had finished it. I got to – I always remember this – thirteen and a half pages.'

'You must have a longer version than...' Warner said, seeing that Kinne now seemed to be enjoying the story.

'Oh, it was a beauty!' Kinne said, 'and they kept wanting to see it, and I kept writing. The commander got very impatient.

They tried to pull it away, but I kept my elbows on it. They got it, and the interpreter started to read it. He read it and read it. Then he started to read it to the commander, who was a tiny little pretty lookin' guy. The commander got furious. They made me stand to attention. I wouldn't. They held my legs together. The commander said, "You *must* write a confession." I refused. This went on forward and backwards, real childish, for about ten minutes. Then the commander went outside and told the Chinaman (his superior at the camp), and he came in angrily. He came at me. I stepped forward, and I hit him. And he went down. So they all jumped on me, and we fought...'

Warner was dumbfounded as Kinne continued his extraordinary story. He was handcuffed and roped up to the ceiling again for another fifty-six hours on end. He was beaten with fists and rifle butts every day. Later he escaped and was recaptured and sent to a Korean jail – called the Wooden Boxes – for another month of solitary. Kinne said he could communicate – by whispering – with other prisoners. At the end of the long filmed interview, Warner understood why Kinne had been awarded the George Cross for his enormous courage as a POW. This erratic character was unique.

Warner was inspired to make the extra effort in his search for witnesses. Later, at the Herald apartment, he tried to reach those Vietnamese defectors. Finally, after three hours of international calls, he reached the Vice-President of South Vietnam. He said it would be difficult to find these men in time. Warner became belligerent and demanded that he find and send the two men to Sydney, immediately. Using every bluff he could think of, Warner at least got the Vice-President to promise he would do something.

In court next day, Cooper asked Burchett to give his version of the North Korean POW incident on the football pitch. Burchett recalled the speech he made there but claimed it had been a straight discussion about the way the peace talks were going at Panmunjon. There was no hostility from assembled POWs, he said.

Kinne was sitting next to Peggy Warner in the public gallery as Burchett spoke. She saw that Kinne was shaking. He had slipped to his knees beside her. Peggy became worried. She reached for Kinne's hand and held it throughout Burchett's version of the incident. Burchett recalled only that a POW

came up to him after his speech and asked for a 'match'
or 'map'.

Burchett was stood down while the judge conferred with
Traill. Burchett got the judge's attention.

'Would you please stop that person from staring at me!' he
said, pointing at Kinne. The judge had apparently noticed his
odd behaviour.

'Mr Kinne,' Taylor said firmly, 'would you please leave the
courtroom.'

Kinne stood up and without taking his eyes off Burchett
made his way out.

At the adjournment for lunch, Burchett left the court flanked
by Cooper. Suddenly Kinne leapt from behind a pillar. He
grabbed Burchett by the throat and brought him down on the
court steps.

'Remember me, you bastard?!' Kinne shouted, as he pushed a knee into Burchett's chest and gripped his neck. 'Remember me?'

Burchett wrestled Kinne down several steps. Peggy Warner
rushed to them and tried to haul Kinne off. Cooper joined
her, and moments later a half dozen people had separated the
two men.

Photographers arrived, but only in time to see Cooper
bundle Burchett into a taxi and speed off.

The incident shook the defence even more than Burchett's
side. Such attacks could lead to a re-trial, and Kane was not
optimistic about his chances, especially in trying to pull
together the international witnesses again. Kinne had to be
restrained. His brother happened to be living in New South
Wales. Could he help take Kinne away for at least a day or two?
The brother agreed. He took Derek into the country and then
decided to take him on a tour of his workplace. But this did
not help settle Kinne down at all: his brother was a prison
warder.

16. A Solitary Darkness

Former US Air Force Lieutenant Paul Kniss was next to be put through his paces by the indefatigable Traill, who had already read his US military intelligence top-secret debriefing. Traill wanted to iron out any testimony anomalies with both Americans before subjecting them to the courtroom ordeal.

The straight-shooting Kniss, with his All-American good looks, had been a commercial pilot for two decades. He seemed calm enough and repeated his claim that he was not after revenge. He even felt a little sorry for Burchett, whom he regarded as a misguided individual who had become carried away with his role as a communist propagandist in Korea.

Kniss liked Jack Kane and wanted to help him in his struggle. On the night before his appearance in the witness box, Kniss went through his hellish experience for an attentive Traill, who hardly interrupted him.

'Bail out! Bail out! Bail out!'

Kniss could hear the other bomber's pilot screaming through his earphones. But he didn't think he had been hit despite the heavy flak of 20 mm shells from Russian MIGs all around him. Kniss made a sharp descent. The other US bomber pilot followed him down and warned that his tail section was on fire. He had to jump. Kniss took all emergency precautions. His cooling radiator had been hit, and soon ethylene glycol flooded the cockpit. Kniss's eyes were burning with the vapour. The MIGs followed him down and five of them made swoops, all guns blazing. They had a hit, and each enemy pilot wanted a kill. Kniss shot back at two of them. He hit one. It was a kill. He saw it spiralling away, ablaze. But the engine began to splutter. He kept it running for two more minutes with his primer, but was still 30 kilometres short of the south coast of Korea.

The other pilot – Lieutenant Massey from 12th Squadron's 18th fighter-bomber wing – kept yelling that he should bail out; the plane was burning. The engine stopped. Kniss trimmed his aeroplane and went through bail-out procedure, but just as he stood up in the cockpit, the plane seemed to fall away from under him. He jumped up rather than falling normally and banged his head on the tail section. He was stunned, but conscious, and when he saw the ground he opened his parachute – at about 3,000 metres.

Minutes later he landed in an irrigation ditch in a rice paddy near a Korean house. He was in about one metre of water in a two-metre ditch. Kniss quickly buried his papers in a metre of mud and called Massey on his escape radio. He got through and asked for a helicopter to come in. Massey apologised and said he would have to leave. The MIGs were closing in on him now too. Kniss told him to leave and scrambled out of the ditch. His leg was hurt, and he fell several times as he stumbled towards the hills. But seconds later he was confronted by a Korean pointing a rifle at him. Soon he was surrounded by about thirty Korean civilians.

They moved in and took all his possessions except his watch and a letter to his father, which was in his pants pocket. An old man played with his .45, and Kniss worried that he would kill himself or somebody else with it. The old man finally learnt how to fire it, and he started shooting wildly in the fields until others stopped him. Kniss was taken to a courtyard where the old man waved his gun at him. It was a big laugh for the Korean audience. Then several Chinese arrived. One carried a rifle, another a Mauser pistol and another a tommy gun. They confiscated the .45 and took all his belongings from the Koreans.

The Chinese marched him away and were met by a Russian driving a truck. He got out and argued with the Chinese about who should have the prisoner. Then he walked up to Kniss and punched him in the face. Kniss went down but did not attempt to strike back. The Chinese remonstrated with the Russian and took Kniss away.

The Russian came after them, but he was apprehended by the Chinese who blindfolded him and marched him over a hill. A shot rang out, and Kniss assumed the troublesome Russian had been killed.

Kniss was also blindfolded. Once again he thought he was going to die. He was led to a hut in barracks where several Russian advisers visited him. Despite their presence, it was clear that the Chinese were in charge and that they wanted Paul R. Kniss, USAF, AO1909070, alive.

On 31 May 1952, when the communist world was well into the build-up to a massive germ-warfare campaign, a Chinese interpreter questioned him. Kniss was puzzled when he was presented with a photostat copy of a *Peking Daily* article covering the testimony of the two American B26 bomber pilots, Lieutenants Enoch and Quinn. They had confessed to dropping germ bombs and, although Kniss was not aware of it at the time, this was the beginning of an attempt to force a confession from him.

The article said that Enoch and Quinn had had lectures in Kunsan, South Korea, before flying the germ bomb missions. They begged to be forgiven by the Chinese people and claimed that they had been forced to carry out the bombings by imperialist war bosses.

Kniss was then interrogated by a higher ranking Korean who wanted detail about his commanding officers and how many missions he had flown. He was taken to a filthy room in a village and ordered to sleep in his wet parachute. He was woken three times in the night and taken for further interrogation. Kniss was asked about the B51 bomber that he had been flying and air force information and tactics.

Less than twenty-four hours later, Kniss was interrogated by a Chinese intelligence officer who had seen the letter Kniss had from his father, who happened to work in an Illinois ordnance plant. In the letter, there was a phrase that referred to the bombs Kniss was carrying. It said, 'Would you look on those bombs and see where they are loaded?' The Chinese told him 'those' bombs meant that his father was loading germ bombs and that he, Kniss, was dropping them. Kniss was surprised by the accusation. Then the Chinese claimed that American B26 bombers were dropping germ bombs. Lieutenants Quinn and Enoch had testified that American B26 pilots were responsible for such actions against China and North Korea.

The Chinese worked on Kniss for six hours through the night and hammered him with the words 'those bombs'. To ease the pressure, Kniss agreed that perhaps the B26s had been dropping germ bombs.

For the next five days he had alternating interrogations by Chinese and Korean officers. Kniss was beginning to get an inkling of why he had been kept alive.

There had been little physical abuse by the Chinese, but they kept up a mental barrage by making veiled death threats all the time. They would remark about the chances of his dying by disease and dysentery. Other times they would put pressure on him about being a war criminal because of his bombing of peaceful Korean villages. They accused him of being an enemy spy because he had no identification on him. Kniss argued back that his dog tags had been stolen, with most of his papers, the day he was captured. Would a spy wander around in American airforce flying clothes, he demanded. The Chinese threatened to shoot him over the germ-bomb missions, and when that didn't impress him, they tried bribery. If he would tell them about the germ missions, he would be forgiven and let free.

Kniss was taken to a jail in Sinui ju, North Korea, then to prison camp number 5 at Pyocktong, on a hill. By 14 June 1952, he was in Chinese hands. It was then that he met Burchett for the first time.

The next morning in court, Traill guided Kniss through his encounter with Burchett.

'I thought he was a British POW,' Kniss said. 'He had on an old khaki shirt and a pair of Chinese fatigue pants. Burchett asked me which group I was in, and how I got shot down. When I told him it was a MIG, he commented that it was a fast plane for someone in a B51 to be fooling around with.'

'Did Burchett ask anything about germ warfare?' Traill said.

'He asked what I thought about it, and I said I didn't approve of it.'

Kniss explained that on 18 June 1952 he was taken to nearby camp number 2, where interrogations were expanded to include questionnaires on his background and family, right down to each relative's political beliefs. Then he was put in solitary confinement, where he was quizzed on simple details of bombing missions – the altitude at which bombs were released, for example – and what intelligence, weather and group operations officers had said. It had to be answered in writing. With all American POWs doing the same, Kniss calculated that the Chinese Command was building up an exact picture of how the American Air Force operated.

'And did you give them facts?' Traill said.

'Those I considered useless or harmless,' Kniss said, 'but sometimes I would be accused of lying.'

'What did this indicate to you?'

'That my statements were being checked very carefully, and that whoever was doing so had to know English and American colloquialisms well.'

The questioning became more intense, and Kniss was kept in a hot room for twenty-four hours without being allowed to go to the toilet. The Chinese discovered that he came from a working-class background. When he told them that his father had once remarked that Stalin was a 'man of steel' and 'a good man', the Chinese were pleased. Instead of telling them that he had studied until he joined the air force, he told them that he had done menial tasks. That went down well with his captors, too.

Kniss told how he was worn down by the persistent and isolated inquisition. The threats would come often: 'Spy. No ID. Do you want to see your wife again? Disease. Death...'

Kniss's interrogators kept telling him how bad diarrhoea and dysentery could be. He knew several men who had died from it, and it scared him.

'You caught it, didn't you?' Traill asked.

'I sure did. Vomited three times a day. I became danger-ously ill.'

'Were you given treatment?'

'No. Of course, I kept asking for it. But they used my condition as a weapon. If I co-operated, I would get help. I wrote anything that would please them about, say, names and groups numbers in the Army Reserve. Some bits of fiction were checked; others were not. I would have to correct facts that were found to be incorrect.'

'So, did you get treatment?'

'Eventually, yes, when I was too sick to care. I was given pills and sulphur treatment. It worked, but I was very weak.'

'At this point, what did the interrogators do?'

'Oh, they switched their approach. They no longer asked if I had been involved in germ warfare. They began acting as if they *knew* I had been involved.'

'So they pushed even harder?'

Kniss seemed to falter for the first time in court. The memory was painful as he explained how he was pushed towards a mental abyss. He was told by his inquisitors that he talked in his sleep, and that his conscience was bothering him.

'I said it was not my conscience but the interrogation that was bothering me,' Kniss said, 'but they insisted that because I'd flown germ missions it was hurting me.'

Kniss thought he would face a firing squad if he confessed, and then the Chinese wound up the inquisition a notch, until it was a kind of torture reminiscent of Stalinist methods of the 1930s Moscow and 1940s Eastern show trials. Kniss was made to stand to attention for twenty-four hours at a time. If he slackened, a guard's rifle butt would prod him, not enough to bruise, but sufficient to force him to obey. The interrogators blew cigarette smoke in his face. There would be frequent fits of anger from the interrogators and guards, just to vary the emotional temperature in his hot and stuffy cell.

'I became exhausted, exasperated, mentally disturbed, and frankly I didn't care anymore,' Kniss told the hushed court. 'I had gotten used to the freezing nights, poor food, stomach disorders and unsanitary living, but they were pushing me to the limit.'

'Did you have an Achilles heel?' Traill asked.

'Yes, my wife. I was worried about her.'

When the Chinese discovered this weakness in Kniss, he snapped. He broke down and cried. Then, Kniss recalled, the Chinese knew that they had him.

'One of their aims was to have me corroborate O'Neal's testimony. But as yet no one from my squadron, the 18th, had been implicated. I was their boy.'

'Now they had a deadline,' Traill said.

'Sure. The so-called International Scientific Commission was coming to Korea to answer the communists' accusations that the US had been dropping germ bombs on China and North Korea.'

The commission was the object of the main communist propagandist thrust on germ warfare. Set up by the executive of the communist-backed World Peace Council, the commission met in Oslo at the end of March 1952.

It consisted of six (later seven) scientists of distinction in several fields. Dr Kuo Mo-jo, of the China Peace Committee, asked Professor N. Zhukov-Verezhnikov, who in addition to his scientific duties was also Vice-President of the Soviet Peace Committee; Dr Joseph Needham, who was active in the peace movement, president of the British-China Friendship Association, and among those who believed that the Japanese had used germ warfare in China; Dr Andrea Andreen, director of the Central Clinical Laboratory of the Hospital Boards of Stockholm, and a member of the Swedish Women's Leftist Association; Dr Olivero Olivo, Professor of Anatomy in the Faculty of Medicine at Bologna University, another peace worker; Dr Samuel B. Pessoa, Professor of Parasitology at the University of Sao Paulo, Brazil, and a well-known member of the peace movement; Dr Franco Grazioso, assistant in the Institute of Microbiology at Rome University; and Jean Makterre, director of the Animal Physiology Laboratory at the College of Agriculture in France. Because of their affiliations, all were predisposed towards an anti-American position.

Needham, for instance, was quoted in the *Daily Worker,* Winnington's paper, as saying in April 1952 that germ warfare in Korea 'seems to be apparent from all the evidence we have'. This was before the commission was set up. He was going to be a most useful member as far as the communist cause was concerned. Needham's interest in germ warfare reached back to 1941, when he was a scientific adviser at the British Embassy in Chungking. At that time he received a report from a Professor Chen Wen-Keui, a Chinese parasitologist and plague expert, who had arrived at Changteh in Hunan province four weeks after a Japanese plane was believed to have flown over the town, dropping pieces of paper, wheat and rice grain, cotton wadding, and some unidentified particles. Six days after the plane's appearance, five people developed suspected bubonic plague, and died. Chen was not persuaded that the evidence against the Japanese was conclusive, but in his report to Needham said, 'Suspicion that the enemy had scattered plague-infested material was in the mind of the medical workers who saw the incident on the spot.' Needham reported this to the British government but added that the Japanese had been dropping plague-infested fleas, which Chen had not originally claimed.

Eleven years later, in 1952, Chen claimed that he now recalled the Japanese at Changteh 'were disseminating plague-infested fleas with rice husks and cotton wool'. Chen was to become one of the commission's principal witnesses.

It would be useful to have not only the evidence, which the communists had presented to the world through journalists such as Tibor Meray, but also the culprits who had perpetrated the crime. If the pilots could be pushed in front of the commission, it would be a convincing coup.

After a lunch break, Traill kept the pressure on the issue of Burchett's involvement with Kniss by keeping him on the witness stand. In a second long session with the defence counsel Kniss said that, finally beaten in mid June 1952, he said he would sign a confession. But the interrogator didn't want him to sign anything. The Chinese wanted him to write a confession. This threw Kniss. He did not know how he could do that, if it had never happened. The interrogator left him and went off laughing with the guards. The next day he returned to tell a distressed Kniss to write his confession so that it would corroborate O'Neal's. Kniss refused, and the same old pressures were applied. He was a spy, war criminal, bomber of

North Korean cities. Did he want to see his wife? He was anxious to be reunited with her. He capitulated.

He was left to write something, anything, it appeared, that would seem like a plausible confession. He had only read those of Enoch and Quinn briefly. On 7 July 1952, Kniss began his first fictional essay since high school. He came overseas on such-and-such a date, and reported to the group. The next day he was taken to a secret briefing with a Captain McHugh. He gave the group a lecture on germ warfare. It lasted one hour. Kniss then wrote that he flew a germ mission under orders and against his principles. He hoped all the peace-loving peoples would forgive him.

It thrilled the interrogator. He translated it and rushed off to discuss it with the person or group masterminding this exercise. A few hours later he returned somewhat less enthusiastic. It was not a bad effort, but there were a few discrepancies. Kniss found that amusing, since he had written a total fiction. But he commented with a straight face that he imagined there might be a few inconsistencies. Kniss was told to think harder. Who gave him that lecture about his germ mission, for example? Was it really Captain McHugh?

The interrogator suggested that it might be Captain McLaughlin. Kniss guessed that O'Neal must have given McLaughlin's name. He had left Korea before the dates Kniss had given, so he agreed that it must have been Captain McLaughlin. There were four other things that did not match O'Neal. Kniss corrected his 'mistakes'. The hand re-writes went on for several days and amounted to twenty pages. Each time they would come back typed and edited in English. At the end, Kniss was taken to his editor: Burchett.

Burchett showed him files that he maintained were evidence of American use of germ warfare. He said he wanted to change four things in the 'confession'. Kniss refused. Burchett kept insisting on each point but did not press for too long. After three hours, Burchett tried to cajole the prisoner into having some cognac and Chinese beer. Kniss thought it was a ploy to loosen his tongue, so again he refused. Burchett drank the cognac, and remained 'friendly'. Kniss suspected he was playing 'good cop/bad cop' with him. Burchett gently probed further, asking questions about his being an air-force instructor, the radar studies he had taught, and his former connection with the US navy.

Burchett kept returning to the germ bomb business. He asked what happened in the case of an aborted mission. Kniss had said that he returned to base with the germ bombs, which he felt was so stupid that it had to be picked up if it was ever broadcast or published in the west. Burchett suggested that he had made a mistake. Wouldn't he be more likely to drop the bombs and get a radar fix on them so that if the germs were too close to Americans, a special US infection team could be sent to destroy the germs? Kniss thought long and hard about the odd suggestion. It crossed his mind that giving a radar position could entice the communists to rush out and plant germ bombs on the ground. The press could be called in to view the terrible crime. Yet he did not dare challenge Burchett or the interrogators. They were playing a serious game of make-believe, and it would make things difficult if he conveyed any impression that he knew where things were heading.

Another 'error' by Kniss was to claim that there was no germ spraying from aircraft. Burchett suggested that the planes involved might be in a portion of the South Korean air-base field that Kniss had not seen. He denied it.

The next day the interrogator started asking detailed questions that covered the areas opened up in the chat with Burchett. At the end of a long session, in which Kniss had balked, side-stepped and lied his way as much as possible, the interrogator accidentally left a typed-up sheet of questions in the hut cell. It was signed, W.G. Burchett.

Kniss signed his confession, and soon afterwards, on 25 July, he asked if he could write to his wife, as promised. The Chinese reneged.

Kniss was taken to Pyocktong, where a Chinese reporter, Chu-Shi-Ping, who had worked on an American aircraft carrier in World War II, wanted to record an interview of his confession. The American said no, he had done enough. He wasn't going to record a phoney confession too! The Chinese hated the reference to the confession being false, and they let Kniss know. He was threatened angrily with a 'people's trial'. Kniss gave Chu-Shi-Ping his propaganda 'scoop'. But not to be outdone, Burchett demanded the same kind of question-and-answer radio interview. It seemed to Kniss that this was very important to this zealous journalist, who always seemed to be drunk. During their meetings he would sit and drink glass after glass of cognac, or vodka, or wine. Kniss assumed that he was a chronic alcoholic, and even wondered if Burchett was on drugs. His pupils seemed like pinpoints.

The next demand was for Kniss to appear before the International Scientific Commission. While he was being broken down and 'prepared', the commission was being helped by a Chinese Committee of Reception, which included Dr Li Te-Chuba and Dr Liao Cheng-chih, both members of the World Peace Council. It had begun its research in Peking on 23 June 1952 and left for Manchuria on 9 July, where it worked from 12 July to 25 July. It was taken by the Chinese Reception Committee to North Korea and held meetings – interrupted by American bombing – in Pyongyang from 28 July to 31 July. Finally, it spent two days at POW camp 2 on the Yalu River, where they were scheduled to hear confessions from four Americans who had been kept separate from one another. They were Quinn, Enoch, O'Neal and Kniss.

At this time, Vessa Burchett arrived at Pyongyang from Peking to see her husband and to observe the anticipated historic confessions by the American war criminals. She met Kniss over the only half-decent lunch he could remember during his isolation. There was bread, sausage, fresh tomatoes, and a case of beer. Kniss was not interested in the drink, which he left to Burchett.

The interrogators concentrated on making sure that Kniss was primed before he was to give evidence to the commission. He was even schooled on the questions that went beyond his confession that would be put to him. While the pressure mounted, Kniss was treated marginally better, and he began to dare to think of blowing the whole thing by telling the commission that germ warfare bombing was a pathetic hoax. But just as he was making plans, he was summoned to the formidable General Wang, the overall commander of the POW camps. Wang warned him that he had better co-operate or he would never leave the area. Kniss got the message. There was no way he could avoid being used as a pawn in the biggest communist war-time propaganda effort ever.

At 10 am, on 5 August 1952, just after the threats from the general, Kniss was marched into a big tent to face the members of the commission, who were seated at a long table. There were about forty people there, including ten caucasians. Kniss sat at one end of the table with his main interrogator, Lin Chiu, next to him. Wang sat at the other end of the table, staring. A camera was rolling.

The only time Wang showed a flicker of emotion was in the first few seconds of Kniss's arrival, when the garrulous Professor Needham blurted something about what 'O'Neal' had said. The professor's blunder was not lost on Kniss, despite the nerve-wracking atmosphere. It was his first inkling that other Americans were in the camp facing the commission, and gave Kniss courage. He was not in this charade alone.

The confession was in French, for most of the members of the commission spoke it or had interpreters next to them. Burchett read it to them and announced that a typewritten copy would be given to them at the end of the meeting. He then took a back seat to scribble his way through the questioning. All the time Wang glued his eyes hard on Kniss, who tried not to look at him.

The prisoner's only act of defiance was to take notes and read from them. This had been forbidden by Wang, who wanted articulate spontaneity in front of the commission. Its members asked the questions for which Kniss had been readied, and gave them the answers his captors wanted to hear.

The film and news items that went out to the world from 5 August 1952 shook the US and the west. America was made to look inhumane, and a tremble of collective guilt ran through the world's most powerful nation. The media asked whether the US could have really perpetrated this hideous evil. Suddenly, it seemed so. Its heroes – air force POWs, Kniss, O'Neal, Quinn and Enoch – were saying it was true.

After the meeting, Kniss heard that Wang had approved of his performance, and Burchett made sure that his letter was sent to his wife. But life did not improve for Kniss and the seventy-seven other airmen who had been marked down for germ warfare confessions. The solitary confinement continued. If they had been sent to other camps, their captors knew that the campaign's credibility would have been destroyed. It was bad enough that at one British camp dead rats wearing tiny mock parachutes had been found outside the Chinese commander's headquarters, which implied that prisoners thought the germ-warfare stories were a huge joke.

At the end of Kniss's evidence, Traill again asked for a comment on Burchett's reputation.

'He was a traitor to the allied cause,' Kniss said. 'He was another Chinese interrogator to me and numerous of my friends. I personally felt him to be very high in the institution of the propaganda of this germ warfare. I would place him high in the hierarchy in the group that did the germ-warfare propaganda, by the Chinese...'

Kniss was very worked up. He added abruptly, 'I had better stop there.'

With Burchett's image as a conscientious journalist doing his job still in jeopardy, Cooper felt he had just enough to work with in the restoration job needed in the cross-examination. He skilfully attempted to demonstrate that there was no evidence that Burchett actually knew that the germ-warfare story was propaganda. Cooper jabbed at Kniss with short, sharp questions and tried to make it appear plausible that Burchett was the unknowing 'editor' of the confession that he wanted for professional reasons to broadcast and publish.

The defence was back on the defence. Kniss was kept on a tight line concerning who did what to the confession. Cooper was careful not to accuse Kniss of germ-warfare activities. But he did manage to make the confession seem as if it was all the witness's work.

Cooper was confident now, for he still could use Burchett to refute Kniss's evidence. Burchett, back on the stand, wearing a red tie and the same dark suit, which now appeared crumpled, was his sure-footed self as he gave another angle on the Kniss testimony. Burchett said he did not speak to Kniss about germ warfare at their first meeting, and he denied indignantly editing the confession or giving interrogators lists of questions and answers. He was clear, articulate and unemotional.

The defence feared that Burchett's performance could have confused the court enough to make Kniss's evidence on Burchett's role in the germ-warfare campaign inconclusive.

Bud Mahurin was very pleased to receive an invitation from the American consul for an evening drink at his residence in North Sydney the night before he was to appear in court. He dressed in the smartest clothes he had brought from the US, as did his wife. They were picked up by an embassy limousine from the Wentworth Hotel and driven over the bridge. The evening was warm and muggy, and they were given drinks on the lawn with a magnificent view of the bridge and the Opera House. The consul and his wife were gracious hosts, and the small talk drifted into the reason for the invitation.

The consul asked Mahurin what his 'line' in the witness box was going to be, and Mahurin opened up. He, Kniss and the other witnesses were going to make sure that Burchett got what he deserved. The consul asked a few more questions. Was there enough evidence to prove that Burchett was a KGB agent? Mahurin said he hoped so, that John Traill was gradually building a powerful case against him. Traill, he had heard, might be able to introduce some sensational evidence that would fix Burchett. The consul's manner changed, and no more drinks were offered.

Mahurin and Joan were thanked somewhat coldly for coming, and the car that had brought them to the residence drove them only a few blocks to a taxi rank.

The Mahurins were mystified. On the drive back across the bridge they worked it out. The consul would have been reporting to Henry Kissinger at the State Department on the progress of the trial and would not want Burchett's name to be linked to the KGB. This could reflect on Kissinger, because of the behind-the-scenes dealings he was having with Burchett over the Vietnam war. Mahurin recalled that the US government had offered no help at all to Kane in his bid to get to witnesses.

The consul's manner was a blow for Mahurin, and the situation had ironic overtones. He had not been pleased with the way he had been treated after his germ-warfare 'confession'. Until Korea he had been heading for a brilliant military career, but when he was brought home in 1953, the government did not know how to deal with POWs who had confessed to war crimes. For some time, Mahurin and the others were treated like lepers, and, in effect, the confession finished his military career. The consul's attitude brought back that cruel rebuff and its depressing memories. Mahurin was angered but resolved to give the best performance possible in the witness box.

PART
THREE

An Agent of Influence

17. Moscow Rules

Burchett entered the witness box to be examined on his visit to Moscow in the summer of 1956 – a period that was crucial in the case. He was there to see if he could set up in Russia. If all went well, he planned to return with his family in 1957 to live. In his deposition before Traill and Cooper, Krotkov had said that Burchett had made a big effort to 'sell' himself. He had spoken about his secret membership of the Australian Communist Party and his help to the Chinese, North Korean and Vietnamese communist organisations. Krotkov made it appear that Burchett was a clandestine consultant who wanted to act for the KGB in the way that he had for the other communist organisations. Krotkov again mentioned that Burchett had talked about Maggie Higgins, his love affair with her, her marriage to an American air force general, and the fact that Burchett would find it difficult to travel to the US. The inference that Burchett was proposing blackmail was less apparent than in Krotkov's deposition before the US Senate committee.

Burchett, on the other hand, was suggesting that his visit was in preparation for basing himself as a journalist in Moscow because, after Kruschev's speech, in 1956, denouncing Stalin, it had become the most important place in the world. Burchett had prepared himself well for the Krotkov allegations, and he delivered a determined performance, which turned almost every accusation on its head. Burchett's confident replies were plausible in every circumstance, right down to the nuance of who phoned whom when Burchett arrived in Moscow. He made it sound as if he and Krotkov socialised and spoke like two old journalist friends meeting up after a decade apart.

'Was anything discussed about mutual friends?' Cooper asked.

'Yes. Krotkov asked, "Where is your old friend Eric Borne?" Eric Borne used to be a Reuters correspondent. And I said, "He has left Reuters, and he is now in Vienna, a freelance correspondent." "Where is Jack Raymond of *The New York Times*?" "Jack Raymond is now back on the desk of *The New York Times*." "Where's Marguerite Higgins?" and I said, "Well, I met her in Korea, in Panmunjon, and you will never believe it, but she married an air force general." He thought that was very funny.'

'Do you recall what he said?'

'He said, "I thought you were going to marry Marguerite Higgins," and I said, "Well, she turned me down for an air force general."'

Krotkov had claimed that Burchett had asked him for $150. Burchett said that the Soviet magazine named *International Affairs* (run by the KGB) had sent him a copy of Graham Greene's book, *The Quiet American*, to review when he was in Hanoi. He told the court that he asked Krotkov for payment.

If Burchett was lying, he was treading dangerously but cleverly. If he was not lying, then his memory, like Krotkov's, was working exceptionally well on conversations that had taken place eighteen years earlier.

In one part of the testimony, Burchett's explanation ran close to Krotkov's. Burchett told the court that on a train trip to Warsaw, Prague, Belgrade, and Brioni, returning by way of

Budapest, he had been on an innocent, fact-finding mission.

'Did you have a conversation with Krotkov about your trip?' Cooper asked.

'Yes. In the normal way – "How was your trip. What was your impression? Was the conference in Poland interesting?"'

'And what did you say?'

'I said, "I found the situation in both Poland and Hungary very bad; economically bad, politically, a lot of unrest. The Soviet Union is absolutely not popular in those two countries ..." I said, "We are old friends, and I am going to be frank with you. I think you are in bad trouble in these areas."'

Krotkov inferred that Burchett had passed on vital intelligence to him, and that he had informed the KGB, including names of people in both countries who had been responsible for unrest.

Was Burchett really an independent reporter?

Budapest, July 1956

Tibor Meray received a call from Burchett the day he arrived in Budapest. The two had seen each other only once since the Korean war, and that was in Geneva at the Indo-Chinese armistice talks in 1954. Meray was still working for the newspaper *Szabad Nap*. Burchett began by marvelling that the phone operator at the Hotel Astoria, where he and Vessa were staying, knew who Meray was. His name was not listed in the local directory, but she had found it.

Meray organised a party for his old friend who was staying in Budapest for three days. Sixteen guests were invited to Meray's villa at 8 Mese Utza, on the outskirts of Buda, in an attractive residential area of Budapest. They included distinguished writers and journalists, all of whom were restless for a new Hungarian government to be led by Imre Nagy, the former prime minister. He had been expelled from the Communist Party, but after Stalin's death had started a new political movement.

Meray knew that Burchett had reported the trials in Hungary in 1949 of Ladislas Rajk (the former communist underground leader against the Nazis) and Cardinal Mindszenty. The party had already admitted that at least the Rajk trial was a fake. Not a word of the confessions or the evidence was ture. It had resulted in several executions. Yet Burchett had reported the trial as justice. In his book *People's Democracies*, he had written much in praise of the handling of the trials. Meray wanted him now to hear the truth. He wanted to shock his guest.

Burchett listened for hours and took notes from people who had been jailed – some for more than ten years – on false charges. He took details on arrests, torture and imprisonment. Among the informants were Miklos Gimes, whom Burchett had also met in Geneva, Geza Losonczy, Janos Reisman, Ivan Boldiszar, George Paloczi-Horvath, and Bela Szasz.

But the party was not all desultory. Burchett got pleasantly drunk, and a tipsy Vessa, who had not seemed interested in the Stalinist horror stories, climbed a large tree in the villa's spacious garden, much to the amusement of other guests.

Meray looked after the Burchetts each day of their stay and saw them off on the train to Moscow at Budapest's eastern station.

Meray was fascinated to learn Burchett's impression of the information he had picked up at the party, and it was the last thing they discussed before the train departed.

'Such developments may be unfortunate,' Burchett said, 'but we should never lose sight of the real enemy.'

Now it was Meray's turn to be surprised.

In Moscow, Burchett informed Krotkov of unrest in the Soviet Union's satellites, and the attitudes of the people he met, particularly in Poland and Hungary.

But what was Burchett's motive? Was he passing this on to warn the Kremlin it had to do better in Poland and Hungary? Or was he betraying his contacts? The answer may be in a report he made for the East German paper, *Berliner Zeitung*, in July 1956, when Burchett wrote that economic difficulties in Poland were a cause of Poznan riots. 'There have been justified complaints by the Polish industrial workers... they have had little for their efforts.'

His words contradicted the *Neues Deutschland*, the official organ of the East German Communist Party, which blamed the riots on American secret service organisations.

This backed his claim that he had an independent attitude

to the Kremlin and the KGB. Nevertheless Burchett admitted in court that he reported to Krotkov the riots and the unrest in Hungary.

Whatever his intention, Burchett's information, according to Krotkov, was valuable to the Russians and entered the growing dossier against the Hungarians concerned in the uprising, which occurred a few months later, and within days Soviet tanks rolled into Budapest to put it down. Gimes was arrested and later executed, as was Losonczy, and Nagy. Except for Boldizcar all the others at that 1956 summer party in Buda fled the country in the days following the failed revolution.

According to Krotkov, he assured Burchett that he could come and work in Moscow. It would all be arranged. Less than a year later, in May 1957, Burchett telegraphed that he and his family were coming to Moscow.

In his evidence, Krotkov claimed that when Burchett and his family arrived, Krotkov's KGB chief had changed. Details of arrangements for Burchett's setting up in Russia had been misplaced. Krotkov said that Burchett stormed off to see a representative of the Australian Communist Party in Moscow.

'He – the representative – smoothed the way for Burchett,' Krotkov claimed in his deposition. 'The KGB gave him a smart apartment, and Burchett came under the control of a former senior policeman, Victor Kartsev, who, with Krushchev in power, had become a KGB part-timer.'

Krotkov said that his connection to Burchett then stopped, and that he only came across him once – in a Moscow petrol station.

'Burchett complained that he didn't like Kartsev, not the least reason being his anti-semitism.'

Krotkov said that Kartsev told him, however, that the relationship had no difficulties. Burchett's KGB activities were said to be under the overall direction of Colonel Barsegov, with whom he was on very good terms. Barsegov ran the section of the KGB concerned with foreign correspondents.

In court, Burchett again handled accusations of his KGB affiliations adroitly, continuing to play close to the line.

He admitted meeting two KGB men – Colonel Bespalov and Lt Colonel Kultipin – for dinner with Krotkov at an open-air restaurant in Moscow's Agricultural Exhibition grounds. Burchett had met these two before in Berlin. He stayed with the story that his main aim in Moscow was to gain accreditation from the American communist paper, *The Guardian*. By occasionally agreeing with Krotkov, in between making firm denials, Burchett increased his credibility. He maintained that a 'service organisation' from the Soviet Diplomatic Corps found him a flat 'in one of those Moscow skyscrapers'. It was a five-room place on the ninth floor, and he remembered that it was number 25. Burchett was doing his best to make it sound modest. He told the court:

'We made the five rooms into a living room, a living room and a dining room combined; one was a largish bedroom – large compared to the others – two very small bedrooms, a rather decent-sized kitchen and what had been only a maid's room at the back, which I turned into my office.'

Whether it was a luxury apartment or a modest flat became a bizarre point of controversy in the trial. The Australian journalist Gregory Clark, of *The Australian* newspaper, and formerly a member of Australia's Department of External Affairs, took the stand for Burchett and continued to belittle the living quarters.

'It was much like the old-style Moscow flats,' Clark said. 'It was old and run-down. It had quite a nice parquet floor, which you get in the old flats, but it was below the standard which we diplomats and foreign correspondents...'

Traill objected, and Taylor asked the address, which Clark said he couldn't remember. 'It was facing the Moscow River, the other side of the Kremlin,' Clark said.

Traill's research indicated that the flat was a privileged one, and luxurious by Moscow standards, partly because it was said to provide the best views of the city. It was in Visnotni Dom, a building reserved for the elite. Krotkov's claim that people such as Russian movie stars (in particular, Shared Nishenko) and actors such as Sergei and Clara Lukyenov lived there had been easily checked.

Clark kept plugging the line that it was sub-standard, and it infuriated Traill. The big, sedate man lost his temper and exposed the pressure that both counsel were under.

'You keep saying that, don't you?' Traill snapped.

'Well . . .' Clark began.

'You want to get that message across, do you?'

'It struck me at the time as a rather curious place for a westerner to live, yes?'

Peggy Warner scribbled in her diary, 'Traill is losing his marbles.' At the very least, the defence seemed to be losing its way. The flat had been made to look second-rate and the link to KGB privilege appeared doubtful.

18. Kim of Egypt

Traill's spirits were lifted by the arrival in Sydney of two North Vietnamese communist defectors – Bui Cong Tuong and To Minh Trung – less than forty-eight hours after Warner had 'ordered' the Vice-President of South Vietnam to find them. No one could predict how they would perform in court. The defence team had little time to prepare the two men, and it was difficult because they spoke no English.

Traill was preoccupied with a possible sensational breakthrough about Burchett's connection to Kim Philby. Ever since reading the Krotkov testimony, Traill had wondered about the vague reference to a person coming from London to Moscow. He started with the hypothesis that this could have been either George Blake or Philby (although the latter defected from the Middle East, not London). The only possible link between Blake and Burchett could have occurred when the British spy was a POW in North Korea in 1952 and 1953.

Because of Burchett's special interest in the prisoners, they could have come in contact with each other then. Some sources suggested that this was when Blake was recruited as a Soviet double agent. But the slick KGB operation that allowed Blake to break out of Wormwood Scrubs prison in England came in 1966, at a time when Burchett was mainly in Phnom Phen. Traill would have liked to pursue the connection further, but time forced him to concentrate on the more likely link to Philby, who had defected from the Middle East in early 1963.

During his travels in Australia, England and the US, Traill had raised this possibility. At last, information was emerging that went beyond circumstantial evidence.

Beirut, January 1963

Kim Philby was an alcoholic wreck. British intelligence officers such as Nicholas Elliott had finally hounded him into a confession, as yet unwritten and unsigned. His Moscow links had been cut off, and for all Philby knew they were going to let him rot. He feared a public indictment and trial that would put him away for life. George Blake, the most recent British double agent caught, had been given forty-two years. Philby was terrified of assassination – it would have been a neat way of avoiding all that embarrassment for the British government and the intelligence services – and he was well aware of MI5's capacity to arrange assassination. He had been privy to its consideration of a plan to have Egypt's President Nasser killed during the Suez crisis.

There was also the KGB. If he was kidnapped back to London – espionage was not an extraditable offence in Lebanon – for interrogation, it would be bad for Soviet intelligence. Once the game was up, Philby was not the type to resist what would be an inquisition. Plenty of dead British agents and ruined careers would be brought into account. His Soviet masters would hate it, and his British peers would loathe it. With every bottle of whisky or gin he consumed, the spectre of his assassin or public humiliation haunted him. It was a vicious and hideous spiral. But the more he panicked, the more he drank, and the more he knew his masters on both sides would worry about his stability, and which way he would leap.

Philby had been happy with his fourth wife, Eleanor, in Beirut, where he had been placed as a foreign correspondent in September 1956 in the middle of the Suez crisis, and his children visited him from England from time to time. He filed copy diligently, but was under no pressure as long as he complied with his editors' requests for stories of events in the Middle East. It gave him useful cover for his spying for both sides, and there was not the pressure from Whitehall. He could get blissfully drunk by 10 am on the terrace of the St George Hotel, or at one of his own dinner parties. He would be in good company, with a range of contacts from British diplomats to CIA agents. But he knew that even if his masters let him drift on, sooner rather than later *The Observer* and *Economist* for whom he wrote would be forced to sack him. There was nothing coming in from the Russians. He would have no income, no pension, no livelihood.

In desperation, at ten one night, he took a risk and moved a flower pot on the balcony. It was a signal to the Soviet Embassy that there was an emergency. He had to make contact. Philby knew his fifth-floor apartment on Rue Kantari was under surveillance from locals on behalf of British Intelligence. He had to change taxis several times and go some distance on foot before he reached the sleazy Furn-esh-Shebbak quarter of Beirut and an apartment above a barber shop. There he met a muscular Russian with thinning blond hair known as 'Leo'. Philby explained that he had to leave before the British moved in. He wanted sanctuary at the Soviet Embassy, but Leo thought it would cause an international incident. There was nowhere he could hide in Beirut. The Russians wanted him to stay put for just a little longer. Philby wasn't sure he could, and hoped his concern would force the KGB's hand. It had a good record of looking after its own, and he was gambling on them recognising his unparalleled work for them since 1934.

Two days and nights later on 23 January 1963, he and Eleanor were invited to a dinner party given by Hugh Glencairn Balfour-Paul, First Secretary of the British Embassy in Beirut, for some English and American friends interested in archaeology. Eleanor arrived alone. Her husband had telephoned home to tell her he would join her at the party later. But he didn't. He had disappeared. Some investigators claimed that Philby left Lebanon on foot through the eastern mountain frontier to Syria. Others suggested that he may have boarded a Russian freighter, the *Dolmatova*, at the port in Beirut. Eleanor at first thought he may have gone off on a story. He had done it before without warning her. But this time she was so concerned that she told friends, and the British Embassy. Then Eleanor found a letter from Philby at her Normandy Hotel mailing address. He claimed to be on a news assignment and 'a quick tour of the Middle East' on which his first stop would be Cairo.

In early February, Burchett arrived back at his Moscow base from Hanoi, a man in a hurry. He had only been back a day when he announced to friends, including the English correspondent Martin Page, that he was off on a writing assignment to Algeria because, as he said, he wanted to 'observe the success of the revolution'. His friends accepted this as typical of his romanticism. His initial destination, however, was not Algeria but Cairo.

On 14 February, Burchett checked in at the rustic Shepherd's Hotel in the heart of the Cairo, where Philby had always stayed on his many trips to Egypt. He rang Atta Mahmoud, a senior official of the new canal authority that had been created by President Nassar after he nationalised the Suez on 26 July 1956. Burchett told Mahmoud that he was a journalist for the London *Financial Times*, and various other papers. He wanted to write something big about the improvements since Egypt had taken it over. Mahmoud arranged a meeting at the authority's Cairo headquarters and was so impressed with the visitor's politeness and intentions that he arranged a guide – Gamal Abou-Raia – and a car for a four-day trip along the canal. Burchett seemed keen to see everything, especially Ismailia, the Canal port in north-east Egypt.

The next day Burchett drove many kilometres along the road parallel with the date palm-lined canal. They passed a long line of tankers gliding north to Port Said. Burchett took copious notes. At a watchtower in Ismailia, at the beginning of the eighty kilometre stretch to Port Said on the Mediterranean, Burchett asked questions about the number and types of ships passing through and insisted on being shown the control room. He was most interested in the progress of Russian vessels. A pilot told him that several Soviet tankers passed through each day, but only one Soviet freighter would be through this week, the *Paul Robeson*. This ship was expected to dock at Ismailia to off-load goods and pick up produce before sailing on to Odessa on the Black Sea. Burchett made an inspection of the docks for two hours.

On his return to Cairo, Burchett again interviewed Mahmoud, who was flattered to learn that he would be mentioned in Burchett's article. Mahmoud offered him the car for the rest of his stay, and Abou-Raia, if needed. That night Burchett received and made several international and local phone calls at his hotel.

The next morning, before dawn, Burchett drove east out of Cairo for a second trip to Ismailia in time for the half-day docking of the *Paul Robeson*. On this trip he was seen by several people employed by the city's Research (Canal) Centre, including its director, Dr Ala Fatin, and one of its two female engineers, Isis Abd-el-Hahlim Kamel, who, at twenty-seven, was in charge of the materials testing laboratory. Burchett spent half an hour talking to her.

On 20 February, Burchett asked her out for lunch but later cancelled the appointment. He was seen, however, with an unknown man walking in a municipal garden and at a coffee shop close to the docks.

Burchett stayed until after the Russian freighter had departed and then drove back to Cairo. American intelligence operatives suggested that Burchett's contact could have been Philby.

The night he returned to Cairo from Ismailia, Burchett made contact with an old journalist colleague, American George MacArthur of the Associated Press News Agency, who lived on a houseboat on the Nile. MacArthur was surprised to see him and suspicious of his timing. MacArthur knew the Philbys well and had been invited to their dinner parties in Beirut. He asked Burchett what he thought of the probable defection, but Burchett did not react beyond expressing his astonishment. MacArthur asked what he was doing in Cairo, and Burchett said that he was en route to Algeria. MacArthur was sceptical. After having come from a dangerous assignment in South Vietnam, Burchett was now about to write something about peasants' collectivism in Algeria. It seemed unlikely, unless it was a cover for something else.

During the next few days, MacArthur saw a lot of his old drinking buddy from Korean days and noted that he seemed in no hurry to leave Cairo. He spent much of his time cataloguing some 250 negatives and contacts of shots he had taken in Vietnam, and MacArthur surmised that he must have been in a rush, or at least occupied in Moscow, not to have left them there.

Burchett asked MacArthur to approach the Australian Ambassador to Egypt to see if he could be issued with a passport. MacArthur obliged, but three days later Burchett was told that he had no hope of obtaining it.

Days after Burchett left Cairo, word reached McArthur that Eleanor Philby had received a cable from there dated 3 March. It was purported to have come from Philby. Intrigued, MacArthur checked with the PTT, Cairo's central cable office, and discovered that it had come from the concierge at Shepherd's Hotel while Burchett had been a guest there until 3 March. The concierge later claimed that the cable for Eleanor had come from Burchett via an Arab middleman.

On 30 July 1963, the Soviet paper *Izvestia* announced that the Soviet Union had granted political asylum to Philby, who joined the small nucleus of British spies, including Burgess, McLean and Blake. Burchett moved easily among them, and acted as middleman between these exiles and western correspondents hungry for interviews. He became friends with Philby for the next two years and would often drink with him at his dacha outside Moscow. Burchett often introduced special friends, such as members of the Australian Communist Party, to Philby. Mavis Robertson, for example, met him at the champagne bar in a grocer shop on Gorky Street, Moscow, but Philby was drunk and incoherent.

Burchett's role, as seen by the foreign correspondents, was that of a public relations man for the Soviet Union. He and Vessa would take them under their wings when they arrived and act as convivial hosts who had unlimited stocks of alcohol and fine food at their apartment. And, if they needed a special interview or information, Burchett was someone who would do his best to help. The reporters were grateful for the help and company.

When John Miller of the London *Daily Telegraph* first arrived in Moscow, Burchett took him to a Pakistani restaurant. In the middle of telling him how civilised and friendly the Russians were, two drunks at a nearby table began arguing, until one hit the other over the head with a vodka bottle. Burchett coughed diffidently and went on talking to a bemused Miller as if nothing had happened, even when Soviet militia arrived to drag the injured man from the restaurant.

A similar incident occurred with another *Daily Telegraph* correspondent, Christopher Dobson, whom Burchett took to a Chinese restaurant. Burchett had just finished telling him what a wonderful family place it was, when a fight broke out between two men on crutches, who began using them as weapons. Burchett contained his anger as he and Dobson quickly left. When they reached his smart black Chevrolet car, there was a drunk asleep on the front seat. He had urinated on the floor. Burchett was furious. He hauled the drunk out and dumped him on the footpath.

Occasionally, Burchett would pass on exclusive information to foreign correspondents. Miller, for example, was told by him of clashes of Chinese and Soviet troops on China's northern border. But there was a catch: Miller could not write the story because the Russians would have sent him home once it was published. Dobson accompanied Burchett to Peking in 1959 and was given useful introductions there at the time of the Sino-Soviet split.

Philby and Burchett were regarded by foreign correspondents as part of a strange band of western mutants produced by the Cold War. Writing in the London *Daily Telegraph* of 4 August 1963, Dobson, who became good friends with Burchett and Vessa, said Philby, Burchett and others were given good jobs and flats by the Russian government: 'They are usually welcome in journalistic circles. They are allowed to maintain contact with the west.' This link allowed access to the luxury items through duty-free shops and quick buying sprees in Helsinki, which were not available to ordinary Soviet citizens. Burchett made modest money writing for the *Daily*

Express in 1958, earning 1,775 pounds, and just 1,383 pounds in 1959, under the name of Andrew Wilson.

But the *Express* was uncomfortable about having a left-winger reporting for it. In 1960 Burchett switched to the London *Financial Times* and earned much less. His books written from Moscow collected no advances and small royalties in the west, and gave him roubles, which could not be converted into western currency, and had to be spent inside Russia. In Moscow Burchett wrote for the *New Times*, which was published in about six languages. He also wrote for the pro-communist weekly American paper, *The Guardian*, which paid little but gave him his accreditation in the Soviet Union.

Burchett, Dobson noted, led a pleasant life with his Bulgarian wife and children. He had earned the gratitude of many western correspondents by leading them through the intricacies of Moscow. But Dobson wondered if Burchett was happy. 'Talk with him over a bottle of good scotch – only ten shillings and sixpence a bottle without duty from a Danish company – and Burchett will wax lyrical over Australian beer and the Australian cricketers, things that are lost, possibly forever.'

Dobson sensed Burchett's restlessness in Russia, despite his enthusiastic beginnings reporting for the *Daily Express* on the launching of the first Sputniks. He later wrote books on the Soviet Union. One was *Cosmonaut Yuri Gargarin, First Man in Space*, which received wide publicity. Another was *Go East, Young Man*.

At about the time of the Sino-Soviet split, Burchett became disillusioned. He argued with Vessa – always a hardline pro-Soviet – about the split, and drank more heavily than before. He worried about the nationality status of his family. A second boy, George, had been born in Hanoi in 1955; Anna had been born in Moscow in 1958. The two boys (Peter was born in Peking in 1952) rapidly lost their fluent Vietnamese and spoke Russian, although French remained the family language. Burchett approached the British Consul in Hanoi and the Australian Embassy in Moscow in attempts to have the children registered as Australian citizens. The applications were refused.

From the end of 1962, he began to make more trips to South-East Asia. It was the beginning of the end of Burchett's love affair with life in the country of his boyhood dreams.

In 1962, Denis Warner visited Moscow and was in touch with a man named Rogov, believed to be with the KGB. He worked for Novosti News Agency, and had spent some time in the East. Rogov visited Warner at his Moscow hotel and described Burchett as 'a very unhappy man'. Like many who met Burchett in those latter days in Moscow, Rogov noted that Burchett was drinking too much.

Warner later had lunch with Australia's ambassador in Moscow, Keith Waller. He asked Warner to sign the visitors' book at the embassy. The last signature in the book before Warner's was Burchett's. He had been there seeking his elusive passport. Waller said that it was ridiculous to suggest that Burchett was a communist. He was, Waller said, 'just a woolly-minded idealist'.

With not enough of this information on Burchett's Moscow days documented, Traill wondered how he could introduce it without witnesses. It was too late to bring anyone else to the trial. The defence had stalled long enough over the Vietnamese witnesses who would be introduced at the next opportunity. Just as he had given up hope, a chance presented itself as Cooper was examining a pro-Burchett witness, the journalist Russell Spurr.

Spurr, a big Englishman with white hair swept back and the look of an army colonel, had received a letter from Burchett asking him to help out as a witness. After urging Burchett not to sue because of a belief that journalists should never resort to litigation, the Englishman decided to come. He had never been to Australia but knew of the long feud between Burchett and Warner. He was aware that people in Australia either thought of Burchett as a 'commie bastard' or an 'angel of peace', and that opinions went back twenty years and were deep-rooted. Spurr, a former *Daily Express* correspondent who had since moved into television and now was deputy editor of the conservative *Far Eastern Economic Review*, had an attitude that fell somewhere in between. He saw Burchett as 'the last of the revolutionary romantics and true believers of the extreme left'. On the one hand, Spurr viewed him as a political fanatic. On the other, he saw him as reasonable and likeable. Spurr had always found the fanatics – either fascist or communist – unpleasant.

But to him, Burchett never was. To the contrary, Spurr and his wife Rosemary loved Burchett. Rosemary found him 'charming and wonderful with children'. Spurr said that he truly liked women: 'Not just as "skirt", but as human beings. He charmed them, from eight to eighty. The key was that he understood women and was genuinely interested in them.' For reasons of deep loyalty, Spurr made the flight from Hong Kong.

When he arrived in Sydney, he wished that Burchett had heeded his advice. Spurr was met by Roy Turner, who remarked with typical frankness that the case would have been all right a year ago, but that the political atmosphere had changed: 'Everyone is out to get Whitlam.'

The impressions that Spurr had of Australians from abroad were deepened in the days that followed. He thought of them as incapable of forgiving – people who took their political views and private hatreds beyond those that were acceptable in England: 'You could have mateship on the one hand and hateship on the other.' Spurr acknowledged that the British were hypocritical and didn't say what they thought often enough. But he was certainly more comfortable with that than the Australian way on display in this trial.

Just before Spurr took the stand, Burchett came and sat next to him outside the court room.

'If I lose this case,' Burchett said glumly, 'I'm never coming back to Australia.'

In the witness box, Spurr did a fair job of attempting to restore Burchett's image as a harmless, professional, left-wing reporter.

Cooper became confident with this refreshing witness and even tried to denigrate Warner in order to weaken his testimony.

'Were you and Mr Warner and a couple of other men present at a dinner on one occasion?' Cooper asked.

'That is true, one night in Bandung,' Spurr said.

'Was the subject of the plaintiff discussed?'

'It was.'

'Did you hear Mr Warner say anything about the plaintiff?'

Traill was quick to object, and Taylor rejected the line of questioning. It had been badly prepared, as was a bungled exchange moments later:

'Did you, on behalf of the *Daily Express*, arrange something with the plaintiff?'

Spurr, unrehearsed by Burchett or Cooper, should have replied that he had signed Burchett as a correspondent for the *Daily Express*, which would have given Burchett a touch more respectability. But instead, Spurr said: 'I asked him if he could try and arrange a meeting with Burgess and Maclean.'

As he spoke, Spurr noticed the agonising wince on Burchett's face, and added, 'I flew to Moscow to see him, but ended up seeing Guy Burgess. I didn't see Maclean. Nobody has ever seen Maclean except [the Australian Hong Kong-based journalist] Dick Hughes.'

Traill became noticeably animated. He scribbled on a note-pad and whispered something in Kane's ear. Cooper moved on with alacrity, and Spurr redeemed himself by saying how awful Burchett's apartment was. But Traill was waiting. When the cross-examination began, he moved straight in on the Burgess remark.

'He helped you get this interview with Burgess in Moscow?' Traill said, in an accusatory tone.

'Correct,' Spurr said. He seemed determined not to make another mistake.

'I suppose that was a bit of a scoop for you?' Traill said sharply. He circled for a kill.

'No, we did not print it,' Spurr said, a hint of humour in his ruddy face. 'Burgess was so drunk we could not get the story out of him.'

Spurr's timing and delivery were good, and the spectators burst out laughing.

'And . . .' Traill began, but he was drowned out by continued laughter.

'We . . . we wanted Maclean!' Spurr called loudly. Traill shook his head.

'They were the spies who defected to the Russians from the British Services?'

'That is right,' Spurr said, with a cool shrug. 'They had already been interviewed,' which implied that it was not important.

Traill realised that the moment was lost. Spurr's calculated responses had defused the issue, and it was clear that Spurr was ready to field anything. Although he considered Burchett's apartment as top-class accommodation for Moscow, he managed to make it sound crowded and poor. He even boosted Burchett's reputation by squeezing in that he had a long-standing contract with the respected US CBS television network.

Soon after Spurr appeared, Cooper called an emergency meeting with Burchett. He had heard that Warner had brought two mystery witnesses in preparation for examination of Burchett's Vietnam period.

19. The Mountain Comes to Mohammed

The first of the North Vietnamese communist defectors, Bui Cong Tuong, was asked during his swearing in if he was Christian.

'No,' he explained through an interpreter, 'I am Catholic.'

This brought a laugh from the public gallery. Then Traill got down to the difficult business of eliciting testimony. Tuong explained that he was a defector who now worked for the South Vietnamese. He specialised in encouraging other defectors from the north.

His evidence about Burchett was confusing. Cooper kept the pressure on by objecting. With the need for interpretation, proceedings became so frustrating that Taylor sent the jury out. When they returned, Tuong managed to explain that Burchett was a secret 'director' of the North Vietnamese Communist Party. But then he made the strange claim that Burchett was somehow connected to the New Zealand Communist Party. It was clear that Tuong and To Ming Trung were both in awe of Burchett, whom they referred to as an international comrade soldier, a description reserved for only the elite – people such as Ho Chi Minh – in the communist world.

At one point Tuong said: 'Before Comrade Burchett's arrival in South Vietnam, I was informed from Central Office that a would-be comrade journalist was coming to survey the fighting in the south, to play a part in supporting the cause...'

Both defectors struggled to explain that Burchett was sent from Hanoi to instruct other journalists in the war zone on how to inspire resistance. His methods, writing, and particularly his film, were used to urge people to fight, for example, in the Mol Tan – New Year – uprising of 1967.

Although Burchett became known internationally for his effect on the media in the Vietnam conflict, he was also involved in about twenty films, which were of inspirational value to the Viet Cong in their offensive pushes against US, South Vietnamese, Australian and New Zealand forces. In one film captured from the Viet Cong and obtained from the Australian Defence Department, Burchett is seen with French journalist Madeline Riffaud travelling through the jungles and Viet Cong tunnels of South Vietnam. Viet Cong cadres are seen showing them various primitive but deadly weapons – including spear and boulder booby traps and poisoned arrows – set for western and South Vietnamese troops. Burchett visits improvised hospitals and is viewed as an honoured guest at a rally of several hundred Viet Cong soldiers, who give him a rousing reception. He is seen as a leading symbol of resistance and organisation against the south.

Overall, these former Vietnamese communist witnesses were far less successful than Traill and Warner would have wished, but the defence hoped that the clumsy presentation from these two may have broadened Burchett's reputation in the jury's mind as a clandestine communist operator.

Cooper did his best in the cross-examination to put the emphasis on Burchett as a visiting journalist who travelled in the south with the Viet Cong and wrote books on his experiences.

'While in Vietnam,' he said to Burchett, 'did you ever address any journalists' organisations?'

'I think that after I came into NLF [National Liberation Front]-controlled areas of South Vietnam, I returned to Moscow via Hanoi. The journalists asked me to give them a talk on what I had seen. That was in April 1964.'

'Was any film taken of you while you were in Vietnam?'

'Yes. Wherever I went, there was always a cameraman and photographers. They considered this was a historic visit.'

'Were you a member of the Communist Party in Vietnam?'

'Of course not. I don't think they accept foreigners into their party.'

'Were you a member of the Communist Party of New Zealand?'

'Of course not. I went to New Zealand for the first time in my life last year.'

In Vietnam much was changing. World attitudes were developing against the US, and, in the late 1960s, many opinion-makers had begun to come out against US involvement. Burchett was the most influential figure. He had not changed his anti-American, pro-communist position, but he had learned to make his writings and utterances less polemical. His arch-rival, Denis Warner, acknowledged this when he was examined by Traill on Burchett's Vietnam years.

'There was a change in his writing, which was prolific,' Warner said. 'No longer did he say such things as, "American General Van Fleet's hands were dripping with blood". Some of his books on Indo-China are interesting.' But that was all he would concede.

In reply to a query from Cooper about his dislike of Burchett, Warner said: 'There are many people of his ideological persuasion whom I have friendships with. But I would not tolerate for a moment their behaviour if it had been similar to the plaintiff's – traitorous and inhumane.'

'In Korea?' Cooper asked.

'Yes, and in Vietnam.'

From 1962 to the time of the trial, Burchett wrote seven books supporting the communists in Indo-China. He also continued writing for newspapers, but now, instead of being buried in obscure Marxist journals, he was making front-page news, even in the US. He continued to take photographs and make radio broadcasts, but in this war he made more use of film, because he understood the impact of visual evidence. The American networks were reluctant initially to show anything more than their vetted film, which showed the US war effort in an uncritical light. But when a sense of reality and doubt began to seep into media coverage, Burchett, the only international spokesman for Hanoi, began to break through. He was perfectly placed to take advantage of the US's democratic processes. He had cornered a vast communications market, and he relished it.

With more than a decade of intermittent living and travelling in Vietnam behind him by 1965, he began to find outlets in substantial western publications for his articles. A letter to his father in January of that year reflected his long-awaited recognition: 'This looks like the most triumphal week since I started in journalism.'

In early 1965, a ten-part series of articles was about to appear in Japan, and a thirty-five-minute documentary film that he made in 1964 for the Hanoi-controlled National Liberation Front in South Vietnam was in demand. Burchett made it over many months by travelling on foot, bicycle and boat through the liberated zones. He accompanied National Liberation Front (NLF) guerillas on the attack, and ducked American air raids. The film showed how the guerillas were fighting the war in the jungle. It was bought by about twelve countries, including the US (CBS), France, Italy, Canada, Japan and Holland. The film's revolutionary romanticism touched many nerves in the west and was the first significant propaganda breakthrough in the war. Burchett was delighted. Not only was he doing great things for the communist cause, he was getting paid handsomely by the west in the process.

Burchett's penchant for visiting POWs for more propaganda continued in Vietnam where it had left off in Korea, but it nearly backfired on him.

Traill had information from the Vietnam war concerning many more incidents of American POWs being forced to take part in 'interviews' for film. In 1964, Burchett visited four American soldiers held prisoner by Viet Cong guerillas. One of the soldiers, George Smith, of Chester, West Virginia, said that Burchett displayed a 'communist attitude' about the war but did not try to extract military information from him. In 1965, however, Hanoi began a campaign to extort 'war crimes' confessions from senior US officers. Burchett, the expert in such matters since the Rajk trial in Hungary in 1949, was involved. One case was that of Navy Captain Jeremiah Denton Jr, later a US senator from Alabama, who was interrogated for seven days and nights under the direction of a Major Bai. Denton was repeatedly tortured into unconsciousness. When broken down sufficiently, he was brought out to meet Burchett and a Japanese newsman for a filmed interview. While making the confession, Denton had the presence of mind to blink out the word 'torture' in morse code. The film was used as propaganda for Hanoi until someone spotted Denton's methodical 'affliction.'

Another US pilot POW, Colonel Guarino, was taken blindfold and in irons to be interviewed by Burchett for a film on American war atrocities. Lt-Colonel Thorseness, also a pilot POW, who shared a cell with Guarino, told him that 'he was kept in solitary confinement, in irons and was beaten and maltreated until he agreed to the Burchett interview'. According to Guarino, 'the entire POW community lived in constant fear of being selected by the Vietnamese to see Burchett and others like him'.

Traill was keen to introduce this evidence, but the judge, who had become testier as the trial progressed, had ruled that evidence concerning Burchett's activities beyond 1957 was unnecessary for the case. Taylor had let the two Vietnamese defectors give evidence covering the 1960s, but had expressed his unhappiness about it. Traill knew that he would have to be devious now to introduce material from the Vietnam war, unless it was specific to a Burchett-KGB connection.

By 1967, Burchett's international reputation was intact. He was fifty-six and a key public figure in the most publicised war in history, and his successes for Hanoi were having an effect.

Burchett arranged for a friend, Harrison Salisbury of *The New York Times*, to visit Hanoi. Salisbury wrote to Burchett: 'I need hardly say that I am deeply grateful to you for the aid and assistance that you were able to give in presenting my case to the Vietnamese authorities.'

He filed an article critical of American saturation bombing of military and civilian targets in Hanoi and other towns, which Tass circulated widely. Washington denied it. Burchett wrote that the denial 'constituted one of the most gross lies ever attempted by Washington'.

In a 19 January 1967 letter to his son Rainer (from his first marriage to Erna Hammer), Burchett explained:

'Your suspicions were quite correct in your letter before last, but that is not a thing to talk about. The main thing is the result. As you said, Harrison [Salisbury] said what I have been saying for a long time, but it is much more important that it is said in *The New York Times*.'

His next move, in February 1967, was to interview North Vietnam's Foreign Minister, Nguyen Duy Trinh. This was first broadcast over Radio Hanoi, then written for AP, and published widely. It began:

'Hanoi is ready to sit down with the United States to hold preliminary talks to explore what steps can be taken to end the war in Vietnam. They are also prepared to receive President Johnson in the North Vietnamese capital if this will facilitate ending the war.

'I was told: "President Johnson said he was ready to go anywhere anytime and do anything to end the war. It's up to the United States to act now. The United States must provide its good will in the affair.

'... It has been made clear to me that Hanoi will never agree to talks while bombing is continued...'

The article embarrassed the Johnson administration. Washington hawks saw it as a peace feeler, even a weakening of Hanoi's position. On a visit to London, the Soviet Premier, Alexei Kosygin, referred to the Burchett interview as a possible outline for peace negotiations. This underscored North Vietnam's ploy to halt the bombing raids in exchange for a conditional suggestion that there 'could' be peace talks.

In Paris, speaking with American reporters, the North Vietnamese envoy, Mai Van Bo, further dignified the Burchett interview by calling it the 'Burchett Declaration'. After this a spate of analytical articles in the US attempted to answer the question: Who is Wilfred Burchett? Most were written by veteran war correspondents who remembered Burchett from World War II, Berlin, or Korea. They usually either ignored his Korean record or skated over it now that he had reached some pre-eminence in possible peace negotiations. Few reports were critical. Journalists and editors everywhere wanted good relations with Burchett, who had the power of veto over people wanting interviews with Hanoi's leaders. With a possible eye to the future, Henry Kissinger opened up a communications link to the North Vietnamese through two French friends of Burchett.

The international attention prompted Burchett to approach the Melbourne *Age*'s foreign correspondent, Creighton Burns, to intercede about his passport with the Australian ambassador in Phnom Phen. Burns saw the ambassador. The request was put through to Canberra, but the Liberal government held firm. It had not forgotten Korea, and in Canberra information was coming in about Burchett's activities behind enemy lines in Vietnam, mainly in dealing with American POWs. There were reports of Burchett being protected by large units of Viet Cong guerillas as he travelled the countryside, and that he had access to a large Viet Cong transmitter that could have been used to communicate military information from anywhere in Vietnam to Hanoi and Moscow.

Undaunted, Burchett continued on his way by orchestrating the release of three American GI POWs held prisoner by the Viet Cong. The men were set free at the North Vietnamese Embassy in Phnom Phen (where Burchett now had a villa with Vessa and the children) and were received by Tom Hayden, the US anti-war protester. The communists had asked a 'respectable' American to accept his fellow countrymen. Hayden had arrived in a rush from New York. He had no suit, so he borrowed a jacket and tie from Burchett, with whom he stayed, because the communists insisted that Hayden look presentable for the TV coverage. Burchett held a tight press conference at the Hotel Royale, from where he did most of his business for the North Vietnamese, invariably over drinks. Only seven western journalists with whom he was close friends – George MacArthur of AP was one of them – or those who would not put an anti-Hanoi slant on their reports, were invited. On 28 October 1967, on Burchett's recommendation,

Hayden also made a broadcast over Radio Hanoi directed at American servicemen in South Vietnam.

Burchett's friendly mien with western journalists, and the fact that he was the *only* source from the other side, made him popular. All correspondents experienced his amazing capacity for drink, or his predeliction for savouring exotic offerings from Phnon Phen to Paris: stories of Burchett's desire to tour brothels in the region abounded. A reporter for a quality Fleet Street weekly paper recalled a visit to a whorehouse with reputedly the most beautiful prostitute in town. Burchett and the reporter tossed a coin. Burchett lost the toss; the Fleet Street man got a dose of VD.

Burchett's efforts for Hanoi were having an influence in the US by October 1967. A massive anti-war rally took place in front of the Pentagon, and the writer Norman Mailer and the playwright Arthur Miller turned up to add support. The demonstrators carried placards with large shots of President Johnson captioned 'war criminal', which angered and troubled him. Opinion polls showed then that most Americans still supported the war, although by the end of the year a majority thought it had been a mistake.

A few months later, at the end of January 1968, a Vietnamese lunar New Year, a 'Tet' military offensive took place involving 70,000 communist soldiers. They violated a truce and hit a hundred cities and towns, including Saigon, moving the conflict from rural to urban areas for the first time. Although the southern Viet Cong suffered heavy casualties, the attack shook US confidence. Suddenly, it was possible that the US could lose. The political atmosphere changed dramatically. A leading opponent of the war, Senator Eugene McCarthy, lost to Johnson by only 300 votes in the Democratic Party's New Hampshire primary election. Johnson decided not to run in the 1968 presidential election. Tet had defeated him.

Peace talks began a few months later between the US and the North Vietnamese in Paris, and Burchett moved there to cover them. He was appointed a consultant to the CBS news team, which was run by an old friend, Charles Collingwood, and Walter Cronkite. Burchett was to play the same role he had during the Korean peace talks at Panmunjon, in which he and Winnington accurately informed western newsmen of the communist positions and the talks' progress. This time, however, it was formal, and Burchett, still the communists' solitary source, was exclusive to CBS News, the highest rating news programme in the US. He was fulfilling his desire to 'shape history'. Burchett's activity as a political agent of influence had peaked.

One night in the hot summer of 1968, Burchett was dining at Hotel Lutetia on Boulevard Raspail with Collingwood and his wife when the students' attempted revolution exploded around them. Tear gas drifted through plate-glass windows and cut short the evening. The Collingwoods retired to their room, but Burchett could not resist rushing to the barricades on Boulevard St Germain to observe the rioting. He later told London *Evening Standard* journalist Sam White he was disappointed that French workers had not supported the students and gone through with a real revolution. Burchett thrived on observing radical political change.

His left-celebrated reputation preceded him everywhere now, and people sought his name for projects. Apart from the never-ending demand from newspapers, TV and radio networks, several western countries wanted his comments on anything to do with South-East Asia. According to his early publisher, Joe Waters, Burchett's interest was to be published rather than worry about large payments. (Waters maintained that Burchett didn't need to be concerned because he was paid by communist governments including the Soviet Union and North Korea. Payment would always be in cash. Waters said that Burchett would be given just enough to live well, and no more: 'It was not the paymaster's aim to have their agents retire.')

Whatever, Vietnam had changed Burchett's status, and he began to think more commercially. He was astonished at the amounts being made by Ed Morrisby, who specialised in making documentaries in communist countries. In 1969, he and Morrisby teamed up to exploit Burchett's expertise in South-East Asia, and made films in Cambodia. (At Hanoi airport Morrisby saw Burchett paid in US travellers cheques by North Vietnamese communists who said: *'Un cadeau de vos amis'* when handing over the money. Morrisby did not know who Burchett's generous friends were but suspected the Russians or the North Vietnamese communists. Such payments helped explain something all his friends and contacts noticed. Burchett always had plenty of cash.)

The Vietnam war was becoming Burchett's salvation. He had not changed or mellowed his basic hard-line views, but he found himself on the winning side in the eyes of the world. And his reputation had been restored.

He decided to start a public campaign to have his passport restored, and a Burchett Passport Committee was formed. The Australian Parliament was sent a petition, signed by the 'Who's Who' of the more celebrated western left-wing and liberal fraternity. People such as Jean-Paul Sartre, Jane Fonda, Vanessa Redgrave, Norman Mailer and Arthur Miller put their names to it, as did philosopher Bertrand Russell, who regarded Burchett as 'the greatest historian of our time', because of his writings on Vietnam, Korea, and Hiroshima. The Australian government rejected the petition, but it was wavering: most of the conservative Gorton Cabinet in mid-1969 were in favour of restoring the passport.

The lack of the document caused restrictions on his travels. Burchett was never more aware of this than in the summer of 1971 when he had a meeting with the head of the North Vietnamese Delegation to the Paris peace talks, Xuan Thuy, at the Hotel Lutetia in the Latin Quarter's fashionable Boulevard Raspail. The Vietnamese hoped that Burchett might be able to make a US trip to gauge Washington's attitudes to the war. The Paris talks had reached stagnation, and Hanoi was unsure of Kissinger's intentions. In 1969, the Americans had tried to win the war by bombing Hanoi. In 1970, after the overthrow of Prince Sihanouk in Cambodia, they claimed to be attempting to destroy 'Vietnam sanctuaries' in that country. This year – 1971 – they had ordered the invasion of southern Laos to cut the Ho Chi Minh trail.

Burchett asked Thuy about any recent communications with the American peace talks team in Paris, and Thuy remarked that its leader, William Porter, was not interested in talks. The North Vietnamese did not trust him because of his record as second in command at the US Embassy in Saigon. It was said he hated the northerners. It was impossible to negotiate with him.

Thuy claimed that his team had made some headway with Porter's predecessor, David Bruce, but that Kissinger had sacked him. Burchett liked Bruce and found him 'a good man, like Averell Harriman'. They both had been career diplomats who wanted to extricate the US from the Vietnam quagmire.

Thuy was frustrated and reflected the thinking in Hanoi. He suggested that Burchett could meet Kissinger and attempt to discover his attitudes in the stalemate. Burchett would find a way of encouraging Kissinger to see him. One way would be to make out that he had an offer from Hanoi that could end the war.

Burchett managed to obtain a limited visa for a visit to New York, when he attended a party to celebrate his sixtieth birthday, which featured anyone who was anyone in the American anti-war movement. It had been thrown by the actress Jane Fonda, the writer Noam Chomsky and the paediatrician, Dr Benjamin Spock, as a tribute to the man regarded as the father of the protest movement. Burchett had been railing against American involvement in Vietnam long before President Eisenhower had sent military advisers to Saigon in the late 1950s. Those well-informed among the faithful knew that Burchett had acted as more than just an unofficial spokesman for the Hanoi government and Ho Chi Minh before his death in 1969. Many believed that he was North Vietnam's key secret negotiator with Washington.

One of his most ardent fans at the party was Jane Fonda, whom he had first met in Paris with her husband, Roger Vadim, the French film director. Fonda had become close to the Burchett family, and she and Vadim were regular visitors to their Paris apartment. In the second half of the 1960s as the counter-culture fermented around her, and before meeting Burchett, Fonda had gone through a rapid metamorphosis.

In the 1960s, she met many French left-wing intellectuals, and Burchett. He and his wife Vessa made a big impression on her. The French leftists, many of them armchair socialists, who had never been to the US or Vietnam, often ridiculed her defence of American values and government action. But

Burchett was the expert on South-East Asian politics and had lived in Hanoi, Peking and Phnom Phen for the better part of the last two decades. He wrote with clarity and experience about the Vietnam conflict and did not regurgitate cliches. Although Burchett castigated the American government, he seemed less critical of ordinary Americans, whom he suggested had been misled over foreign policy by every administration since President Roosevelt. Burchett became one of Fonda's most important mentors, as she took on the daunting role of an anti-war activist.

Burchett wanted Fonda to visit North Vietnam. He said he would be delighted to arrange it for her at any time. Fonda had been keen to make the trip but had been cautious because of the reaction it would be sure to get. But Burchett wanted her to go precisely for this reason. He wanted Fonda to make anti-war speeches over Radio Hanoi and a documentary film on American POWs. She suggested that she might be able to make the trip in the summer of 1972, depending on her film schedules. Burchett was delighted. An appearance by Fonda in Hanoi would be the greatest propaganda coup of the Vietnam war.

20. Breakfast at Kissinger's

When Warner was on the stand again, Cooper touched on the late 1971 period by attempting to paint Burchett as the peace-maker and Warner the warmonger.

'Were you not advocating throughout 1971 an increase in the military activity on the part of the Allied forces in Vietnam?' Cooper asked Warner.

'That is not true,' Warner replied. 'I was not suggesting that the Americans should increase their forces there, or anything of that sort.'

'Weren't your policies diametrically opposed to the detente policies of North Vietnam, China and Dr Kissinger?'

'Not at all. I wrote as early as the late sixties of the China problem for a magazine in Washington which set out a great deal of need for bringing China into the community of nations.'

'Were you aware in October 1971 that there was a lot of talk among journalists that Dr Kissinger was seeking a detente on the Vietnam War?'

Warner was about to reply, but Cooper added: 'Were you aware in October 1971 that Mr Burchett had an interview with Dr. Kissinger?'

'I have a good deal of knowledge about that particular incident.'

'Would you answer the question?'

'Yes, I am aware that he saw Dr Kissinger.'

Warner was annoyed about being cut off. He knew that it was Burchett who had tried to see Kissinger, rather than the other way round. Burchett had always implied that Kissinger had approached him. When Warner approached Kissinger to check this, he replied by telex that it was definitely Burchett who had wanted to see him because he had an important initiative from Hanoi. Cooper's cross-examination of Warner showed Burchett as the high-level peacemaker, rather than as a mouthpiece for Hanoi.

New York, October 1971

The phone call Burchett had been waiting for came late one night at his New York apartment. One of Kissinger's aides invited him for breakfast with Kissinger at the West Wing of the White House. Burchett asked about the restriction on his movements, but the aide told him to forget about them. Burchett was pleased. He was going to crack the inner sanctum of the 'enemy' after several months of trying to reach Nixon's key foreign-policy adviser.

Because of the possibility of planes being fog-bound, Burchett took the train for a four-hour ride from Manhattan's Pennsylvania Station to Washington DC. He was still nervous about the forty kilometre radius restriction. Once beyond it, he half expected to be apprehended. But despite the feeling that he was being watched by at least two people in his carriage, nothing happened. He spent Sunday night, 10 October 1971, in an obscure hotel on 17th Street West, and on Monday morning walked to the White House. He was apprehensive as marine guards at the West Wing perimeter guard-house inspected his UN press credentials, and then instructed him to make his way down the drive to a squat building. On his left was the white portico entrance to the presidential residence. All was tranquil in the foggy morning, and the compound seemed empty to the untrained eye. Nixon had closeted some of his key aides, including H.R. Haldeman and John D. Ehrlichman, along with Kissinger, the National Security Adviser, in the small, labyrinthine West Wing.

Burchett was surprised to see Kissinger come into the foyer and greet him with a broad grin. He ushered Burchett into his office adjoining the reception hall. They sat on comfortable chairs and breakfast was placed in front of them on a coffee table. Conversation was hesitant at first. Kissinger, who reminded Burchett of an indulgent headmaster, seemed to be doing his best to put his guest at ease. He complimented Burchett on articles he had written on China and Vietnam, and Burchett indulged in an initial burst of backslapping by saying he found some of Kissinger's writings in the magazine *Foreign Affairs* quite interesting. They were like two dogs circling each other, despite their wagging tails.

Kissinger was waiting to hear what new revelations from Hanoi Burchett had for him. When they weren't mentioned, Kissinger began to probe his guest about his thoughts on the Chinese leadership. They included Chou En Lai, whom he knew was a long-time friend of Burchett's. That done, Kissinger asked Burchett what he wanted to see him about and was disappointed when he repeated Hanoi's peace plan. There was nothing new in the proposals that Burchett put to him, and he wondered if Burchett was there on Hanoi's behalf to assess his resolve and strength.

Kissinger was annoyed. He told Burchett that he thought the Hanoi plan was boring, even with the linkage of US troop withdrawals to the release of POWs. Burchett replied that being stuck with the sort of regime the Americans had in Saigon had to be an even greater bore. Hanoi could not expect the US to dump the South Vietnamese government, Kissinger said. Burchett accused him of doing nothing to change it. Instead, the US was maintaining it in power. Kissinger suggested that Hanoi was too suspicious about the US plan to pull out all its troops. History justified those suspicions, Burchett said. Kissinger reflected on this as he poured the coffee, and took the opportunity to move into less contentious areas in an effort to turn the tables on his guest.

Kissinger asked Burchett some subtle questions about the Hanoi leadership. Kissinger was cunning. He began by giving his impressions, and then tickled Burchett's ego by asking his opinions. Kissinger wanted to know about Pham Van Dong, and Burchett said that he was 'very impressive, similar in a Vietnamese way to Chou En Lai'. What about Le Duc Tho, Kissinger asked, was he really more important than Xuan Thuy? Burchett thought he was and said why. The conversation continued in this manner until Kissinger received a call from President Nixon about his coming trip to the Soviet Union. Burchett noted the contents of the call.

Soon afterwards, the meeting was finished, and both men left it thinking it had been worthwhile, although strained at times. Kissinger was pleased that he had got first-hand assessments of the Hanoi leadership, which he needed, he had resolved, if he were to save the US's position in the war. Burchett, on the other hand, felt he had got important information to report to Xuan Thuy and the rest of the Hanoi leadership and had scored a scoop on Nixon's decision to go ahead with a trip to the Soviet Union.

Burhett's next meeting with Kissinger was in early 1972 in China when Nixon made his historic visit. Burchett disapproved of the trip. In articles for major papers east and west in early 1972, he played it down by calling it a cynical vote-scoring gimmick in a presidential election year and by pointing to the massive US TV network live coverage. In private, Burchett was ill at ease with events unfolding around him. His neat view of South-East Asian political affairs was looking frayed. He was finding it difficult to reconcile the emerging relationship between China and the US. Burchett had personal ties to both China and North Vietnam, with whom the US was still at war. How could Peking play footsie with the arch-imperialists? His only way of dealing with the new situation was to attack American motives and imply that 'rapprochement' was US instigated and bound to be short-lived. Yet Mao Zedong and Chou En Lai had held out for mediation with the US since before they took power in 1949, despite the US's having backed the forces against the communists.

When the question of Burchett's connection to China arose in court, it became important to Cooper's argument that Burchett could not have been a KGB agent. He would be unlikely to serve the KGB and side with China when it was in conflict with the Soviet Union.

'Is it true that you were an expert on the Sino-Soviet split in 1959–60,' Cooper asked him.

'I was knowledgeable on that period, yes,' Burchett said.

'And what side did you support?'

'I travelled between Moscow and Peking at the time. It was rather important to stay neutral in making an analysis of the issues of difference between the two countries.'

If he were pushed by Traill on his attitude to the break-up between the two biggest communist powers, Burchett was considering referring to a letter he wrote to his father in March 1963. If anything, it indicated that he was secretly pro-Chinese:

'I am very glad that you and Clive [a communist union organiser and the oldest of the three Burchett brothers] have been supplied with literature. There is no doubt at all that this side [China] is 100 per cent right. The fact that some high-ranking Australians [amongst the ranks of the Australian Communist Party]...only confirms what I have thought for a long time...in my own position I have to be extremely careful as you can imagine, and you should show this letter only to a few really good friends. And those should not gossip about it...'

In cross-examination, Traill pounced on the China question: 'When President Nixon made his historic visit to Peking in 1972,' he began, 'you were there to monitor it for Hanoi, were you not?'

'No,' Burchett said, shaking his head. 'I represented several papers. There was –'

'Didn't you fear a repeat of China's sell-out of the North Vietnamese at the 1954 Geneva Convention?'

Burchett said that the Chinese were urging the North Vietnamese to concede a quick settlement of the war in order to get the last American troops out of Vietnam. Burchett said he and Hanoi were against anything but a complete, unconditional reunification of Vietnam.

'Wasn't this in line with Kremlin thinking?' Traill asked. 'After all, it was Vietnam's biggest arms supplier.'

'The Soviet Union took Hanoi's position,' Burchett agreed.

The Nixon–Kissinger visit to China further illustrated Burchett's influence. He moved with the huge contingent of reporters who were following them in their ceremonial talks with the ageing Mao and their more substantive discussions with Chou En Lai, China's prime minister. Vietnam was near the top of the agenda, and Chou En Lai, who had hoped that a long war in Vietnam would retard the US and allow the Chinese to exert more influence in South-East Asia, now felt the growing threat from the Soviets. Chou En Lai wanted a quick end to the conflict, but he had to be careful how he pushed it. He didn't want the Soviets and the Vietnamese to become too close, and consequently at the banquet for Nixon, he urged an early peace, without endorsing North Vietnam's political demands.

Chou En Lai consulted Burchett on two occasions and made Hanoi's position clear.

The second-last banquet was given for the presidential party at Hangchow. At a cocktail gathering before dining, reporters mingled freely with the politicians. Nixon took delight in introducing Chou En Lai to members of the US press corps, including Walter Cronkite of CBS, and Stanley Karnow of the *Washington Post*. He called each his 'good friend'. With a mischievous look, Chou En Lai tugged Nixon by the sleeve and led him to a group of reporters in one corner of the crowded room.

'And this is my good friend, Mr Burchett,' Chou En Lai said, introducing him to Nixon.

'I know you,' Nixon said. 'You're the Australian.'

Burchett wished him every success on the trip and remarked that it was an historic moment. Nixon drew nervous laughs when he replied that no doubt he would read what really happened in Burchett's articles, and closed the discussion by asking Burchett to give his regards to 'your Prime Minister'. Burchett grinned, but was unsure if Nixon was mocking him or not.

One journalist who had witnessed the introduction was intrigued. He asked Burchett why Nixon implied he knew a lot about him. Burchett replied, 'Nixon knows his enemies better than his friends.'

Burchett's power and influence was still manifest in the 1972 presidential election year. Opposition to the war had been forged in the turbulent 1968 elections, which had seen Richard Nixon just defeat Hubert Humphrey. Four years later, that opposition was strong and united, but the US had still not pulled out of the war. The anti-war movement wanted to keep the pressure on Nixon as he strode towards his second term in office. It backed the challenger, George McGovern, who promised to end his country's intervention in Vietnam.

Burchett had recommended to Hanoi that several American citizens be allowed to visit North Vietnam and speak on Hanoi radio. They included the radical American anti-war protestors, Stokeley Carmichael, Eldridge Cleaver, and Tom Hayden. Instead of making broadcasts himself, Burchett made sure that an even spread of talented people on the left had a say in speaking to the American troops. POWs were used in a propaganda film to say how well they were being treated and to plead for an end to US involvement. A steady stream of specifically designated guests were invited to Hanoi until 1972. All of them had a predictable, cumulative influence in the US, but none received the kind of publicity that would sharpen opinion for or against the war.

In January 1972, Jane Fonda went to Paris to make 'Tout Va Bien' for Jean-Luc Godard. The film co-starred Yves Montand and was a Marxist soapy born of the 1968 attempted revolution. It was co-scripted by Godard and Jean-Pierre Gorin, but ended up as a bore with actors turning to the camera to explain things to the audience. If Fonda was irritated by the lack of explanation of the film's text, she was cheered by being in Paris and catching up with old friends, including the Burchetts. A trip to Hanoi was again discussed, and later Burchett and Tom Hayden, a veteran of two Hanoi pushes, discussed details for a July visit. All of them realised the enormous value of a trip by her.

The biggest itinerary prepared for an American visit was planned. Fonda would make at least eight broadcasts over Radio Hanoi and visit as much of the bombed areas around Hanoi and the countryside as possible. A Burchett specialty – American POW pilots – would be used in a film to be shown on Fonda's visit in Paris, her first stop after the trip. And Burchett planned to attend a press conference in Paris to make sure that the story ran ahead of the second stop in New York.

Fonda arrived in Hanoi on 8 July 1972, and her trip became a media event for TV viewers worldwide. On 14 July, a Vietnamese broadcaster introduced her speech as for 'all the US servicemen involved in the bombing of Vietnam'. Fonda launched into an attack on US 'terrorist tactics' and accused it of bombing civilian targets. She said:

'I implore you, I beg you to consider what you are doing. In the area I went yesterday, it was easy to see that there are no military targets... no important highway... no communication network... [and] no heavy industry... All of you in the cockpits of your planes, on the aircraft carriers, those who are loading the bombs, those who are repairing the planes... please think what you are doing.'

Three days later, in another broadcast, she said:

'This is Jane Fonda speaking from Hanoi, and I'm speaking particularly to US servicemen who are stationed on the aircraft carriers in the Gulf of Tonkin, in the 7th Fleet, in Anglico Corps in the south of Vietnam.'

'Anglico' – the US's Air-Naval Gunfire Liaison Company, was a shore detachment composed of marines and sailors, which handled air and artillery strikes from off-shore naval ships. This specialist reference was typical of the careful scripting organised for Fonda.

On 19 July, in another address, she appealed to US troops:

'What are your commanders telling you? How are they justifying this to you? Have you any idea what your bombs are doing when you pull the levers and push the buttons...

'How does it feel to be used as pawns? You may be shot down... even be killed, but for what, and for whom... We are afraid of what must be happening to you as human beings. For is it possible to destroy, to receive salary for pushing buttons and pulling levers that are dropping illegal bombs on innocent people without having that damage your own souls...

'Tonight, when you are alone, ask yourselves, What are you doing? Accept no ready answers fed to you by rote from basic training on up, but as men, human beings, can you justify what you are doing? Do you know why you are flying these missions, collecting extra combat pay on Sunday... I know that if you saw and if you knew the Vietnamese under peaceful conditions, you would hate the men who are sending you on bombing missions...

'All of you know the lies. You know the cheating on the body counts, the falsified battle reports, and the number of planes that are shot down and what your targets really are. Knowing who are doing the lying, should you then allow these same people and same liars to define for you who your enemy is? Shouldn't we examine the reasons that have been given to us to justify the murder that you are being paid to commit? If they told you the truth, you wouldn't fight, you wouldn't kill... You have been told lies so that it would be possible for you to kill.'

Fonda called for a halt to bombing and accused the US administration of lying about the air war's purpose. Fonda endorsed Hanoi's seven-point peace plan, which Burchett had tried to sell to Kissinger months earlier. She spoke of US war crimes, of US treaty and international law violations, and of the inevitability of North Vietnam's continued resistance and eventual victory.

Fonda's performances were impassioned and full of the conviction that had marked her sudden conversion to social causes from 1969. Cries of 'traitor' and 'Hanoi Jane' were rife, and some US senators made noises about trying Fonda for treason, but her country had not declared war on Vietnam.

When Fonda arrived in Paris, Burchett was there to bolster her at a tough news conference, and she was very pleased to see him. The questions about treason were sharp, but Fonda was well prepared.

'What is a traitor?' she responded angrily. 'I cried every day I was in Vietnam. I cried for America. The bombs are falling on Vietnam, but it is an American tragedy...The bombing is all the more awful when you can see the little faces, see the women say, "Thank you American people, for speaking out against the war." I believe the people in this country [the US] who are speaking out are the real patriots.'

Fonda seemed surprised at the hostility of some reporters. Wasn't she seeing only one side of the issue?

'There are *no* both sides in this question!' she said, and then stressed her unshakeable belief that America was totally at fault. One journalist suggested that she was being used by the North Vietnamese for propaganda purposes.

'Do you think the North Vietnamese blow up their own

hospitals? Are they bombing their own dikes? Are they muti-
lating their own women and children to impress me? Anyone
who speaks out against this war is carrying on propaganda –
propaganda for peace, propaganda against death, propaganda
for life!"

Burchett, in a white sports jacket, black shirt and black and
white tie, stood in the second row of the journalists on one
side of Fonda. He scribbled page after page of notes but asked
no questions. He didn't need to. Fonda, choked with emotion,
was giving the performance of her life. Yet she meant every
word she said, and she would repeat the performance in New
York the next day. When she was challenged about stories of
North Vietnamese torturing Americans, denying what was an
accepted truth, Fonda asserted that only the North Vietnamese
were tortured.

An ebullient Burchett congratulated her warmly after the
film show that followed the news conference. It was from the
heart, for having worked for an American defeat in two wars,
he considered he had just witnessed a triumph. Decisive
moves would follow quickly to ensure a North Vietnamese
victory on the battlefield.

Burchett's links to celebrities such as Fonda had also restored his standing. His enemies were now more cautious
about moving against him, and he had legally muzzled those
like Warner.

Vietnam had given Burchett his place in history.

Vietnam had also given Burchett his world fame, especially
among activists and left-wing intellectuals. By the time of the
trial it was at its peak, and it posed the biggest problem for the
defence in its bid to portray Burchett as unworthy and disreputable. Opposition to US involvement in the war was popular now in Australia, and Burchett was closely associated with
such opposition.

In the countdown of the trial's final days, Traill and the Kane
team decided to focus again on the Korean war, this time with
emphasis on the last months from the middle of 1953. In
preparation, the defence lawyers concentrated on the strange
relationship between Burchett and General Dean, the highest
ranking American captured during the war.

21. The Defection Attempt

General Dean had spent sixteen months in a North Korean POW camp hut in which he could not stand up straight. He was not allowed to exercise outside the hut and had nothing to read. Although he was not tortured, he was often threatened with it. His food ration was small and of poor quality. His living conditions had deteriorated to a point where he contemplated suicide. Then one day, in the mid-winter of 1952, a group of Chinese and North Korean journalists and cameramen arrived with Burchett. Dean was interviewed by Burchett, who gave him news of his family and promised to write to his wife. Later the photographers went to work taking pictures of them. Dean even did some calisthenics. He was very excited by Burchett's visit, for he had not seen another westerner for so long. The 'little Australian with the receding hairline,' as he put it, seemed a reasonable man.

A few days later Burchett returned and said that he had sent the letter to Dean's wife. They talked alone for two hours, and

Burchett insisted on knowing if Dean had any complaints or requests. Dean was reluctant at first to divulge too much for fear that he was in some way being conned, or that this new contact might not return. But Burchett persisted and returned two days later. Dean asked for writing materials and something to read. He complained about the food and lack of exercise. Within another week, Dean felt as if some magic had been performed. His guards stopped pushing him around and became respectful. He was allowed out for regular 'walks' and exercise. The walk was a four metre stretch between his hut and the latrine. He was thankful for this and on his first day tried to march the equivalent of a kilometre. But it was too much. He slipped on the frozen ground and cut his head open.

Dean feared that the walks would be stopped, but they continued. Mats were provided for his calisthenics, and the food improved in quality and quantity. Burchett brought him beer and books. Most of them were in some way ideological, but Dean didn't care. He wanted to exercise his mind. In the next year he was to build a small library that would include a short-story collection by Jack London, and another of his works, *Love of Life*, the history of the Communist Party in the Soviet Union, *Anti-Duhring*, a text in which Engels restated and clarified Marxist doctrine, issues of the magazine *Soviet Literature*, a book including all of Stalin's Orders of the Day, issued on special occasions during World War II, *Stalin as a Military Leader*, *Stalin's Lessons in Leninism*, *Gentlemen of Japan*, by Havens, *Dollar Diplomacy*, published in 1925, copies of *Masses and Mainstream*, an American communist periodical, a very boring British Labour Party paper, and not so boring but infuriating copies of the London *Daily Worker*.

Burchett brought most of the non-propaganda material, but Dean read it all; he wanted to understand the enemy. Writing materials were sent to the hut, and Dean was soon scribbling letters to family and friends. Later he also began to receive mail. Alan Winnington appeared on 5 April 1952 and interviewed Dean. He enjoyed that, too, although it was spoilt by the fact that both men suffered from dysentery.

In a photo session, a bench was brought in, and Dean posed on it. It was the first piece of furniture he had been near during his captivity, but it was taken away at the end of the picture-taking.

Winnington came again with whisky and chatted about many things. But he did not endear himself to Dean as Burchett had done. Winnington seemed aloof and less outgoing.

Dean appreciated that there was no direct propaganda introduced at his meetings with Burchett. Nevertheless, Burchett discussed the possibility of Dean taking a Corps Command in the Chinese army, or a political post in China. The conditions were made to sound most attractive, but Dean respectfully declined.

Dean noted in a diary that he found Burchett a sad figure:

'I feel sorry that he is where he is and sees things as he apparently does,' he wrote. 'This kindly man has cut himself off from his own people for the sake of strong beliefs.'

Dean's last meeting with Burchett was in mid-1953 on the eve of his repatriation. Burchett arrived with a large retinue of Chinese and North Korean journalists and photographers. A feast was prepared at the cookhouse, and throughout a heavy drinking and eating session, the cameramen continually took shots for more useful propaganda about Dean. Burchett expressed sorrow that Dean was about to be released, because it would be the last time he would have a chance to eat with him, and Dean thanked him. He wrote later that Burchett never explained either his choice of the communist side in the Korean war or why he had shown special kindness to him.

Traill had discovered that Dean was the first of several POWs that Burchett 'befriended' or made contact with not long before their repatriation in 1953. Traill though that this was evidence that Burchett had tried hard at the last minute to improve his standing in the west. Why?

Soon afterwards, Burchett expressed doubts for the first time about the germ-warfare campaign. He told one US journalist that it might just be possible that the Chinese rigged the evidence. He may have been gullible enough at the time not to question it. He also remarked to George MacArthur that the germ-warfare episode was the major regret of his professional life. These two comments were not an admission that it had all been a hoax, but other communists were also beginning to have serious second thoughts about the affair. Among them was Tibor Meray.

In August 1953, eighteen months after viewing the germ-warfare evidence, Tibor Meray began to doubt the truth of what he had been shown. Sol Tchang Sik, a Korean poet who had worked as an interpreter at Kaosong, was tried as a confessed American spy. Meray knew him well and refused to believe the accusations. Events in Hungary began to turn Meray against communist ideology, and he became one of the would-be revolutionaries who succeeded in overthrowing the Soviet-controlled regime in Budapest in October 1956 – but for just ten days. When the Kremlin countered, and Soviet tanks rolled in and put down the uprising, Meray fled to Paris, where he had time to re-think his communist experiences. He decided to probe into the germ-warfare episode, which had worried him for more than four years. He consulted several French experts, including Professor Jean Rostand, a leading biologist; Professor Seguy, the director of France's Institute of Entomology; and Dr Gallut, of the Pasteur Institute, who was a world authority on cholera.

Seguy told Meray that a bacteriological attack to cause cholera using insects was impossible, and that communist claims of evidence were scientific nonsense. The professor said that insects constantly cleaned themselves, and that any microbes on them would be destroyed. Seguy thought the germs would have died when the bombs hit the ground, and they would not have withstood the extreme mid-winter Korean temperatures. Dr Gallut, the cholera specialist, confirmed these observations.

In his investigations Meray found no one, with the exception of Burchett, who had ever seen the insects dropped. (Meray was surprised by Burchett's claim, because he had never mentioned it in Korea, where the two men had been in contact daily for more than a year.) A Hungarian doctor, who had visited a North Korean village where flies had been found, was told by local peasants that the flies had been planted by Chinese soldiers. Then there were the mystery clams that had been eaten by the husband and wife. No one had seen the planes that were supposed to have dropped them. There had been no witnesses to the clams. Indeed, no one had even seen the unlucky couple.

Meray wrote a twelve-part series of articles for the French newspaper *Franc Tireur*, in March 1957, entitled, 'The Truth about Bacteriological Warfare.' He completely reversed his position and concluded that the campaign had been a brilliantly organised hoax.

While Burchett and Meray were re-thinking events in August 1953, General Dean, now free, told General Mark Clark, the Commander of all UN forces in Korea, of his feelings about Burchett. Clark wondered if Burchett could be persuaded to defect. He considered it would be a major victory to have Burchett switch sides and denounce the germ-warfare business as a big communist lie. Clark asked the CIA to approach him.

He continued to move among the UN prisoners of war in an attempt to influence them to stay with the communists and not move to Kaesong for repatriation. It was one propaganda battle the communists were losing badly. Many more North Korean POWs were happy to stay south, but very few South Korean and UN prisoners opted for communism.

Burchett was enlisted by General Wang to convince POWs about the benefits of becoming communists. He spoke of Russia's being a worker's paradise and of his belief that the spread of communism would end all war. Conflict in Korea, he said, was the US's fault. The American fascist government, as he put it, was responsible for prolonging the war and for exploiting working people.

Predictably, few were converted. Most had been repulsed by what they had seen of communism in the camps.

Early in September, Burchett made a special effort with Bud Mahurin, who had been the most important prize for the communists in the germ-warfare exercise. He had been the highest-ranking officer who could have been in a position to order the claimed bombing missions. Mahurin had been shot down in May 1952. After 16 months in solitary confinement, he was a shell. His weight had dropped from 73 to 43 kilograms, he spoke a gibberish mixture of Chinese and English, and he looked eighty. Because of his rank and importance he was one of twenty American fliers who had endured extreme physical and mental torture. He was feeble, and what was left of his nerve was nearly shot with the terror of waiting to be repatriated on the last day of the exchange of POWs. He was worried that he would not make it, although his freedom seemed tantalisingly close, because he was in a tent with a few other waiting POWs. They were the first caucasians Mahurin had seen in his period of solitary, apart from two men: Winnington and Burchett.

An armed guard came into the tent late at night and ordered Mahurin out. He was taken a few hundred metres to another tent. Inside, and seated at one end of a long table covered with green felt, was Burchett.

Mahurin was just alert enough to notice that the guard took orders from Burchett as if he was an officer, and it had an alarming effect on the unstable prisoner; he felt that Burchett had complete power over him. He was aware that about thirty other American airmen were dead or missing after long periods of captivity and torture. Mahurin feared he might not be repatriated if this man did not like him or what he said. Burchett, however, was friendly. He introduced himself and said: 'I was a war correspondent in South-East Asia during World War II, assigned to MacArthur's staff. You and I have several mutual friends.' Among them was Maggie Higgins.

Mahurin was shaking. He could not be sure Burchett was whom he claimed, and it crossed his torture-shocked mind that his host could be anything, even Russian. Mahurin's fears surfaced when Burchett began to discuss germ warfare. He asked him how he felt about dropping germ bombs on an innocent population. Mahurin did not dare go back on his confession.

'I was a soldier doing my job,' he said.

Burchett spoke about the consequences of Mahurin's return to America. There would be a revolution in the US within twenty years, he said, and people with his background would suffer. The communists would take power, and he would be in trouble because of his military efforts in Korea. Burchett wanted him to change sides. Mahurin refused.

Burchett mentioned Winnington, and Mahurin reacted. It was the Englishman who had sat on a tribunal with two

Chinese and sentenced the American to death for his supposed war crimes, for which Mahurin had been marched out of solitary confinement at night to be shot. On several occasions a revolver was put to his head and the trigger pulled.

Burchett returned to the tent minutes later and said that Winnington had left for Peking with his Chinese-European wife. Then he delivered a long harangue about the US efforts to contain communism, but he was careful not to threaten Mahurin who later told the *US News & World Report* that Burchett on that last night – their first and only meeting – was 'very pleasant to me. Very pleasant. No military business at all.'

The meeting with Mahurin was all part of Burchett's deliberate plan to have a high profile among American and Australian POWs at the time when he was negotiating his future with the west.

General Clark's intermediary, an American reporter, approached Burchett and discussed his defection, but Burchett would only consider making the move under certain conditions, which centred on the Australian government's granting him a complete amnesty.

Clark's people approached the Australian Embassy in Tokyo, and embassy staff sent a telegram to Canberra on 8 September 1953, two days after his meeting with Mahurin, which said:

'The United States Army would be willing to agree to joint interrogation with the Australian Army if we so desire it and would arrange for interrogation to take place in Korea, or Okinawa if we do not desire that Burchett travel to Japan.

'Please advise urgently:

(a) whether Burchett would be allowed to enter Australia;

(b) whether he can be given an assurance that, subject to good behaviour, he will not be liable to proceedings or other actions in Australia;

(c) whether you wish the Australian Army to be associated with the United States Army in his interrogations;

(d) whether his repatriation would be at the Australian government's expense or whether we should accept United States' Transport authorities in the event of Burchett not having funds.

'General Clark hopes we will treat this matter as one of

considerable urgency since the opportunity for continued personal contact with Burchett through the American press correspondent in the demilitarised zone may be interrupted in the near future and any delay in reaching a decision will, therefore, reduce prospects of bringing Burchett out at all. Obviously, any leakage to the communists of Burchett's desire to leave North Korea would prejudice the whole operation.

'According to the United States Army Intelligence, Burchett has a Czechoslovakian wife and one child in China. So far as is known Burchett has not raised the question of his family and may not do so.'

The response of the Menzies government was swift. A top secret cablegram reply two days later, on 10 September, from the Department of External Affairs read:

'Matter has been considered at the highest level. For your background information, recent return of (Ernie) Thornton raised storm as to why government allowed him to return. Public opinion finds it difficult to understand and accept legal position that the government had no power to keep out an Australian citizen. If now a second and even more notorious communist sympathiser returned – particularly with government assistance or guarantee – there would be public outcry, especially from men who fought in Korea or their relatives.

'Specific answers to your questions are:

(a) government has not the least desire that Burchett should return. It may not have the legal power to exclude him, but it will do what it can;

(b) under no circumstances will government give Burchett any assurance he will not be liable to proceedings or other action in Australia;

(c) and (d) government will make no contribution to his repatriation and will grant him no facilities. If nevertheless Burchett leaves North Korea and is interrogated by Americans, the government would be prepared to consider sending from Australia some special security officer to assist interrogation.

'You can explain background to General Clark, make it clear to him that his own interest in the case led to matter being seriously considered here at the highest level.'

The Australian government was already investigating if Burchett could be tried for treason.

The American High Command was disappointed, and its

plan received a further setback when the intermediary had to leave Korea. General Clark, however, asked Major General Blackshear Bryan, a senior US negotiator at Panmunjon, to see if a defection strategy could still be devised. Bryan approached another journalist, Edward Hymoff, bureau chief for the International News Service in Seoul. Hymoff had been a US intelligence officer in World War II. Bryan inferred that he had information that indicated that Burchett was ready to switch sides. Hymoff, who was not privy to previous negotiations with Burchett, was sceptical because he could not see Burchett leaving Vessa and their recently born child, Peter, in Peking. Burchett was very proud of them both and 'never stopped talking about them'. Bryan indicated this complication would be catered for.

Days later, Hymoff was contacted by a 'Colonel Jones' of the CIA, and they drafted a plan in which Burchett would be offered $100,000. Hymoff, however, wanted his own deal. If he was to make the offer to Burchett, the CIA had to give him the scoop of the defection. And Hymoff demanded that the CIA get information on two newsman friends, Donald Dixon and Richard Applegate (who had daily greeted Burchett and Winnington by saying, 'Hi, traitors'). They had been captured by the Chinese in March 1953 while on a journey from Hong Kong to Macau in a yacht owned by Applegate, a Hong Kong-based correspondent for NBC News, and a former war correspondent in Korea for United Press. The yacht had been intercepted by a Chinese patrol boat. Everyone on board was imprisoned in Canton. Hymoff had tried for months, without success, to get news of his friends from Burchett, Winnington and other communist newsmen representing the Chinese at Panmumjon.

Colonel Jones said that the offer should be put to Burchett, that he had already been prepared in earlier discussions with the other intermediary. Burchett was aware that the Menzies government was not interested in any amnesty.

After a peace talk negotiating session on the morning of 19 September 1953, Burchett and Hymoff strolled along the dirt road leading to the UN negotiators' tents. The road was flanked by jeeps, one helicopter occupied by a waiting pilot and soldiers. If he was going to defect, he had to shout 'sanctuary' and dash for a waiting helicopter. A tense Hymoff turned to Burchett.

'General Dean has been offered $50,000 by the *Saturday Evening Post*,' Hymoff said. 'We will pay you $100,000 for your story and take good care of you.'

Burchett hesitated, and laughed nervously.

'I'm serious!' Hymoff said. Other journalists were only a few paces away. Burchett glanced at the jeeps and the helicopter but said nothing. Then the two men parted. Burchett had made his choice. There would be no turning back.

Burchett was a marked man. Even before the end of September 1953, ASIO had prepared a legal opinion on whether or not there was a case for trying him. He could not be charged with treason under Section 24 of the Federal Crimes Act because it could not be used outside Australia. ASIO considered, however, that it could possibly prosecute Burchett under the English statute and common law on treason. Action might be brought in the Supreme Court of Victoria. But it would have to be proved that Burchett owed allegiance to the Queen; that he had 'adhered' to her enemies – giving them 'aid and comfort'. The main question was whether or not the Chinese and North Koreans could be regarded as the Queen's enemies. Technically, Burchett's British passport meant that he owed allegiance to Elizabeth Regina II. The government and ASIO were also confident that they could prove he had given much 'aid and comfort' to the Chinese and North Koreans. There were his radio broadcasts, articles, books and speeches, and the more contentious area of Burchett's activities in the POW camps.

In November 1953, two ASIO officers were sent to Japan and Korea to gather evidence from high-ranking American military officers.

After all the repatriated POWs returned to the US, in late 1953, Burchett gained notoriety when a spate of articles analysing his part in the propaganda campaign appeared. Instead of being a hero who saw the error of his ways and defected from the evils of communism, Burchett was vilified in a concerted effort by the US media.

Typical was a lead story in the right-wing *US News & World Report* headlined: 'Strange Case of Two Traitors.' It went:

'Two newspapermen from the British Commonwealth are

being viewed with a jaundiced eye by American diplomatic and military officials.

'These two men, during the Korean war, worked actively for the enemy. They played major roles in the "germ-warfare" campaign that did much to hurt the United States. They processed "confessions" extracted from American aviators by torture. One of the men [Winnington] sat on a tribunal that tried a colonel in the Air Force of the United States.

'One of the men is Alan Winnington, an apple-cheeked Briton, correspondent for the London *Daily Worker*, and a member of the British Communist Party since the mid-1930s. The other man is a hatchet-faced Australian, Wilfred Burchett, correspondent for the Paris communist daily, *L'Humanite*...

'Both of these men aided the enemy in Korea. Both did their best to undermine and bring defeat to United Nations military forces. Yet both write dispatches that are featured in papers of nations with troops in Korea. For doing less, William Joyce, Britain's Lord Haw Haw, was tried and hanged at the end of World War II...

'Evidence so far gathered indicates that these two newspapermen were not the "bully boys" who obtained confessions, but were willing tools and top aides who provided the air of authenticity to the words that came from the mouths and pens of American fliers. They did the faking of confessions that convinced much of the world that American pilots were conducting germ warfare...

'Winnington and Burchett were heard in sound recordings, and seen in a propaganda moving picture, which was widely distributed. One man had a British accent and the other, an Australian accent. They talked calmly with American air officers – some of high rank – who said they had dropped bacteriological bombs on areas occupied by Chinese and North Korean peasants and soldiers. Recordings and movies appear believable because the men questioning the westerners, were westerners themselves.'

After this, Winnington had his British passport confiscated for twelve years. He was to fade into obscurity as a hack communist correspondent, writing the occasional novel and non-fiction book, from China and East Germany. But for Burchett it was part of his mounting confrontation with the US in every world troublespot in which it was involved. For many influential Americans, Burchett emerged from Korea as international public enemy number one. Several POWs such as Kniss and Mahurin watched his progress with varying frustration, until their day in court.

The US now agreed to hand over its intelligence on Burchett's activities in the Korean war, which included US military intelligence interviews with thirty-five American POWs (including in mid-1954 'germ-warfare confession' pilots Kniss, Mahurin, Quinn, Enoch and O'Neal) who had spoken to Burchett. By December 1954, there was still a possibility that Burchett would be charged with treason and brought to trial. But since he was not likely to appear in Australia, he had to be arrested overseas.

Burchett, however, was not about to be picked up easily. He moved from North Korea, to Peking and then to Vietnam in 1954. This kept him clear of possible action by Australian, British or American agents. Winnington had had his passport removed, and Burchett knew that he was in trouble if he set foot on British Commonwealth or American soil. His forced retreat to the communist world had its advantages. His efforts in the germ-warfare campaign had enhanced his status on the left. The North Koreans decorated him, the Chinese offered him permanent sanctuary, and Ho Chi Minh became his friend. Burchett, then, was in the right place to witness another key event in the twentieth century: the battle of Dien Bien Phu between the French and the Viet Minh. Burchett was able to report the final victories over the French and accompany Ho's victorious troops into liberated Hanoi.

Warner was also in Vietnam at the time, taking advantage of the French fall. He had often predicted that the French might lose the war in Vietnam and so was banned from entering the country. He heard that Burchett was arriving with Ho's troops and rushed to leave Hanoi on the same day that his rival marched in, remembering Burchett's promise to 'get him'.

In early April 1955, Burchett was scheduled to fly with the Chinese delegation, including Chou En Lai, on the Indian

Airliner Kashmir Princess to Bandung for the Afro-Asian Conference. At the last moment the North Vietnamese delegation decided to hire its own Dakota, and Burchett left with them. Chou En Lai also made a last minute decision to switch planes so that he could meet the Egyptian leader Gammar Abdul Nasser in Rangoon.

During a fuelling stopover in Hong Kong, a time bomb was placed in one of the petrol tanks of the Kashmir Princess. (According to Burchett, a Kuomintang agent from Taiwan put it there. Russell Spurr – also at Bandung – claimed that the CIA station chief in Hong Kong was behind it.) The plane later exploded and crashed into the sea south of Hong Kong. Thirty Chinese officials were killed.

Meanwhile, Burchett's Dakota, a short-range aircraft, made a fuelling stop in Rangoon, then flew on to Penang and Singapore before making for Jakarta. At the Singapore stop, Burchett refused local authority instructions to leave the aircraft. The plane was delayed for an hour while officials tried to persuade him to leave with other passengers. Finally, Burchett's passport was checked by airport police.

This incident was reported to the British charge d'affaires in Jakarta, Ronald Parkes. He initiated moves to detain Burchett on his return trip through Singapore, and ASIO men rushed there to wait for him. Warner, a friend of Parkes, knew of the plan in advance. So did three others. One of them tipped off Burchett.

At the end of the conference, Chou En Lai's plane flew directly to Nanning, in Kwangsi province near the Vietnam border. Burchett went from there to Hanoi by train and car, with a few days stopover at a rest-house inside Vietnam. When he reached Hanoi, Burchett claimed that his passport was missing and blamed it on 'CIA agents recruited from Vietnamese who had previously worked for French Intelligence'. The disappearance of the vital document sealed Burchett's exile from his home country for the next fifteen years and drove him even more firmly into the communist camp.

That was early in May 1955. Coincidentally, in early May, Denis Warner suggested to an Australian diplomat, Sir Keith Shann, that Australia should do something 'about muzzling Burchett by having his passport withdrawn'. Shann noted Warner's suggestion in a memo dated 9 May 1955.

22. Reason and Treason

Treason was the underlying thrust of the trial from day one. Burchett had prepared a defence against the charge based on the case of Frenchman Alfred Dreyfus (1859–1935). In 1894 he was accused of selling military secrets to a German military attaché, then arrested, convicted and sentenced in a military court to life imprisonment on Devil's Island.

Public opinion and the French press welcomed the verdict and sentence for anti-semitic reasons. The French army's majors Esterhazy and Henry invented evidence and forged documents that were used against Dreyfus. In 1898, the novelist Emile Zola wrote an open letter, which was published on the front page of Clemenceau's paper *Aurore, 'J'Accuse'*. It accused the army of covering up its mistaken conviction of Dreyfus and of acquitting Esterhazy on the orders of the Ministry of War. It split French opinion in two.

Dreyfus was re-tried in 1899 and found guilty again, but this time was pardoned. In 1906, a civilian court of appeals cleared him and reversed all previous convictions. A sharper alignment of political and social forces followed, leading to the separation of church and state in 1905, and a cleavage between right-wing nationalists and left-wing anti-militarists, which continues. The controversy destroyed the cohesion of French life for more than a generation. Mistaken loyalties, repeated stupidities, base forgeries, and extremism had inflamed a crisis.

Burchett saw similarities in his case. He felt the Australian military had made him look like a risk to national security after Korea, and this had led to his exile.

Burchett felt that, like Dreyfus, the local media had turned public opinion against him after Korea. Burchett's 'J'Accuse' came from liberal and communist friends taking up his passport cause, which became popular during Vietnam. The passport issue also became one of national security versus international socialism. Burchett argued that it was a case of his right to support what he liked politically against the state's concept of what it saw as the interests of security. Australia's active involvement in Vietnam and Korea had also become a question of right-wing nationalism versus left-wing anti-militarism. Although Burchett may have welcomed a national crisis over his rights, it did not reach those proportions. But opinion was split.

The Kane camp used the traitor element by attempting to make comparisons between Burchett and William Joyce, who was tried in 1945. In the Joyce case, the only doubt was whether he was 'British' at the time he broadcast for the Nazis. Joyce had been born in America, which gave him American nationality. He became a German national in July 1940, and the question arose whether he was British before then. But he was found guilty and hanged. There was no popular emotional support for his right to support his chosen ideology, which happened to be fascism, against the interests of the British government. He was executed because he had gone beyond intellectual support for Nazism to give all his energies to backing Hitler.

In Burchett's case, the question was how far he had gone beyond intellectual support in his backing of other countries that were engaged in fighting Australian troops. Because both the Vietnam and Korean conflicts were not officially declared as wars by either side, he and his supporters felt that he had every right to his views and actions. Furthermore, Burchett was not widely hated in Australia because its involvement in Korea, and Vietnam particularly, had strong opposition.

Traill also pointed out that both Joyce and Burchett wanted radical political changes in their respective countries. Joyce dreamt of returning to a Hitler-conquered United Kingdom, with some dictatorial role for himself. Burchett's letters and utterances suggested that he would have returned happily to an Australia convulsed by a communist revolution, and that he would have expected a role in communist government. He spoke often of the inevitability and desirability of such an upheaval in Australia (and the US). The dreams and writings of radicals could not be considered by law as treasonable, however, unless they were translated into action, and Traill was further restrained by the political atmosphere created by Whitlam's 1972 victory and the increasing unpopularity of the Vietnam war in Australia. Yesterday's potential traitor had become tomorrow's heroic patriot.

23. The Judgment

Traill decided to finish off the defence case with an important reminder of Burchett during the Korean war by putting Walker 'Bud' Mahurin in the witness box. Evidence of his experiences should, Traill felt, be fresh in the jury's mind when it deliberated.

Mahurin leaned forward in the witness box, hands clasped. He described himself as an 'executive vice-president' and looked on edge but in control. He was an impressive figure, with his wisps of grey at the temples, perfectly tailored light-coloured wool suit and fashionably wide, dark brown tie. His wife Joan, the most photographed person the court-house had seen in years, sat confidently in the gallery. Her ebullience had helped her husband who, like Kinne, had been deeply affected by the trial. A year earlier, when Jack Kane had reached across a restaurant table in California and asked, 'Well, will you be in it?' Mahurin had fallen for his rugged Irish charm and no-nonsense attitude. Yes, he would come to Australia and help.

Now he was here and, regurgitating those horrific days, he was close to a breakdown. The resilient Joan, however, was doing her best to bring him down to earth. She was enjoying Australia. Why couldn't he try to relax and love it too?

Like Kinne, Mahurin was an oddity to the court – an air ace with twenty-two medals bestowed by the US, the UK, France and Belgium. Traill read them out in detail and so increased the credibility and prestige of the defence. It seemed to work. Three jurors were wearing Australian Returned Services League badges. Both camps noticed them. Cooper, however, feared that all this heavy artillery from the defence might push the trial into a jingoistic, partisan battle, which could work against Burchett.

Mahurin was tense as he spoke firmly of his first sighting of Burchett.

'Have you seen either of the two Caucasian men who were at Pyocktong here today?' Traill asked.

'Yes,' Mahurin said, pointing dramatically. 'That man there!'

The witness then described seeing Burchett and Winnington with the four Chinese interrogators as he was being transferred between camps.

'The men chatted, and I could not hear anything, I was too far away. They were smiling. Burchett stared at me like a snake would stare at a mouse.'

That simile became the headline of the trial. Reporters rushed to cameras and microphones to repeat it, and every paper splashed it. Mahurin had rehearsed it and managed to work it in under a lather of words about the Chinese interrogators who started to work on him soon afterwards. Cooper objected, but too late. Taylor intervened:

'Was Mr Burchett there when they did this?'

'No,' Mahurin said. 'He was not.'

Traill led Mahurin through his experiences to his meeting with Burchett. Cooper speared in several objections and effectively kept deflecting Traill, but the story came out more or less as the defence hoped it would. Judge Taylor, however, drew the line at Mahurin's saying that he had met Winnington when he 'had been under intense brain-washing'. It was stricken from the record, as was Mahurin's attempt to say that he had tried to commit suicide. But the canvas was bleak enough, and Traill was pleased with the American, who had been a secondary witness because of his limited contact with Burchett. His evidence had been less complicated. If the jury members had been confused by the detailed Kniss testimony, they would have had fewer problems with Mahurin's.

Traill managed to have an article in the London *Daily Worker* of 7 September 1953 entered as a case exhibit. Despite Cooper's objection, the witness was able to say that the article, by-lined Wilfred Burchett, had statements attributed to him that were not true.

Traill spent much time attacking every paragraph in the piece, which he treated as a crucial piece of evidence. The article appeared in the London *Daily Worker, L'Humanite*, and the Sunday 6 September 1953 edition of Radio Malaya Special News Service, the Monitoring Digest of news from Peking, Taipeh, Vietnam and Moscow. In the Digest news from China the article was headed:

'Highest US Authorities Planned Bacteriological Warfare, says Burchett.' The piece began:

'Three key senior officers of the American military hierarchy were among the twenty-five American airmen handed over here this morning [6 Sept.] who have admitted taking part personally in germ warfare in Korea and China, writes Wilfred Burchett, *L'Humanite* correspondent, from Panmunjon. He continues:

"The three full colonels are Walker F. Mahurin, former assistant executive to secretary for Air Finletter...

'"Mahurin told me last night that the great 'error' the [American Joint Chiefs of Staff] planners made was complete under-estimation of the organisational ability of the Korean and Chinese peoples, and of the speed and efficiency with which they are able to take effective counter measures.

'"At the time Mahurin was shot down, he was commanding the 51st Fighter Wing in Korea, one of the two fighter wings flying F-86 Sabre jets. 'As far as the man in the airplanes is concerned,' he said, 'it's just a matter of pushing a button.'

'"Mahurin... emphasised that he 'had no complaint whatsoever' about the treatment from the time he was captured...

'"Both he and Schwable [another American airman captured] roared with laughter when I told them that the American authorities had charged that...a technique was used to 'extract' admissions from them. 'I suppose they would be putting us in straight jackets and taking us home in padded cells,' Schwable commented. Mahurin added that he 'could not figure out why the Americans waged germ war'.

' "He said he was 'deeply convinced that the Koreans and Chinese authorities were motived by a purely humanitarian reason' in their painstaking investigations into germ warfare in order to have it banned, and this was the reason why he co-operated in exposing American germ warfare activities and the part he had personally played..." '

There were frowns and glances between Cooper and Burchett at Burchett's table. Burchett shook his head.

'Never met the man,' Burchett whispered. 'He's mistaken or lying. Maybe he mixed me up with Winnington, too.'

Traill threw out fifteen fast questions.

'Did you ever say to Wilfred Burchett anything about a great error the planners had made?'

Each time, Mahurin replied with characteristic certitude.

'No, certainly not.'

'Did you ever say anything to Mr Burchett about dropping bug bombs?'

'Not to Mr Burchett. That was part of my confession.'

Traill ended with a familiar probe.

'What, to your knowledge, was the plaintiff's reputation, as at 1971, and prior to that?'

'I based my knowledge on the fact that I have been exposed as President of the American Fighter Pilots Association to the prisoners in Korea,' Mahurin began. 'I consider Mr Burchett to be a petty, conniving communist propaganda hack. I believe that his reputation throughout the free world is of that kind, and I base that on my own personal contact with newspaper men and government leaders throughout the United States, and Europe and in the Orient.'

Traill then asked Mahurin to say that Burchett was seen as a despicable individual in the US, but the point of the witness's feeling had already been given. In his eagerness to use him, he was in danger of overkill. Just when Taylor was about to intervene, Traill ended his examination.

The strain showed on Cooper as he began the cross-examination. As with Kinne, the defence had left Cooper with little chance for refutation. But he had to try. To leave such a witness unchallenged would leave the jury with the thought that all Mahurin had said was accurate.

'Did anybody approach you and ask you to give evidence?' Cooper asked sharply.

'I volunteered to give evidence,' Mahurin said, nervously.

'To whom?'

'To Mr Kane. Not Mr Kane himself. The first contact I had was with Mr Traill, and Mr Traill was directed to me by an Ed Hunter in Washington DC.'

Cooper later flayed about with other questions that were directed at showing that the witness was biased, but they were rebuffed, although he did score a point when Mahurin contradicted himself about what Burchett had been wearing when he was said to have stared at him, like a snake would a mouse.

'Did he have a star on that uniform?'

'That is correct. I could see it.' Earlier, during Traill's examination, when asked if he had seen any insignia on Burchett's clothing, the witness had replied, 'No, I did not'.

Inexplicably, Cooper did not follow through. After asking him if he was terrified at the time, Cooper said:

'I put it to you that it was not the plaintiff you then saw.'

'As God is my witness,' Mahurin said, 'that was the plaintiff!'

'And is it not the fact that over the years you have wanted to get, what you call "get even", with Mr Burchett?'

'I have no feeling of revenge,' Mahurin replied, with less conviction.

'You say you wanted to come here and give evidence?'

'Absolutely, for justice.'

Based on Burchett's word that Mahurin had not seen him, Cooper repeated the assertion that the witness had been mistaken. Again, Mahurin was adamant:

'Absolutely not. I saw two white men all the time I was in Korea. He was one, and Alan Winnington was another. I could never forget, never.'

The cross-examination ended soon after, and the defence appeared to have come out on top. Burchett continued to show his bewilderment, but Cooper realised that the damage had been done.

Cooper's solution was to use Burchett in a long final examination, covering the most contentious areas in a last bid to limit Traill's openings. Despite the strain, Burchett performed well and could not have failed to leave the jury with an improved impression. He was questioned for several hours. Then Traill began a gruelling cross-examination that was to last for nearly a day. In typical fashion, Traill started out slowly in his chronological run-through of Burchett's career. Burchett looked and sounded as if he was still being quizzed by Cooper. In the first hour or so, which took the court to a lunch break on Wednesday 29 October, he did not hesitate in his responses, and it appeared as if the defence was attempting to string out the cross-examination in the hope that the jury would be left with a poor image of Burchett, along with tit-bits of his communist connections. It wasn't working. Taylor was looking alternatively annoyed and frustrated. The jury was plain bored, and the public gallery seemed irritated or half asleep. The snoring gentleman was using a small pillow as a head rest, and his steady grunts punctuated any lulls in proceedings.

In the post-lunch session of Traill's long quizzing, Taylor began to show his attitude to Traill's tardiness, and intervened several times. Then just as it seemed that Traill was losing control, Burchett admitted that he had made an error when arguing with the Australian Korean war POW, Hollis, about the quality of the food prisoners were given. In days of testimony it was his first concession.

'He [Hollis] made some unpleasant remarks,' Burchett began, 'and I made a remark that I should not have made. I said "Well, the next time you go abroad to kill communists you make sure you go abroad to kill communists in a country where steak and eggs is the staple diet." I should not have made the remark, I know now.'

If it was a tactical comment to give the appearance of honesty, or simply a sincere comment, it may have worked against him, for the callousness of the words to a POW, no matter what the provocation by Hollis, was consistent with the defence line throughout the trial that Burchett was 'on the other side', and not the impartial observer he claimed to be. Burchett had so far denied ever referring to 'your side' or 'our side', or of ever indulging in the Cold War rhetoric of the time. His admission, observers noted, put this in doubt.

*The many faces of Burchett. The French look. He was based
in Paris from 1968 until 1983*

Comrade Burchett greets his old friend Uncle Ho on a visit to Hanoi in 1967

'If I kiss you, will you turn into a frog?' Burchett greets Cambodia's Prince Sihanouk in Phnom Penh, 1965

Burchett and his counsel, Harvey Cooper, leave the court looking wary. Earlier POW Derek Kinne had tried to strangle him on the court-house steps

Those boring Stalinist Show Trials. Burchett had trouble keeping awake during the trial of Laszlo Rajk in Hungary in 1949. He took Benzedrine to stay alert

Burchett the actor. In 1948 in Berlin he made a short film on how the black market operated

Traill moved on to question Burchett about Mahurin. Burchett had denied ever meeting the American war hero. Traill produced the contentious article in the London *Daily Worker*. It was the interview with Mahurin, and it carried the by-line Wilfred Burchett.

'I am puzzled about this,' Burchett said, frowning, 'because I was not writing for the *Daily Worker* at that time.'

'Do you have any recollection now of a conversation with Colonel Mahurin?'

'To the best of my knowledge I saw Colonel Mahurin for the first time in court.'

'Were you at this time the correspondent for *L'Humanite*?' Traill asked.

'At that time, yes.'

'I show you a certified copy of the *Daily News Release*, the Hsinhua Newsagency, Monday, 7 September 1953…'

Cooper objected. Taylor, a hand propping up a weary head, allowed Traill to continue his reference to the Mahurin interview.

'Did you write that story?' Traill pressed. Burchett took a sip of water. His hand was shaking.

'I must have written that story,' he said, reluctantly.

Traill kept pushing and Burchett tried to side-step the issue. Taylor intervened again.

'Did you write that article?'

'I have no recollection of writing an article, but if it is in the *Daily News Release*, I accept I must have written it. But I have no recollection of the event.'

Traill read out passages from the article, and each time asked Burchett if he wrote it. Burchett accepted that he had. Traill became more forceful as he recited the piece, until Taylor told him he was only entitled to prove that Burchett had spoken to Mahurin.

Traill switched to other extracts from Burchett's book on Korea, *This Monstrous War*. Again Judge Taylor cut Traill off and ruled it inadmissible. Traill was furious.

'Obviously, if various statements are written which are all slanted one way,' Traill said, 'it goes to the issue of whether or not he was working for the Chinese!'

'It does not, in my view,' Taylor said, and ordered Traill to show him any further extracts before attempting to read them.

Traill asked him to look at a certain passage. Taylor rejected it. Traill turned his back on the judge and made great play of lying *This Monstrous War* down on the defendant's table. The book was still open at the passage he had wanted to read out. Traill paused as if he were counting to ten.

'Did you,' he began in a whisper that betrayed his frustration, 'during the period you were in Russia, write for the magazine, *New Times*?'

Burchett said he had.

Traill asked more questions about his connection to the magazine, which he believed was under KGB control and had mainly agents writing for it.

'Did you get paid for your contributions to *New Times*?'

'Of course.'

'Did the state run the publishing house for which you worked?'

Cooper objected. Taylor rejected the question, and Traill sighed. His next question would have explained that the KGB had control of the publishing house. It was a ploy to educate the court about the complicated apparatus of propaganda control in the Soviet Union, but the defence had fallen short of its aim.

Traill was forced to change his line for the fourth time in a few minutes as he tried to prove that Burchett was employed by the North Vietnamese and Chinese. That took Traill into the post-1957 period, and Taylor got tough. He admonished Traill for going beyond his ruling. With help from Cooper, and Taylor's growing irritation at the defence, Burchett had managed to hold his position.

Cooper kept him in the stand in an attempt to demonstrate to the court that Burchett had not mentioned germ warfare in a book published many months before the orchestrated communist campaign against the US, which had begun early in 1952. Burchett now claimed that he recalled that he had written the introduction to *China's Feet Unbound* in 'July or August 1952'. Even though the book's publishing date was July 1951, Burchett and Cooper were implying that his introduction had been added at the last minute – after the germ-warfare campaign had begun. It was not a convincing end, and Burchett looked weary and stunned as he left the stand. Most chapters of his life had been open to the world in an intriguing, bitter and probing eight days in court.

Taylor absented the jury so that he could talk with first Cooper and then Traill. Cooper wasted no time in pinpointing that the use of the word 'blackmail' in the *Focus* article was in bad faith and had defamed his client. The judge read the article again:

'Burchett had a close relationship with Colonel Barsegov, the head of the KGB special branch dealing with foreign correspondents. HE PROPOSED THE BLACKMAIL OF AN AMERICAN AIR FORCE GENERAL WITH WHOSE WIFE HE HAD A "VERY CLOSE INTIMATE RELATIONSHIP".'

'There is no evidence that the plaintiff proposed blackmail of a United States Air Force General,' Cooper said. Taylor looked over his glasses at Cooper and shook his head.

'I am against you on that,' he said. 'I think that is a jury matter. If a man says...'

Cooper made a shrewd move. Instead of tackling Taylor head on, he referred to Krotkov's evidence from the examination that he and Traill had made earlier in the year in the US. In it Cooper had effectively cornered Krotkov on the issue of Burchett's supposed blackmail offer when they met in Moscow in the summer of 1956.

The passage from page 125 went:

'*Cooper*: And amongst the correspondents you asked about was Marguerite Higgins?

'*Krotkov*: Now that was not – that was a special case, but that wasn't the situation...

'*Cooper*: Well isn't the situation that Marguerite Higgins was only one of a number of correspondents mentioned between you in that conversation?

'*Krotkov*: Yeah, but there was only one correspondent who married the American general. There was no other.

'*Cooper*: Well now, to you as an agent, or as a co-opted agent of the KGB, it was of special significance?

'*Krotkov*: Well, together with all the situations was a special situation. It was actually the first little hint of a possibility of espionage.

'*Cooper*: To you?

'*Krotkov*: Yeah, because there's no other possibility of getting to know a General of – what? – the Air Force?

'*Cooper*: Well, now to you in your co-opted capacity as an officer of the KGB, that had special significance?

'*Krotkov*: Yeah, and my first suspicion about this totally

different area than journalism was when we told them about Peenemunde. [Krotkov referred here to the claim that he and Burchett had connived in 1947 to mislead the British Admiralty over the Peenemunde German rocket site.] In that case, another military power was involved. There was nothing general about that.

'*Cooper*: Well, now, we're not going into what your thoughts were. You didn't communicate any thoughts about the special importance of Marguerite Higgins to Burchett, did you?'

'*Krotkov*: Well, now, when he mentioned it, I thought it was something special.'

'*Cooper*: But you did not tell Burchett you thought it was something special, did you?

'*Krotkov*: Why would I need to tell him that?'

'*Cooper*: Did you or didn't you tell him that?'

'*Krotkov*: No. I repeat it wasn't said so directly. It was all hinted. He said, "Well, by the way, she married..." He didn't say he was able to go and take the documents from the safe of the general. That wouldn't have been an intelligent game. He [Burchett] is an extremely intelligent man.'

Cooper had gone on to show that Burchett had not actually suggested blackmail, although it was clear that Krotkov was sticking to his explanation that Burchett was in Moscow to show that he would be valuable to the KGB. Krotkov was expounding on his impressions, the nuances of which were lost in the transcript. Without a tape of the actual meeting in 1956, or the appearance of Krotkov in court to explain what had occurred, Cooper's line that there was no direct evidence of a blackmail offer swayed Taylor.

Cooper claimed that it was only in Krotkov's mind that there was 'some sort of sinister significance' in their discussion about Higgins.

'You do not have a tittle of evidence that he [Burchett] ever got any money from them [the KGB],' Taylor said to Traill.

'There is evidence that he asked for introduction to people who could put him on the KGB payroll,' Traill protested. 'There is evidence from Krotkov...'

'Not admissible evidence,' Judge Taylor snapped. Traill's round face flushed. After all the years of investigation, he had not been able to link the KGB evidence strongly enough to influence Taylor, who would be sure to sway the jury. It was a bitter blow.

Burchett's table was elated. It was Cooper's finest moment.

The night before Judge Taylor's summing up and the jury's deliberations, Burchett threw a party at Mavis Robertson's apartment to celebrate the expected victory. He rang Vessa to tell her what had happened, and then the party went on into the early hours. The Herald apartment, by contrast, was like a wake. Traill was still confident that after his enormous effort the jury would see it differently from the judge. Kane was nervous but philosophical. He thought Traill and the rest of the defence team had fought a good fight. The Warners braced themselves for the worst. If Kane lost, they would be Burchett's next legal target.

Judge Taylor began his long summing up by reminding the jury of the law of defamation.

'Defamation is any imputation concerning any person, by which the reputation of that person is likely to be injured, or by which he is likely to be injured in his profession or trade, or by which other persons are likely to be induced to shun or avoid or ridicule or despise him.'

Taylor reminded the attentive twelve men that the *Focus* article should be judged not as a verbatim report but as a summary. They had to make up their minds if it was a substantially fair and accurate report. The emphasis was on 'substantially'.

'You are not concerned with whether it is true or not,' Taylor said. 'You are concerned with its accuracy. Is it a fair and accurate summary of what went on? If it is, then it is no libel. It is protected. That is the matter which you have to determine.'

Taylor did some summarising himself and gave his pen sketch of most of the witnesses. It gave both lawyers heartburn. Cooper suffered in silence because much of the damning evidence was regurgitated. When referring to Derek Kinne's testimony, for instance, Taylor said:

'The only really material part of the evidence is that you accept that Burchett said he could have him shot. That could

be some evidence that he was a bit more than a war correspondent. I am not saying you accept this witness. It is your
responsibility. You saw him. You heard him cross-examined.
You saw him in the witness box. You realise his position. He
came from America to give evidence in this case. It is for you
to say whether you accept him as a witness of truth.'

Although Traill was pleased that Kinne had had such an
impact on the court, it was a reminder that the defence had
been at a disadvantage without Krotkov present. He would
have been the star witness. It was underscored when Taylor
reminded the jury that Cooper claimed that the defence had
not provided a 'tittle' of evidence that Burchett had been on
any KGB payroll, or that he had ever received KGB money.

A list of twelve questions were handed to the retiring jurors of
which they were asked to reply to two of them.

The first was: 'Has the plaintiff satisfied you that the [*Focus*]
article is defamatory of him?'

If the jurors said no, Kane would be the winner. If the
answer were yes, the jury would be asked to decide on another
question: 'Has the defendant satisfied you that the article is a
fair report published for the information of the public of the
proceedings of the Senate?'

A reply of 'No' to this would give the case to Burchett.
A 'Yes' would have left a verdict to the judge. The jury left,
and the court waited. The packed public gallery remained.
Some talked; others read or slept. The defence and plaintiff
tables sat quietly. Occasionally lawyers slipped in and out,
but the counsels and their clients were patient. The first hour
crawled by, then the second and all concerned had time to
consider their worst fears. The tension began to etch itself
in the weary faces of the participants, particularly Kane
and Burchett.

After exactly three hours, at 2.53 pm the jurors filed back in.
Burchett looked apprehensive but confident. Kane was stoney-
faced but calm.

The judge's associate asked: 'How do you find in relation to
question one? Has the plaintiff satisfied you that the article is
defamatory of him?'

The jury foreman was standing. He cleared his throat. 'Yes,' he said.

The court was strangely silent, but Burchett and his supporters grinned. They had expected it, yet it was a great relief to have it confirmed.

'What do you find in relation to question ten? Is the article a fair report of the Senate proceedings?'

'Yes,' the foreman replied.

There was a confused buzz in the courtroom. The onus of decision was now with the judge.

'Then, on those findings, Mr Traill,' Taylor said, 'do you want a verdict?'

'Yes, Your Honour,' Traill replied. 'I ask for a verdict.'

'In accordance with that finding, Mr Cooper,' Taylor said, 'I will enter a verdict for the defendant.'

Burchett went white, but remained expressionless. Someone slapped a bewildered Kane on the back. Some people clapped the decision, but the gallery seemed stunned. The jury filed out.

'I order there be entered a verdict for the defendant,' Taylor said, 'and the plaintiff to pay the defendant's costs.'

Kane smiled for the first time.

Burchett gathered up papers, dumbfounded.

It was not just a decision against him. It would exile him.

24. Exile

The verdict did not stop the *Burchett* v. *Warner* case entering its fourth decade. It hastened it. The cost of Kane's defence approached $100,000. Burchett was soon soliciting help to pay it off and fight on.

'I am defeated,' he told Vessa in a call to Paris, 'but we'll appeal. We can still win this.'

He was to be disappointed. Very few of his communist connections and other friends opened their cheque books, as promised. He had lost, and they had deserted him. Mavis Robertson helped organise two appeals, but the money raised made little impression on the amount owing. Explaining the problems of raising the money to Winston, who put up the initial bond money for the trial, Robertson noted in a letter:

'It was clear that there were people who had and would back Wilfred, e.g. [Clive] Evatt, [businessman Gordon] Barton and I think, the [North] Koreans and others. There were also the lawyers in the case who were prepared to act in the case, even to the extent of visiting the United States at their own expense...

'As soon as practicable after the verdict we set about establishing a support committee. Tony Reeves, Alan Ashbolt and Bob Duffield, all well-known journalists, acted as the spokesmen for the committee. In that time money was raised in Australia, Japan and the US – about $4,700. At Wilfred's request some of that money was sent to him to help cover his out-of-pocket expenses and some went for the [Supreme Court] appeal [against the verdict] bond.'

Of that $4,700, there were several American contributors including C. Lamont ($2,000), and the US Civil Liberties Union ($1,000). In the second money raising effort, the Australian Communist Party, Robertson and a few other communist supporters collected another $550. Robertson commented: 'There is nothing we can do about the Koreans or Barton – he lives in Holland now – but we will seek to see Evatt...'

Burchett showed typical tenacity by deciding to take his appeal to the New South Wales Supreme Court. He had been encouraged by the jury finding that he had been defamed and thought more litigation was worth the trouble, despite the setback.

He had hoped for a 'jackpot' from the trial that would have set him up for retirement. When it didn't eventuate, he found himself in financial difficulty. According to his close friend Rewi Alley, a New Zealand journalist who lived in Peking, Burchett was left with three income sources in the mid-seventies: Russia, Cuba and Vietnam. In 1975, the Russians asked him to go to Angola. In Peking, just before Burchett went to Africa, Alley asked him, 'What on earth do you want to go to Angola for?'. It was clear that he had to do what the Russians demanded. Burchett once more had been thrust into a key area of conflict between east and west. The US, through the CIA, was backing the UNITA and FNLA Angolans, whereas the KGB supported the eventual winners, the Marxist MPLA. Burchett wrote for the US *Guardian* and sent back some stories to the Paris-based *Afrique-Asie*. Other journalists covering the civil war noted that Burchett spent most of his time moving around Angola with the Soviet-backed Cuban troops. (Burchett denied that the Soviets had directed the Cubans to Africa. He preferred to push Castro's line that Cuba was Latin-African, rather than Latin-American. The Cubans were in Africa in response to a request from one of their ancestral homelands.)

Even his *Afrique-Asie* editors did not understand why he was there. He was, in fact, acting for the Russians as a counter to the CIA activities of people such as former agent John Stockwell. Angola was the end of his long, and sometimes silent support for the Chinese who were backing UNITA, the third group battling for ascendancy. Burchett had little choice but to dispatch several articles critical of Chinese foreign policy in Angola – at the direction of his Russian paymasters. It meant that he would never be welcome in Peking again.

Anticipating a fightback by Burchett after his loss in the court case, Warner was producing a filmed interview with four other Kane witnesses – Kinne, Kniss, Mahurin, and Hollis – the day after the trial ended. Warner would not let up. He published anti-Burchett articles in the US and Japan, and fed Ed Hunter information for his extreme right-wing Washington news magazine, *Tactics*. The article in Japan, where Burchett's reputation was high, was entitled 'The Spy Who Came in for the Gold'. A similar piece appeared in the US *National Review* on 11 April 1975 under the title, 'Australian Lord Haw Haw'.

Warner and Kane were again forced to sweat out Burchett's legal threats when his appeal reached the New South Wales Supreme Court of Appeal for decision on 16 May 1976.

Burchett's challenge centred on the claim that Judge Taylor had erred in leaving to the jury the question of whether or not the *Focus* report was a fair summary of the Australian Senate proceedings. It was turned down. Two of the three presiding judges argued that it would be unfair for Kane to have a re-trial because it would be difficult for him to bring all his seventeen witnesses – especially the six from overseas – back to a Sydney court. Burchett now had to pay the costs or be exiled permanently from his homeland.

The battle flared once more in late 1977 when Burchett managed to get a visa for a fund-raising lecture tour of the US. The Carter administration was far more generous towards him than previous administrations, which had limited his travel to a radius of forty kilometres outside the UN building in New York. Burchett's tour was sponsored by the *Guardian* and the Wilfred Burchett Support Committee made up of American radicals such as Dave Dellinger, William Kunstler, Noam Chomsky, Cora Weiss, Ossie Davis and Jane Fonda. *The New York Post* claimed that the tour had been helped by Henry Kissinger in return for Burchett's efforts as a middleman during the Vietnam peace talks.

He began his tour on 21 October at Washington High School, New York City, with a lecture entitled, 'The World Struggle Against Imperialism'. About 600 of the socialist faithful were there to hear three tirades against 'American imperialism' as a warm-up to the main event of Burchett. The last speaker before him was the Vietnamese Ambassador to the United Nations, Dinh Ba Thi. He railed against the US, then finished with an undisguised plea for financial help from it: 'We have received assistance from many countries...it is regrettable that the United States does not undertake its obligations.'

Burchett followed. He spoke for an hour on the 'new Vietnam' and mentioned the success of other countries with communist governments, such as Angola, North Korea and Cambodia. He swiped hard and often at imperialism. He emphasised the totality of the US military defeat in Vietnam, and the crowd loved it. At a question and answer session he was asked:

'What is the truth about *The New York Times* reports of a million killed in Cambodia by the Marxist Pol Pot regime?' After the boos had subsided, Burchett said:

'I don't believe it at all.'

He was helped out by another *Guardian* representative, who said that the reports were 'peddled by the same people who have peddled atrocity stories about every peoples' revolution that has ever occurred'.

Burchett continued on his seven-week, thirty-lecture tour across the country he had never seen, but had made the target of his distaste for thirty years since he first wrote about 'American spies' being involved in unsettling the new 'People's Democracies' in Eastern Europe in the late 1940s. It was to be an eventful experience.

It did not take long for the US right to react with outrage.

In a concerted response, the John Birch Society, the Hearst Press, and Rupert Murdoch's New York *Post* went on the attack. The White House was asked to explain Burchett's easy movement, and the State Department was forced to defend its action in granting him a visa. It pointed out that Burchett had never been found guilty in a court of law of KGB affiliations or of torturing and brainwashing American POWs. Murdoch's *Post* was not satisfied. It kept up the attack in a series of investigative articles and editorials and confronted Burchett at the fashionable New York restaurant, Elaine's.

In a letter to Winston about the incident, Burchett wrote:

'My New York publisher, Michael Roloff of Urizen Books, gave us our final dinner at the Elaine restaurant – noted haunt of writers, columnists and such like. It was intended to be the most intimate, midnight "Last Supper". A newspaper pimp spotted us there and phoned a certain character known variously as Murdoch's "hatchet man", "blood and guts" [Steve] Dunleavy, etc. etc. [an Australian who had worked in New York as a journalist for a decade]. He turned up to grossly insult me at our supper table, apparently his specialty. I replied with what I hope was a more dignified but telling riposte. It was a sort of "name your weapons" confrontation. His choice was a photographer from Murdoch's New York *Post*. Mine was acceptance of a suggestion by proprietress Elaine, to leave through the kitchen exit. Dunleavy bursts in to try to attempt to stop our discreet exit, pushes my terribly, impeccably respectable publisher around. Police are called. Dunleavy appears in a New York court on Jan 25 [1978] on three charges of assault, harrassment and menacing behaviour! Charges preferred by publisher Roloff. Vessa and I give sworn depositions as witnesses just before we left. Never a dull moment!'

Burchett was once again inspired to attempt a defamation action, this time against Kane's friend Rupert Murdoch for the accusations in the *Post*. But his experience with the Australian courts caused him to drop the idea. Burchett's litigious days were over.

A popping sound like firecrackers saw all the people in the back of the van hit the floor. The assassin wearing a red headband ran forward, propped and fired a rifle. The driver's head snapped forward. He had been hit in the neck. The van swerved and caused three rockets fired at it to miss it by feet and fly into the surrounding hills. The assassin fired twice more. The driver, blood streaming from the bullet wound, managed to steer the van clear. He kept going to a Vietnamese checkpoint down the road and some ninety kilometres east of Phnom Penh. Thanks to the courageous driver, Burchett and an Australian film crew in the back survived the attack.

For the second time in 1980, Burchett had been the target for assassination by Pol Pot's Khmer Rouge. They had waited in ambush, for his recent writings east and west had been damaging to their murderous cause. The wheel had turned full circle, for Burchett had been a feverish supporter of the hardline Marxists in Cambodia when, in 1975, they first swept to power and pushed the last of the Americans out of Phnom Penh and South-East Asia. He had been keen to write a book on them and was only distracted from it by Moscow sending him to Angola. It took Burchett four years to write a word condemning the Pol Pot regime, and by then it was too late. In one of the worst genocides in history, the regime – based on a warped mixture of Marxist, Leninist and Maoist concepts – murdered three million Cambodians. Burchett ignored and ridiculed reports from refugees fleeing to the Thai border. It was the greatest failure of his career, and his pushes into the country after Pol Pot had been deposed seemed to be motivated by a drive to correct the record. He even resigned from his beloved New York *Guardian* over the issue, for the weekly continued to ignore the truth about the Khmer Rouge.

Burchett expressed his confusion and bewilderment over unfolding events in South-East Asia. Everything had seemed perfect when the Americans, by 1975, had been driven out of Vietnam and Cambodia. But without the great imperialist enemy to unite them, the communist Asian neighbours began to butcher each other.

Hundreds of thousands of refugees fled Vietnam as Hanoi imposed its repressive measures on the south. Pol Pot did his worst in Cambodia. Then these two countries began fighting, and China clashed with Vietnam. Burchett wrote in 1979 in his second autobiography, *At The Barricades:*

'Now my Asian friends were at each other's throats – each waving the banner of socialism and revolution – and I was again in the thick of it. It was a shattering blow for a vision of things acquired during the previous four decades, including my certainty as to the superior wisdom and morality of Asian revolutionaries.'

It seemed as if this naive, revolutionary romantic was finally disillusioned. Burchett had kept his dreamy vision of revolution alive by being on the spot when new communist governments took control. He bounced from the Eastern bloc countries to China, then to Korea, followed by Laos and Vietnam, Algeria, Cambodia and Angola. This partly explained his unquenchable enthusiasm when others, who had started with his zeal for communism, had long since tempered their views.

Burchett, by contrast, became a paid consultant to the communist governments of Bulgaria, North Korea, Vietnam, Cuba, Russia and China, according to many people who were all friends or communists. They included Joe Waters, Edwin Morrisby, Rewi Alley, Ken Gott, Yuri Krotkov and other defectors, Ivan Lazerev (Hungary), Josef Frolik, (Czechoslovakia), Wladyslaw Tykocinski (Poland), and Bui Cong Tuong and To Ming Trung.

For this reason, Burchett never gave himself time to reflect and analyse critically. His role was unique, yet he was not the independent observer he claimed. A true independent who had witnessed what he had would not have supported Stalinist show trials in Eastern Europe. He would have had something more to say about the 1956 attempted revolution in Hungary, which he denounced. He may have considered being other than mute on Czechoslovakia in 1968, or even Afghanistan in 1979. He might also have written with some insight on the trial and execution of a big section of the North Korean leadership in 1953. Instead, he received decorations, accolades and payment from its brutal leadership for thirty years.

Burchett was privy to Mao's crazy Red Guard purges, but he told the world nothing. He knew as much about the Sino-Soviet split as anyone but not a word of revelation was punched out on his battered portable. Because of his tremendous impact during the Vietnam war he could have had some influence on events in Pol Pot's Cambodia soon after. But he chose to ignore the carnage until it was too late.

Yet had he attempted an independent view of any one of these events, it would probably have been his last, as he realised when the Khmer Rouge assassins ambushed him. The CIA also considered assassinating him, and may have tried. Burchett did open up against the Nazis, fascist Japan, the atomic bomb, and US mistakes in South-East Asia. But his price for the privileged observation of a great deal more iniquities of history was silence.

Burchett at seventy made a trip to Vietnam in late 1981 with a French TV team as part of the international production of a series of programmes on the country. By early 1982, his health had deteriorated. French doctors had warned him against a liver collapse, and he was off alcohol. There was some disagreement over whether this, or a slow cancer picked up at Hiroshima, was the problem. Illness had curtailled his prodigious output, and he was struggling to make ends meet in expensive Paris. Burchett's usefulness to the communist governments, which had kept him running in the past, was diminishing. He was relying more on ad hoc arrangements with western TV companies ready to use him for his expertise on Vietnam. He invested in one film himself and lost about $7,000 when he needed it.

TV stories necessitated travel when he should have been relaxing to recuperate. He went to Japan for RAI (Italian radio and TV) for a one-hour documentary on Hiroshima. Japanese TV also filmed him, and he made several speeches. Later he visited North Korea for more public relations work for the government.

Burchett was forced to borrow from Winston and the rest of the family in Melbourne, and reluctantly, he and Vessa had to move to Sofia in Bulgaria. They still owned their beautiful villa on the edge of a forest at Meudon just outside Paris, but their high-living, generous days were over.

Despite his rapidly failing health, Burchett fought on. By chance, he was useful to the KGB and the Bulgarians in early 1983 in the flare-up over the rumoured involvement of KGB-controlled Bulgarian assassins in the attempted killing of Pope John Paul II. Burchett wrote a piece for the London *Guardian* headlined, 'No Bulgarians Under the Bed', which was meant to debunk the idea of the KGB-Bulgarian conspiracy. He wrote similar stories in the Bulgarian review *Otecestvo*, and was touted in Sofia as the hot source on the Bulgarian connection to the assassination attempt. Burchett also wrote a public relations book on Bulgaria, which was not published in the west.

Fortunately, he had time for a last, long overdue stab at Hiroshima that had been inspired by his visit there in May 1982. He wrote *Shadows of Hiroshima,* a book that took up where his 1945 article for the Daily Express – 'I write this as a warning to the world' – left off. It looked at the political, sociological and medical after-effects of the bomb.

He collapsed into a coma with the edited proofs of the manuscript in his hands, and was never to recover. He died on 27 September 1983. According to Vessa, some of his doctors in France and Bulgaria suggested that his death had been caused by the lingering effects of the radiation sickness he had been first to describe at Hiroshima.

Perhaps cancer had achieved what Japanese bombs and assassins in Vietnam, Laos and Cambodia had failed to do. But long after his death, Burchett's influence over his passionate causes will remain.

Bibliography

Barron, John, *KGB*, Bantam, US.

Boyle, Andrew, *The Climate of Treason*, Hutchinson, London, 1979.

Burchett, George, *He Chose Truth*, Australasian Book Society, Melbourne, 1950.

Burchett, Wilfred, *At the Barricades*, Macmillan, Australia, 1981.

Burchett, Wilfred, *Catapult to Freedom*, Quartet Books, London, 1978.

Burchett, Wilfred, *China's Feet Unbound*, World Unity Publications, Melbourne, 1952.

Burchett, Wilfred, *Democracy with a Tommy Gun*, Cheshire, Melbourne, 1946.

Burchett, Wilfred, *Grasshoppers and Elephants*, Urizen, New York, 1977.

Burchett, Wilfred, *North of the 17th Parallel*, Red River Publishing House, Hanoi, 1957.

Burchett, Wilfred, *Passport*, Thomas Nelson, Melbourne, 1969.

Burchett, Wilfred, *Shadows of Hiroshima*, Verso, London, 1983.

Burchett, Wilfred, *The China Cambodia Vietnam Triange*, Vanguard Books, Chicago and Zed Press, London, 1981.

Burchett, Wilfred and Derek Roebuck, *The Whores of War*, Penguin, London, 1977.

Burchett, Wilfred and Sihanouk, Norodom, *My War with the CIA*, Penguin, 1973.

Burchett, Wilfred and Winnington, Alan, *Plain Perfidy*, The Britain-China Friendship Association, London, 1953.

Burgess, Pat, *Warco*, Heinemann, Melbourne, 1986.

Dulles, Allen, *Great True Spy Stories*, Castle, US, 1986.

Herman, Gary and Downing, David, *Jane Fonda – All American Anti-Heroine*, Omnibus Press, London, 1981.

Hudson, Christopher, *The Killing Fields*, Pan, London, 1974.

Irving, David, *Uprising*, Veritas, Australia, 1986.

Karnow, Stanley, *Vietnam, A History*, Penguin, 1984.

Kiernan, Ben, *Burchett*, Quartet, London, 1986.

Knightley, Phillip, *The First Casualty*, Quartet, London, 1978.

Krotkov, Yuri, *The Nobel Prize*, Sphere, London, 1982.

Maclear, Michael, *Vietnam: The Ten Thousand Day War*, Thames Methuen, London, 1981.

McCormack, Gavin, *Cold War, Hot War*, Hale & Iremonger, Sydney, 1983.

Meray, Tibor, *The Enemy*, Secker & Warburg, London, 1958.

Moorehead, Alan, *The Traitors*, Hamish Hamilton, London, 1952.

Page, Bruce, Leitch, David and Knightley, Phillip, *Philby*, Andre Deutsch, London, 1968.

Philby, Kim, *My Silent War*, Panther, London, 1969.

Pincher, Chapman, *Inside Story*, Sidgwick & Jackson, London, 1978.

Pincher, Chapman, *Too Secret Too Long*, Sidgwick & Jackson, London, 1984.

Revel, Jean-Francais, *La Nouvelle Censure*, Robert Laffont, Paris, 1977.

Seale, Patrick and McConville, Maureen, *Philby – The Long Road to Moscow*, Penguin, 1978.

Spada, James, *Fonda*, Dolphin, New York, 1985.

Sterling, Claire, *The Time of the Assassins*, Angus and Robertson, Sydney, 1984.

West, Rebecca, *The Meaning of Treason*, Penguin, London, 1965.

Whitlam, Nicholas, *Nest of Traitors*, University of Queensland Press, Brisbane, 1985.

Winnington, Alan, *Breakfast With Mao*, Lawrence and Wishart, London, 1986.

Wolton, Thierry, *Le KGB En France*, Grasset, Paris, 1986.

Index